Teaching for Educational Equity

Teaching for Educational Equity

Case Studies for Professional Development and Principal Preparation
Volume 2

Jane A. Beese and Jennifer L. Martin

ROWMAN & LITTLEFIELD
Lanham • Boulder • New York • London

Published by Rowman & Littlefield
A wholly owned subsidiary of The Rowman & Littlefield Publishing Group, Inc.
4501 Forbes Boulevard, Suite 200, Lanham, Maryland 20706
www.rowman.com

Unit A, Whitacre Mews, 26-34 Stannary Street, London SE11 4AB

British Library Cataloguing in Publication Information Available

Library of Congress Cataloging-in-Publication Data Available

978-1-4758-2190-1 (cloth : alk. paper)
978-1-4758-2191-8 (pbk. : alk. paper)
978-1-4758-2192-5 (electronic)

∞™ The paper used in this publication meets the minimum requirements of American National Standard for Information Sciences Permanence of Paper for Printed Library Materials, ANSI/NISO Z39.48-1992.

Printed in the United States of America

Contents

Preface

"A belief is just a thought you keep thinking" (Hicks & Hicks, 2009, p. 17). This book was written with the focus of changing our thoughts and beliefs through compassion for all. We are not here to lead the reader down a specific path, but instead we support the reader on a journey toward deeper understanding of the issues that are pervasive in our society and schools.

With the foundation of compassion, our sole purpose is to develop understanding and awareness of one another. We do this through the use of story, blending literature, theory, and current issues, as a tool to bring clarity and insight. Our goal is to challenge the status quo, and to problematize the attitudes that contribute to the disparate treatment of students in our current educational milieu and that contribute to unfair treatment based upon race, gender, sexual orientation, language status, disability, and other identity markers.

It is our hope that this second volume will continue to highlight the pressing need for multicultural education, and to expose all educators to culturally responsive pedagogical practices, particularly in light of the pervasive notion that we live in a post-racial society, despite glaring evidence to the contrary: the shooting of Walter Scott, the Charleston AME church shootings, the shootings inside Pulse nightclub in Orlando, Florida, the bathroom laws in North Carolina.

The cases are based on real stories of students, teachers, and administrators gathered from interviews, our memories, and research. Although some of these cases are based upon real events, all of the names and places have been changed to ensure anonymity. In the context of the social, political, and economic issues we face, if we can begin to put ourselves in the shoes of others, perhaps glimpsing how the world appears from other points of view, only then can our response to our children be based in truth rather than on a limited set of beliefs and assumptions.

REFERENCE

Hicks, E., & Hicks, J. (2009). *The vortex: Where the law of attraction assembles all cooperative relationships.* Carlsbad, CA: Hay House.

Acknowledgments

> To bring about real change, our efforts must be collective and harmonious, based on love and respect for ourselves and each other, our ancestors and future generations. If anger at injustice is what we use as the source of our energy, we may do something harmful, something we will later regret. . . . compassion is the only source of energy that is useful and safe. That is why love must always go together with understanding. Understanding and insight show us how to act.—Thich Nhat Hanh

We are cognizant of the fact that violence, and gun violence in particular, often masks deeply rooted issues of bigotry and oppression. We hope that this small volume makes a difference for the cause of social justice that is so pressing in our world.

We dedicate this volume to the victims of police shootings in the summer of 2016: Alton Sterling, Philando Castile, Deborah Danner . . . We know that this list is incomplete, and we firmly stand against state-sanctioned violence in all communities. #BlackLivesMatter and #SayHerName must be acknowledged.

As a student and a teacher, I have found case studies to be an important tool in the classroom. They provide the context for complex problem solving, and help guide teachers and administrators in the decision-making process. Case study pedagogy provides a method of application, when supported by discourse and reflective practice, that enhances students' understanding and intensifies the learning process.

I have been blessed with the support of many. First, I want to thank my institution, Youngstown State University. I thank my colleagues for their constant encouragement, and the example they set by the compassion they show toward their students. I also want to thank my three children, Jonathon, Jacob, and Emily, for their understanding of the long hours I have put into writing and for their love.

A special thanks to Dr. Truman Hudson Jr., who, as a practitioner in the field, took the time to review several cases and provide feedback based on his many years of experience and expertise. Next, I want to express my gratitude to my writing partner and friend, Jennifer Martin, for her talent and dedication to this project. Through our many writing endeavors, we have challenged and supported each other. Jennifer, you have made me a more thoughtful practitioner—thank you. Finally, I want to thank Rowman & Littlefield for believing in our vision.

I challenge readers to consider the vast implications of social injustice and their role in making a difference. Every small act has the capacity to manifest great things. It is every educator's responsibility to make their classroom, school, or district a safe and just place for our children—a place where teachers and children are inspired to use their intellect and creativity to reach their fullest potential.

—Jane A. Beese

In my first year of teaching, I had a student named John. He was in eighth grade. He was bright and funny, but he did not care too much about school. When I inquired about him, another teacher informed me, "His grandmother is Native American. She has taught him not to care about school." At that time, my knowledge of multicultural education and the history of oppression in American education were nascent at best. In ninth grade, John was sent to the alternative school in our district, but soon dropped out.

I still think of John all of these years later. I did not know then about the history of American boarding schools for indigenous American populations, devised to "kill the Indian, but spare the child," but I bet John's grandmother did. I wish I would have known better to ask the right questions then, to meet John's grandmother, and to hear her point of view. I wonder if she taught John to preserve his identity, an identity that she perhaps thought the school was killing. I wish . . .

And I hope . . . for better teacher education programs so that our future teachers do not, whether knowingly or unknowingly, marginalize, minimize, or erase their students' beliefs, thus damaging their identities. I hope that they will take the time to truly know their students as people, so that they can create the best educational experiences for them. I hope . . .

I dedicate this volume to John and to April. April is a student who I remain in touch with, ten-plus years after she left my classroom, for as I hope she has learned from me, I continue to learn from her. April Little, you force me to remember . . .

I have many others to thank for their support of my work. I thank my institution, the University of Mount Union. I thank my students, past and present, for challenging me to do a better job every single day. I thank my friends and my family for understanding my need to do social justice work, despite the repercussions that undoubtedly affect them.

Extra special thanks to BaFa BaFa facilitators Brianna Boehlke, Victoria Nash, Caitlin Shimp, and Clinton Simmons.

I thank my coauthor, Dr. Jane Beese, for leading this portion of our project, and for providing me with guidance, critique, and support.

I also thank Dr. Thomas F. Koerner, Vice President and Publisher of the Education Division at Rowman & Littlefield Publishing Group, and

Bethany Janka from Rowman & Littlefield for believing in this project from the beginning.

—Jennifer L. Martin

Introduction

The first ten chapters of this book are based on specific topics such as gender identity and expression, gender, race, socioeconomic status, refugees, whiteness, special education, sexual harassment, and school violence. Beginning with a story composed to showcase issues related to social justice, the authors carefully selected literature pertinent to each topic, embedding theory into the case and providing even more noteworthy and specific information in a Teaching Notes section that details a themed trail to resolve certain aspects of the case.

There are also questions for discussion and additional activities provided for class discourse and further study. The last two chapters of the book contain supplemental resources for teachers and administrators on social justice and multiculturalism. While some of the cases are loosely based on headline news, personal experience, or the lived experiences of educators, the names of the places and the people in each case are fictitious.

Teachers and school leaders are confronted by various issues pertaining to social justice every day. The cases in this book were written to help school leaders handle these issues ethically, and are intended to be used by administrators for the professional development of teachers, teacher leaders, and aspiring principals.

This volume can also be used in the higher education classroom in order to prepare current and aspiring teachers and administrators to lead for social justice. This volume utilizes the case study approach, which has been found to "sharpen problem-solving skills and to improve the ability to think and reason rigorously" (Harvard Graduate School of Education, 2013, n.p.).

There are cases pertaining to race, class, gender, sexual orientation, discrimination and harassment, culturally responsive pedagogy, intersectionality, et cetera. Each case requires readers to look beyond the facts, by providing guidance on current research and policy guidelines. Each case provides readers with additional information that will assist them in making informed decisions. Additionally, each case provides facilitators with guiding questions to assist them in their pedagogy and for subsequent class discussion.

We present issues that enable leaders or professors to assist their teachers or students in examining and grappling with the issues facing teachers and administrators today pertaining to social justice. The subject matter will challenge the strategies teachers and school leaders employ as they meet head-on both the problems of day-to-day instruction and school leadership and more unexpected situations and issues through the case study approach.

By utilizing the case study approach, this volume will focus on problem solving as an opportunity for future teachers and leaders to focus their efforts on issues that matter through communication, policy formation, organizational systems, and attention to/reflection on the core work of schools, and on the legal/ethical responsibilities of teachers and administrators. In this way, the text seeks to develop teachers' and school leaders' abilities to respond to the issues and opportunities that arise in their daily practice.

Additionally, each case draws on the appropriate foundational theory, as well as applicable research and policy, to underscore why the strategies contribute to effective practice and school improvement. By exploring these complimentary areas of practice, this text seeks to enhance the social justice understanding of teachers and school leaders concerning their problem-solving skill set and knowledge base.

Understanding how organizations work and the methods school leaders might effectively use to address problems pertaining to social justice in their school organization is central to professional development.

This volume rests on the assumption that the heart of teaching and leading lies in the decisions one makes daily and strategically in relation to the problems the organizational context presents. In an effort to define the niche for this proposed volume, two sets of related literature have been identified: (1) the broader organizational theory literature, and (2) the more focused social justice literature.

We envision that this work will serve as the primary source for professional development workshops and/or undergraduate and graduate classrooms. By focusing on social justice and multiculturalism as a broad construct, it has the potential to serve a wide variety of educational practitioners involved in the problem-solving process.

Should the book be chosen for use as a book study or workshop, leaders will find it to be attractive in that it offers educators concrete and applied examples of problem solving in educational settings. The focus on strategies to enhance the problem-solving efforts of school leaders provides these leaders with practical source material for daily problem-solving activities in school settings. The resources included in the text also support individual or team learning by providing opportunities for reflection on current practices as well as alternatives for future efforts.

The book also can be used as a primary or secondary text for classrooms, as the topics align with classes such as Multicultural Education, Organizational Leadership, School Culture and Governance and/or Decision Making, Curriculum and Instruction, and Policy and Law. The text is informed by knowledge of standards for school leaders and a theoretical knowledge base. In this way, the text offers readers problem-solving strategies for daily practice within school contexts, linking theory to best practice in engaging and practical ways.

This work is unique in that it offers not only strategies for organizational leadership and practice relative to the problem-solving process, but also the potential for understanding and developing problem-solving skills, which are of paramount importance for prospective and practicing school administrators.

PRACTICAL APPLICATIONS OF THIS VOLUME

There are many ways in which this book may be used in classrooms and professional development seminars. The following are some suggestions, but it is recommended that facilitators of these cases use their personal pedagogical styles.

Pedagogical Suggestions:

1. Ideally, have students/participants read the case at home, asking them to take notes not only on the facts of the case, but also on their perceptions of the best course of action.
2. Assign additional resources (most cases have additional readings at the end) as homework as appropriate.
3. In a large group discussion, facilitating with a whiteboard or chart paper, list the facts of the case as students/participants share their thoughts.
4. Ask clarifying questions and encourage debate about the facts among students/participants.
5. Break students/participants into small groups and have them answer the questions at the end of the case(s), and engage in additional activities as appropriate.
6. Share results of small group work as a large group discussion. Ask clarifying questions and encourage debate among students/participants.
7. As a culminating whole group discussion, ask students/participants to identify the optimal course of action for all key actors in the case.
8. Additional work/homework: Ask students/participants to write a reflection on this experience. Adjust pedagogy based upon these responses.

As a follow-up to classroom discussion, students can be asked to write a case analysis and compare their analyses in a small group discussion. As a guide, students are recommended to ask these generic questions: (1) Who are the key actors and what role do they play in this case study? (2) What happened in this case? Identify the plot line. (3) What are the issues of this case? (4) What were the causes and effects of each action? What actions (if any) served to escalate the situation? What actions (if any) served to remedy the situation? (5) What theory can you draw upon to explain what happened in this case? (6) What appropriate actions should be taken by the key actors in this case?

REFERENCES

Hanh, T. N. (2016, November 13). To bring about real change (Facebook post). Posted to https://www.facebook.com/thichnhathanh/posts/10154302665729635

Harvard Graduate School of Education. (2013). Women in education leadership. *Programs in professional learning*. Cambridge, MA: Harvard Graduate School of Education.

ONE

"What Are We Going to Do about the Bathrooms?"

Transgender Students: Civil Rights or Local Control?

According to Orr, Baum, Brown, Gill, Kahn, and Salem (2015),"Transgender describes a person whose gender identity is different from what is generally considered typical from their sex assigned at birth" (p. 6). Because of a lack of knowledge about transgender individuals and the concept of gender in particular on the part of many teachers and administrators, the idea of making accommodations for transgender students can create legal problems for schools. Although the population of transgender students is a very small percentage of the overall student population, a growing acceptance of gender fluidity has encouraged many students to "come out" at younger ages than in past years. The culture seems to be progressing faster than schools and school policies.

Federal decisions affecting transgender students in public schools are becoming more common. The Obama administration's position on allowing transgender students to use the restrooms and locker rooms that correspond to their gender identities has been asserted in legal briefs and civil rights agreements in school districts in recent years (Blad, 2016). However, many state and local policymakers, as well as local school district officials, have disagreed with the Obama administration's stance on transgender school policies, and schools have recently been found in violation of federal civil rights guidance because, for example, they did not allow a transgender student access to the restroom corresponding to their gender identity.

There is a recent trend of state courts and civil rights panels siding with transgender students on questions of access to school facilities.

While schools can lose federal funding for noncompliance, civil rights guidance does not carry the full force of law. Because of this, schools and districts sometimes bide their time in making these accommodations for transgender students, and thus do not have policies in place to protect them. As federal civil rights officials put pressure on districts to accommodate transgender students, many districts continue to question their responsibilities to students whose gender identities do not match the genders they were assigned at birth.

This dilemma may be reduced to one ethical question: should school districts do the bare minimum to reach civil rights compliance, or should they go above and beyond, and do as much as they possibly can to accommodate and protect all of their students? School districts often wait until they experience legal problems, such as being sued by families for civil rights violations, instead of getting ahead of lawsuits by creating policies protecting the civil rights of all students. Teachers and administrators should in fact accommodate the rights of transgender students by, for example, using their preferred name whether or not the students have had their names legally changed. Some districts create a two-tiered system, with the legal name of the student in a computer system and the preferred name of the student on classroom documents, to ensure that the student is not "outed," which may put them at risk for harassment. Districts should have policies in place for this, and for other issues facing transgender students.

However, some district leaders are often at a loss about what they are legally required to do for their transgender students. This is not because the information is not there; they are just not seeking it out, or do not know where to look. This case examines the nuances of accommodating transgender student needs and the legal requirements for schools, as well as the practical implications of these requirements.

THE CASE

Robert (Bobby) Gonzalez, formerly Susan Gonzalez, was a gifted student at Shirley Chisholm High School in the Springfield Heights School District. The gifted coordinator, Dawn Adams, did not know Bobby personally yet, as he was a new transfer student, but she did recognize a mismatch with Bobby's name on the course rosters (Robert) and the official computer system (Susan). After some investigating, Ms. Adams learned that Bobby's gender was listed as female (F) in the computer system as well. As the school typically used a student's name and gender as listed in the computer system when mailing information home, which relied upon recorded birth certificate information as their source, Ms. Adams was unsure what to do. She did not know if this was a mistake: Was this student mixed up with another with the same last name? Or was this a transgender student?

She quickly searched the Internet to find if there was a standard for transgender student name change policies because she wanted to be informed. She learned that when a transgender student transitions, there are many opportunities for a student's previous name or sex assigned at birth to inadvertently appear on documents generated by school systems (Orr et al., 2015), which can have negative consequences for the student. She also learned that although there are ideal standards to which schools can adhere in order to protect transgender students, such as using their preferred name and preferred pronouns, there is not a universal standard.

New to the school and unfamiliar with all of the district and school policies, she decided to consult the school administrator, Principal Romeo. Ms. Adams asked for the story on this student. Principal Romeo replied, "Bobby's gender identity is male. Everyone in the school is aware of Bobby's gender identity and expression, that he is male. However, simple things like taking attendance or enrolling in classes often can compromise a student's privacy. We do what we can, but these legal documents still pose a problem for us."

Principal Romeo indicated that since Bobby's name was never legally changed, she could not place the name "Robert" on the forms; instead, she had to use the legal name of Susan. Ms. Admas ruminated on this. An issue such as this was something that she had never thought of. On the one hand, she thought, "What's the big deal? It is only a letter, M or F, and it is only the paperwork that is mailed home. How bad can that be?" On the other hand, she thought about the logical extension of this issue. She wondered, "What is the worst-case scenario here?" She thought about a teacher inadvertently calling a student by the wrong name (and thus gender) when taking attendance, she thought about teachers unintentionally outing students in front of their peers, and she thought about bullying. What she did not think about was the intentional outing of a student by a teacher. She then came to the following conclusion: "We should always think about the worst-case scenario when making decisions impacting our students."

Ms. Adams shared this idea with Principal Romeo, and he nodded. They both verbally agreed that they would need to seek district support to create better and more inclusive policies to protect transgender students.

Ms. Adams was not happy about Principal Romeo's direction for her to use the student's legal name for home mailings, but she complied, understanding that this was a case of policy lagging behind rapidly changing social norms. She expected that more of these issues would present themselves.

As Ms. Adams took her leave, another thought occurred to her. She stopped in her tracks and turned around to face Principal Romeo. "This is my first experience working with a transgender student," Ms. Adams began. "This is my first experience as well," Principal Romeo concurred. "So . . ." Ms. Adams paused. "What are we going to do about the bathrooms?"

District History with Transgender Students:
John F. Kennedy High School

Two years previously, a very outspoken high school student new to John F. Kennedy High School in the Springfield Heights School District, Trevor Martin, who was born a biological female but identified as male, indicated that it was discriminatory to force him to use the girls' restrooms or locker room at school. After moving to the Springfield Heights School District at the end of his eighth grade year, Trevor's parents, Fred and Joann Martin, were in frequent communication with Principal McAfee over the summer to discuss Trevor's name change, his registration as a male student, his access to the boys' restrooms and locker rooms, and his eligibility for boys' sports teams.

However, at this time, Principal McAfee had no experience with transgender students, and no training. Although he consulted with other building principals in his district and in the surrounding area, and with his own central office administration, he found no easy solutions. The central office administration in the Springfield Heights School District dictated that this student would use the bathrooms and locker rooms for "her" biological sex, and that "she" would be referred to by "her" name, per the legal documents.

Fred and Joann Martin respected Principal McAfee, and they knew that he was trying his best, but they also needed to advocate for their child. They pleaded with Principal McAfee to devise a solution that would benefit everyone. Principal McAfee thought about it and believed he could "get around" the district mandates without getting anyone into trouble.

Prior to the beginning of the school year, Principal McAfee met with all of Trevor's teachers and explained the situation. He indicated that although Trevor's name would appear as Brittany on the class rosters, they should always refer to him as Trevor, and to refer to him using the male pronoun, as he preferred. Most of the teachers were empathic and readily agreed, except one.

Mr. Ward said nothing as Principal McAfee explained Trevor's situation. But the look on his face made his opinion about the situation more than clear. However, no one looked. Mr. Ward had a reputation for being stern, traditional, and hard on students. He had previously been taken to task by the union for proselytizing with evangelical views in class.

On the first day of school, all went well for Trevor, until the last period of the day: Mr. Ward's social studies class. When Mr. Ward took attendance, he called for Brittany Martin over and over. When no one responded to this name, Mr. Ward walked over to Trevor's desk. He stood in front of the desk, looked Trevor in the eye, and stated, "I know you go by Trevor now, but your legal name is Brittany, so I need you to respond when I call you. Otherwise, I will mark you absent."

At this stage, Mr. Ward did nothing else. He simply continued taking attendance, and then he went on with the first day's lesson.

Trevor ran home that day. When his parents arrived home from work that evening, he explained what happened, and they called Principal McAfee, but he was already gone for the day.

The next day, Trevor did not experience any fallout from Mr. Ward's confrontation in sixth period, yet he still dreaded attending that class. He considered hiding in the bathroom instead, or ducking out a side door and walking home early. But, instead, he steeled himself and walked into Mr. Ward's class early, ready and willing to educate his teacher.

Trevor entered the class at 1:01 p.m. on Tuesday. There were still four minutes before the bell would ring, signifying the start of class. Trevor figured that he had two minutes to speak to Mr. Ward before his classmates began filing in. Trevor found Mr. Ward at his desk, organizing papers that he presumably had collected from the previous class.

"Excuse me, Mr. Ward. Can I talk to you before class starts?" Trevor began. Mr. Ward looked up at Trevor over the top of his glasses. He sighed. "Yes?"

"I am not sure what you think of me, but my name is Trevor. I would appreciate it if you could call me Trevor. If you have any questions about anything, I will answer them. I am not sure if now is the best time, but I will tell you anything to help you understand. Just please call me by my name." Appearing brave in his stance and in his words, Trevor was crumbling inside. He had never had to speak to a teacher like that before. At his previous school, all of his teachers complied with his requested name change. Trevor transitioned in middle school. His problem was not with his teachers. On the contrary, they were empathic and supportive. He had problems with some students who knew him as Brittany and could not or would not understand his transition, and therefore made his life hell. Such experiences pushed the Martins to move districts.

"Hon," Mr. Ward began, "I am sure you think you know who you are, but you're just a kid. You're in ninth grade. I am going to do my job as I always have. I am going to read off my roster, which is a legal document, by the way, just as I always have. If you do not respond to your name, you will be marked absent."

As Trevor stood in front of Mr. Ward's desk in disbelief, the one-minute warning bell rang. It was 1:04 p.m. Trevor contemplated whether to run out or to sit down. As the seconds clicked by, students began to file in. Trevor felt as if he could feel their stares, as assuredly as he could hear the ticks of the clock's second hand. He chose to sit, so as not to draw any more attention to himself.

At 1:05 p.m. the bell rang, and Mr. Ward began to call roll. When he heard the name Brittany Martin, Trevor again was silent. But Mr. Ward was not.

"Class," Mr. Ward began, "I want you to know that we have a student who will not respond to her name." Mr. Ward approached Trevor's desk as he continued, "This student, a girl, named Brittany Martin, thinks she's a boy named Trevor." Now Mr. Ward was standing in front of Trevor's desk, facing him. "I guess I am not allowed to, what do they call it these days?" Mr. Ward paused for a moment. "I have it! I guess I am not allowed to 'out' this student," he continued sarcastically, "but what about my rights? Our rights? What about free speech? What about the bathrooms? This is a slippery slope, folks. If I am made to call a girl a boy, what's next?" Mr. Ward looked around as if to gain support from the students, but he found none. The students appeared dumbfounded.

As if by divine intervention, Principal McAfee's voice sounded from the intercom speaker on the wall: "Mr. Ward, please send Trevor Martin to my office immediately."

Mr. Ward smiled. "Brittany, you heard him. Go!"

Trevor left the classroom at 1:10 p.m., never to return.

Principal McAfee had finally returned the Martins' call just prior to the start of sixth period. Attempting to do his due diligence based upon their claims of what Trevor had experienced the previous day, Principal McAfee called Trevor down to the office, listened to what Trevor experienced both on Monday and on Tuesday, and subsequently transferred him to another social studies class.

Principal McAfee silently praised the students in the class for not taking Mr. Ward's bait. Principal McAfee felt he had dodged a bullet here. He made a pledge to himself to be cognizant of the needs of transgender students, and to always err on the side of caution. He also pledged to himself that he would provide training for all of his staff and students on LGBTQ+ students and their needs, including their legal rights and the school's legal responsibilities. He was willing to fight central office administration if need be. He was now committed.

His first charge was to report Mr. Ward's inappropriate behavior to the district administration. By Friday of the same week, Mr. Ward was suspended pending an investigation. After much legal wrangling, Mr. Ward was relieved of his duties, and Principal McAfee considered himself a full-fledged advocate for LGBTQ+ students.

Now, at the start of each school year, Principal McAfee conferences with each transgender student and their family to discuss any possible issues or concerns the family and student might have. Principal McAfee knows how difficult transgender situations can be because as the administrator, he is not permitted to tell anyone about the student. That would be considered "outing" someone. He has to rely on the parents and students to share their situation with teachers.

During the conference, transgender students are provided the choice of using the bathroom and locker room of their birth gender or a private bathroom and locker room set aside for their use. Students have thus far preferred to use a private bathroom. Because these issues are addressed in an honest and open manner, and because students are provided choices, Principal McAfee has not faced any additional issues up to this point.

Current Situation: Shirley Chisholm High School

Shirley Chisholm High School honored Bobby's request to be treated as a male in all respects except access to the boys' restrooms and boys' locker room at the school. However, Shirley Chisholm High School did not have a principal advocate like JFK had in Principal McAfee. Because of this, the school and the district relied on a board decision and subsequently offered Bobby a single-stall unisex restroom and a private changing station in the girls' locker room, which, according to Superintendent Brown, "appropriately serves the dignity and privacy of all students in our educational environment." Anne and Frank Gonzalez expressed dissatisfaction with that arrangement, stating, "This will ostracize our son and draw attention to the fact that he must change separately." They also complained about Bobby's lack of access to the boys' locker room as a student in a gym class.

The Gonzalez family expressed their dissatisfaction with the board's decision to Principal Romeo and Superintendent Brown. They also consulted an attorney and wrote an appeal to the decision that they submitted to Principal Romeo and Superintendent Brown as well as to the board. However, the decision remained firm. At this point, the Gonzalez family filed a formal complaint with the civil rights office in their region.

The civil rights office subsequently filed suit on behalf of the Gonzalezes' claim of discrimination based on gender. The issue was tied up in court for the rest of the academic year, and it was not until Bobby's sophomore year in high school that he was finally permitted access to the boys' locker room and restroom.

Soon after that, some parents and a minority of board members staged a protest of Bobby Gonzalez's use of the boys' locker room. A board member was overheard saying that transgender students suffer from a "mental disorder" and that it's not "a real thing." The board member stepped down in the aftermath of his comments. Despite all of this, the district still had not formulated a policy addressing transgender issues. Although district leaders were pressured by national LGBTQ+ groups and empathic parents and students to support transgender students, they also felt challenged by some parents, students, and community groups who argued that issues related to transgender bathroom and locker room use threatened the rights of other students.

This conflict caused many students, parents, teachers, and community members to take a side. What could have remained a private issue between the Gonzalez family and the school became a political issue, which led to the outing of Bobby's transgender status. Bobby then faced teasing and harassment from several students, which caused him severe anxiety, stress, and decreased academic performance.

Additionally, in the wake of this policy wavering, the US Justice and Education departments sent letters to the Springfield Heights School District instructing that transgender students should be allowed to use the bathrooms, showers, and locker rooms of their choice (matching their gender identity). Violations of this dictate could result in the loss of federal education funding.

The district ignored this guidance and, instead, sued for an injunction preventing the US Department of Education from enforcing the rule allowing students to access bathrooms and other facilities based on gender identity. The Gonzalez family elected to sue on the side of the government, indicating that the Springfield Heights School District had discriminated against Bobby and violated his right to privacy.

The Gonzalez family argued that the "drop your trousers" policy, which would result if these informal and discriminatory policies were allowed to continue, was ridiculous and unconstitutional. As Mr. Gonzalez argued in the press, "No one would know anything about biology unless they got down and peeked under the stall divider. What about the right to privacy?"

Despite protests from Principal McAfee, the Springfield Heights School District submitted a brief with the Supreme Court to find that the US Department of Education does possess the authority to dictate their bathroom policies (i.e., that they should not be compelled to allow transgender students to use the bathroom of their choice). The Springfield Heights superintendent was well aware that districts across the country were struggling with how to accommodate transgender students, so he desired to attempt to benefit from this confusion so as to appease his board. He was also well aware that some state legislatures had passed laws requiring bathroom usage to accord to biological sex. He desired to ride that wave.

The Springfield Heights board members decided that their policies require them to treat students based on the gender recorded at birth. They decided that they would sue the US Department of Education if they were found in violation of Title IX, which prohibits sex discrimination (including sexual harassment based upon gender identity and expression) in any education program or activity receiving federal funds.

TEACHING NOTES

Educators may have concerns about their own abilities to support their transgender students, or become hesitant because of personal feelings or from fear of negative reactions from the community. Similarly, families and caregivers are sometimes unsure of the support their child needs in school, or they may question the school's commitment to their child's well-being (Orr et al., 2015). This dynamic can create adversarial relationships between schools and families who must work together to meet students' needs. Finally, transgender students often struggle with fears of social rejection, bullying, and harassment from peers.

When transgender students are bullied or harassed, learning becomes less important than feeling safe in school and on the way home from school. Students who are bullied or face harassment are less likely to be successful in school (Kosciw, Greytak, Palmer, & Boesen, 2014). Harassment resulting from stereotyping and bias increases the risk of school absences (Kosciw et al., 2014), substance use, emotional distress, and suicide (Toomey, Ryan, Diaz, Card, & Russell, 2010). A school climate survey conducted by the Gay, Lesbian and Straight Education Network (GLSEN) found that students who experienced high levels of victimization based on gender expression face long-lasting negative effects on their mental health and life satisfaction as young adults (Toomey et al., 2010).

According to the National Transgender Discrimination Survey (Grant et al., 2011), 78% of the 6,450 respondents indicated that they had been harassed in school because of their transgender status. Thirty-five percent report being physically attacked, and 12% reported being sexually assaulted. Research indicates that clear school policies help to ensure that transgender students are protected (Grant et al., 2011).

Bullying, harassment, and discrimination against transgender students are covered by Title IX, a federal law, which prohibits sex discrimination in schools (National Center for Transgender Equality, 2016). The US Department of Education, through the Office for Civil Rights (OCR), enforces Title IX, which applies to all K–12 and post-secondary schools that accept federal funds.

Further, many states such as California, Colorado, Connecticut, New Jersey, Oregon, Vermont, and Washington have laws and school district policies that prohibit discrimination in schools based on gender identity or expression as well as sexual orientation. Other laws that offer protection for transgender and nonconforming students are as follows:

- The Equal Access Act requires all school-affiliated student organizations, such as a Gay–Straight Alliance, to be treated equally.

- The Family Educational Rights and Privacy Act protects personal information about students in school records, and in most circumstances prohibits the release of information without consent.
- The First Amendment of the US Constitution protects the right of students to free speech and freedom of expression, including of one's gender identity.

The student, family, and school must work together to establish the most positive scenario for the student—planning is essential. The plan may include professional development for students or faculty.

QUESTIONS FOR DISCUSSION

1. What is the underlying conflict/issue in this case? Please explain your answer.
2. What do you think about the differences in advocacy between Principal Romeo and Principal McAfee? Should principals go above and beyond the minimum legal standards in order to protect their students, or wait until the law "catches up?" Please justify your answer.
3. Do you think schools' Title IX obligations related to transgender students are clear? Has this been an issue in your school?
4. What is the evidence that the district is in violation of Title IX for subjecting Robert (Bobby) Gonzalez to different rules of behavior, and subjecting him to different treatment on the basis of sex?
5. District leaders may argue that by providing a student with a private area to change and use the restroom, they are respecting the rights of all students. How is this a violation of law?
6. All students deserve the opportunity to participate equally in school programs and activities—this is a basic civil right. The district can provide access to this student while also respecting all students' privacy. We encourage the district to comply with the law and resolve this case. What is the best solution to safeguard the rights of transgender students under Title IX and the rest of the student population's rights?
7. Would a principal in a state that passes a law prohibiting transgender students from using the bathroom that matches their gender identity be in violation of federal civil rights laws if they abide by that new state law? Explain your answer.
8. A student's transgender identity can easily be disclosed by student records. For example, a substitute teacher may call out names from an attendance sheet that has a student's legal name on it. Consider other records or documents that may cause distress. What solutions can you provide that would allow compliance with school

recordkeeping and reporting requirements and also safeguard a transgender student's privacy?

ADDITIONAL ACTIVITIES

1. Read the following policy guidance for protecting transgender students provided by GLSEN (2016): https://www.glsen.org/sites/default/files/Trans%20Model%20Policy.pdf. Examine your own school/district policy (provided one exists), and compare it to the guidance provided by GLSEN. What are the areas of need/weakness in your district policy? What changes would you make? If your school/district does not have a policy, create one based upon the guidance provided by GLSEN.

2. Review your school/district-wide dress code. Does the school have a specific dress code that is sex segregated? Would a transgender student be allowed to wear the clothing that corresponds to their gender identity, regardless of their assigned sex at birth, the gender designated on their birth certificate, or other legal documents? What changes would you make to the dress code?

3. Read the following two articles:

Barnes, R., & Balingit, M. (2016, August 29). School board, sued by transgender student, asks for Supreme Court review in bathroom case. *The Washington Post*. Retrieved from: https://www.washingtonpost.com/local/education/school-board-sued-by-transgender-student-asks-for-supreme-court-review-in-bathroom-case/2016/08/29/7c5c5fc4-6bc3-11e6-ba32-5a4bf5aad4fa_story.html

Rinehart, E. (2016, September 26). Federal judge rules in favor of transgender student in case against Highland school district. *The Columbus Dispatch*. Retrieved from: http://www.dispatch.com/content/stories/local/2016/09/26/judge-sides-with-transgender-student-in-case-against-highland.html

Discuss how these current events coincide with this case. In small groups, discuss your views on these two recent stories.

4. Examine the following three websites:

Lambda Legal. (n.d.). FAQ about identity documents. Retrieved from http://www.lambdalegal.org/know-your-rights/article/trans-identity-document-faq

Grant, J. M., Mottet, L. A., Tanis, J., Harrison, J., Herman, J. L., & Keisling, M. (2011). *Injustice at every turn: A report of the National Transgender Discrimination Survey*. National Center for Transgender Equality. Retrieved from http://www.thetaskforce.org/static_html/downloads/reports/reports/ntds_full.pdf

Lambda legal (n.d.). Transgender youth. Retrieved from http://www.lambdalegal.org/know-your-rights/article/youth-transgender. How would knowledge of this guidance have helped the actors in this case?

Work in small groups to gain understanding of the rights of and issues facing transgender students in our schools.

REFERENCES

Barnes, R., & Balingit, M. (2016, August 29). School board, sued by transgender student, asks for Supreme Court review in bathroom case. *The Washington Post*. Retrieved from https://www.washingtonpost.com/local/education/school-board-sued-by-transgender-student-asks-for-supreme-court-review-in-bathroom-case/2016/08/29/7c5c5fc4-6bc3-11e6-ba32-5a4bf5aad4fa_story.html

Blad, E. (2016, May 27). Transgender students and bathrooms: What should schools do? *Education Week*. Retrieved from http://www.edweek.org/ew/articles/2016/05/27/transgender-students-and-bathrooms-what-should-schools.html

Blad, E. (2015, November 11). School districts confront transgender student policies. *Education Week*. Retrieved from http://www.edweek.org/ew/articles/2015/11/11/school-districts-confront-transgender-student-policies.html

Blad, E. (2015, April 21). Duncan on transgender students: Ed. Dept. has 'Tried to be as clear as we can.' *Education Week*. Retrieved from http://blogs.edweek.org/edweek/rulesforengagement/2015/04/duncan_on_transgender_students_ed_dept_has_tried_to_be_as_clear_as_we_can.html

GLSEN. (2016, February). Model district policy on transgender and gender nonconforming students. National Center for Transgender Equality. Retrieved from https://www.glsen.org/sites/default/files/Trans%20Model%20Policy.pdf

Grant, J. M., Mottet, L. A., Tanis, J., Harrison, J., Herman, J. L., & Keisling, M. (2011). *Injustice at every turn: A report of the National Transgender Discrimination Survey*. National Center for Transgender Equality. Retrieved from http://www.thetaskforce.org/static_html/downloads/reports/reports/ntds_full.pdf

Kosciw, J. G., Greytak, E. A., Palmer, N. A., & Boesen, M. J. (2014). *The 2013 national school climate survey: The experiences of lesbian, gay, and transgender youth in our nation's schools*. New York: GLSEN.

Lambda Legal. (n.d.). FAQ about identity documents. Retrieved from http://www.lambdalegal.org/know-your-rights/article/trans-identity-document-faq

Lambda Legal. (n.d.). Transgender youth. Retrieved from http://www.lambdalegal.org/know-your-rights/article/youth-transgender

National Center for Transgender Equality. (2016, May). Transgender and gender nonconforming students: Your rights at school. Retrieved from http://www.transequality.org/sites/default/files/docs/kyr/KYR-Schools-May-2016.pdf

Orr, A., Baum, J., Brown, J., Gill, E., Kahn, E., & Salem, A. (2015). Schools in transition: A guide for supporting transgender students in K–12 schools. Retrieved from https://www.genderspectrum.org/staging/wp-content/uploads/2015/08/Schools-in-Transition-2015.pdf

Rinehart, E. (2016, September 26). Federal judge rules in favor of transgender student in case against Highland school district. *The Columbus Dispatch*. Retrieved from http://www.dispatch.com/content/stories/local/2016/09/26/judge-sides-with-transgender-student-in-case-against-highland.html

Toomey, R. B., Ryan, C., Diaz, R. M., Card, N. A., & Russell, S. T. (2010). Gender-nonconforming lesbian, gay, bisexual, and transgender youth: School victimization and young adult psychosocial adjustment. *Developmental Psychology, 46*(6), 1580–1589.

TWO

The Social Justice English Teacher

This case is written from the perspective of Ms. Jade, an English teacher who tries to protect her female students from the sexism and the sexual harassment that is so prevalent in this particular school culture. After several twists and turns, we find Ms. Jade at crossroads. Should she press for educational interventions that would benefit her students and the school, despite the fact that they may cause initial discomfort and resistance? Should she challenge the status quo that has been detrimental to the female student population? Or should she acquiesce to the status quo? Students are asked to associate the requirements of educational leaders under Title IX as well as the rights of students under the law as they relate to the case.

THE CASE

Ms. Jade is an eight-year veteran teacher, with undergraduate degrees in English Education and Women's Studies and two master's degrees in Women's Studies and Literature. She teaches at an alternative high school for students labeled "at-risk" for school failure. Her students have been removed from the two traditional high schools in her district for behavior issues: multiple suspensions, expulsions, and juvenile incarceration.

Throughout her day-to-day teaching Ms. Jade always tried to be inclusive; she was known for teaching for social justice. As an English teacher, she judiciously selected an equal number of novels written by women as by men. As her experience taught her, girls never question narratives written by and about boys or men; however, many boys would question the reading of narratives by and about girls and women. Her male students would make statements like, "This has nothing to do with me."

"This does not relate to my life." "Why do we have to read this?" Did she face this with any book? Yes, but the scenario was heightened when questions of gender were broached.

Ms. Jade brought up this topic in district meetings with other English teachers to share her struggles and elicit advice from veteran teachers. A teacher who had previously worked with this population informed her, "Yes, I have had that problem too. It is just easier to read books about boys or men. They are universal. You don't have to fight that fight. So that is what I do." Ms. Jade decided then that the resistance was probably normal, and that she was up for the fight. Such an unjust scenario set the tone for her teaching; Ms. Jade was unwilling to accept the status quo just because it was easier to do so.

Historically speaking, school cultures have traditionally been based upon the conventions of (cis gender) male privilege. For example, most high school traditions are based around male sports. Homecoming is associated with football, and "coming home" is often paired with male basketball games. It is only recently that female sports have cheerleaders at their games. In fact, in many school districts, the cheerleaders (female) cheer only for male sports. These traditions stem from a time when women were not thought capable of participating or excelling in athletics (pre-Title IX). The implications of these historical traditions are still with us.

Ms. Jade's classroom became the barometer for social justice. As stated, the culture of her school was steeped in male privilege. Ms. Jade saw it and was victim to it. The male students thought they could push boundaries, question her authority, and sexually harass her. The male students in the school viewed the females as objects, for they had learned throughout their life experiences that women were not to be respected. Ms. Jade understood that this was the case and was prepared to call her male students out on their overt sexism. However, she questioned whether the school was prepared to deal with the questioning of male unadulterated privilege. Was the administration prepared to fight the "battle of the sexes?"

In this particular school context, there was little parental involvement for a variety of reasons: some parents themselves had negative experiences with schools in their adolescence, so they avoided all contact with the school if they could help it; other parents were overtaxed in working multiple jobs so that the hours of the school's operations did not coincide with their flex time; and/or the norms of the school were anathema to their norms and values.

Ms. Jade tried to be vigilant in protecting her female students from the sexism and sexual harassment that was so prevalent in this particular school culture. When she would question the sexist practices of the male students or interrupt sexist jokes made during her class, she was accused by her male students of being sexist herself. Her male students could not fathom their male privilege being questioned. In fact, they never had.

Subsequently, male students questioned Ms. Jade's sexuality because of her questioning of male privilege. Ms. Jade never responded to questions or accusations about her sexuality. However, Ms. Jade was aware that because of her own white heterosexual privilege, she possessed the freedom to question the privilege of others. Had she not possessed this privilege, she questioned whether she would have been so bold, since, in her experience, sexual minorities and people of color did not possess the same degree of privilege and job security.

Despite the aforementioned concerns, at the forefront in Ms. Jade's mind was the small number of girls struggling within this majority male population: 10–20% when Ms. Jade first arrived.

Sexual harassment was rampant. Boys ruled, and girls grappled for a position; this phenomenon was made overt in the overall endorsement of the culture of degradation: the majority of the girls implicitly endorsed the harassment of other girls, for this meant that they were momentarily safe, a reprieve from the daily assessments of their appearance—the comparisons and ratings, the rumor mill about their desirability, their attractiveness. Rumors flew; sexual gossip was prevalent. Or, if they were accepted into an overt relationship with a boy, which was most often fleeting, they enjoyed momentary status within the culture, typically to be tossed aside, which inevitably involved their vulnerabilities being exposed.

Toxic teenage girl themes of pleasing males played out: the ultimate goal of the boyfriend—the ultimate in male approval—was the quintessential acceptance; this narrative of social validation of girl existence played out in the school. The girls had been groomed for it since birth; the school validated it, fairy tales and Disney movies prepared them for this, teenage romance novels reminded them of it. These ubiquitous narratives were a training for silence, for the go-along—for the selling out—for something that they could never truly be included in, for something in which they could never truly take part. And this Ms. Jade understood.

Other indignities the girls typically faced were unwanted touching and salacious propositions for sexual favors, all shrouded under the coverture of "prison silence"—because "snitches get stiches" in this school culture. Many girls would go to Ms. Jade in private and in tears, indicting their male counterparts in the litany of indignities they faced daily. Ms. Jade counseled the girls and implored them to report what they faced.

Although the teachers would report the sexual harassment that they witnessed, the perpetrators were savvy; most were smart enough to engage in such behaviors out of direct sight: on buses, by lockers, in hallways, etc. But those tears spoke to Ms. Jade (they were reminiscent of her own high school tears), as did the girls' complicity in the culture of silence—which was also her teenage complicity, or ignorance. Ms. Jade knew that her silence long ago signified a similar resignation. But as an adult, she knew that more could be done, and needed to be done.

Ms. Jade wanted the girls to know the value of women, and thus of themselves. But, initially, the girls were not buying. Although upset at the treatment they faced, they simultaneously communicated total resignation, a lack of control. Although many of her female students had come to her in tears, relaying their experiences with sexual harassment, they were also fearful of being in a room with other women who experienced the exact same problems.

Many of the girls who experienced sexual harassment also communicated the general sentiment that sexual harassment was "normal," something that girls and women have to face and about which nothing can be done. In other words, most of Ms. Jade's students possessed an external locus of control; they expressed the fact that they had little control over what happened in their lives—their life experiences had taught them this. One's perception of the degree of control one has over situations has much to do with sexual harassment (Jordan, Price, & Telljohann, 1998; Schwartz, 2000).

Moreover, Ms. Jade's students would take on a victim-blaming stance when learning of other students' experiences of sexual harassment; they did not have empathy for girls who experienced the same issue. This sentiment is not without precedent; according to De Judicibus and McCabe (2001), women who possess sexist beliefs ascribe more self-blame and other-woman blame for sexual harassment than do women who possess feminist beliefs. Many of Ms. Jade's students would express satisfaction when other girls were harassed because that meant that they were momentarily safe. In sum, her students did not see their collective problems as women; their lives and the lives of their forbearers had taught them otherwise.

Feminism had been transformational for Ms. Jade in her younger years because she realized the world did not have to be this way. She knew that there could be something more, that women could resist what the culture transmitted as reality, as normal. Having a background in feminism and women's studies, Ms. Jade did extensive research on the issues her female students faced. She examined the impact of women's studies courses. No research existed at that time on the impact of feminism on girls. She researched sexual harassment and curriculum for high school students and found many programs and materials for young people, but no intervention studies analyzing the impact of said programs existed.

Ms. Jade created her own program, a semester-long English elective, in an effort to raise awareness in the minds of the girls that they shared a common problem and that they could in fact possess a sense of control over their own lives—that they were not at the whim of the males around them.

On that first day of class, twenty-two girls were in the room. The maximum was twenty in a classroom because of the "at-risk" label, and because of the student disengagement with school. Despite these pedagogical difficulties, on the first day of class Ms. Jade's students were rapt; they listened to her without a negative comment, and they seemed genuinely interested as she reviewed the syllabus. They would be studying the writings of famous women, learning about women in history, and learning about sexual harassment: its causes, strategies for combating it, etc. The students would participate in both self-defense and assertiveness training.

Soon after, the counselor, Ms. Waze, came in to assess the students on their knowledge and experience with sexual harassment and administered a measure of locus of control, or a measure of the degree to which students felt they had control over their lives. Ms. Jade wanted to investigate whether this level would change as a result of the course. The first day went off without a hitch. Ms. Jade had high hopes for a successful class, and she hoped that this intervention would assist in changing a toxic school culture. But she was ill prepared for what happened next.

The very next day, Ms. Jade learned that many of her students were signing up to speak to Ms. Waze in order to transfer out of her class. Ms. Waze found some tearful responses to the surveys she administered for Ms. Jade; however, she never shared this with Ms. Jade. Ms. Waze felt that the girls were not emotionally prepared to answer questions about the harassment they faced. Instead, they responded to the surveys with anger and dissention, and this, in turn, angered Ms. Waze.

When Ms. Jade learned from several students that they desired to drop her class, she was shocked. In her estimation, nothing had even happened yet. She wondered what could have occurred in twenty-four hours of which she was not aware, causing many of the girls to want to drop a course that was specifically designed for them. Ms. Jade consulted Ms. Waze, who informed Ms. Jade that she would have to personally convince all of the girls to stay in the course; if she was not able to do so, Ms. Waze would transfer them to other classes. Despite Ms. Jade's inquiries, Ms. Waze would not reveal why the girls desired to drop Ms. Jade's course.

Ms. Jade did eventually convince all the girls to remain in the course. The reasons the girls provided to Ms. Jade, when she asked them why they desired to drop the course, included the following: "All my friends are guys," "You can't trust girls—they talk too much stuff," and "There's too many girls in here. It's not safe." Ms. Jade immediately realized that she needed to interrupt these three sentiments by gaining wisdom through and with the collective.

By presenting factual information about sexual harassment and its impact, effects, and consequences for victims, Ms. Jade hoped to enable students to rethink their positions, to ultimately share their stories, as difficult as that was, which required a building of trust among the other female students in the course, and finally finding strength as a collective.

Connolly et al. (2015) argue that between 59% and 90% of urban students in grades 6–9 reported experiencing at least one incident of sexual harassment. Such experiences result in school adjustment issues and issues of emotional distress such as depression, anxiety, and lowered self-esteem, and can negatively impact school performance and achievement (Connolly et al., 2015). Ms. Jade's hope was for a successful intervention that involved peer support and interaction. According to Connolly et al. (2015), "Peers have a substantial influence on aggressive behavior" (p. 407). Ms. Jade envisioned girls talking back to the sexual aggression they faced, as peers can mitigate social norms (Connolly et al., 2015).

Ms. Jade realized that she had to work with her students to undo many misperceptions that they held not only about feminism but also about each other. She also had to emphasize how they could gain strength through bonds with other women; prior to the course they overwhelmingly held only negative perceptions about the prospect of creating lasting friendships with other girls, whom they had previously seen only as competition for male attention. Friendships were beginning to be made, and trust was being built within the class. At that point, Ms. Jade felt that she could then go on to unpack the difficult experiences that the girls faced outside of the classroom.

Ms. Jade also realized that it was important for her to recognize her own privilege, as the teacher and as a white woman. She subsequently moved herself to the side so students could ultimately lead the class. For in order for students to be willing to take classroom risks, teachers must first do so themselves (hooks, 1994; Ochoa & Pershing, 2011). Ms. Jade exposed herself by sharing her own stories of vulnerability and experiences with sexual harassment. Her students were transfixed, as in, "If it could happen to her, why not me?"

Girls would rush into class, not at first but eventually, to share a microaggression that they had faced that day, and students would stay long after the bell had rung to dismiss class—necessitating the banging on the door of male students who were actually eager to get in to catch a glimpse of what was occurring. The boys in the school were beginning to get an inkling of the cultural change within the school, and many were not happy. Some would try to listen at the door or knock during class, pretending they needed something. But the girls were adamant that they should be excluded, for they were doing important work that involved determining how to dismantle the toxic culture of which they were a part. Class time became devoted to interrogating ideas and theories, challenging opinions, bridging content to lived experiences, and critiquing said experiences.

Providing accurate information about sexual harassment, its causes, its prevalence, and its effect on victims had profound positive effects on Ms. Jade's students; the information also made them angry, but they experienced this anger together. About halfway through the semester, the students led a protest about the unfair dress code and wore boxers on the outside of their pants. They were upset that boys received no consequences for their underwear showing when they sagged their pants; they were simply told to pull their pants up, while girls were told to put on a sweatshirt (the school housed many) if they wore a shirt with spaghetti straps. This changing of dress, in adding a sweatshirt, necessitated girls missing time away from class to go down to the main office in the school to obtain a sweatshirt when directed to do so by school staff. The girls realized that this was an inequitable practice—and one not experienced by the boys in the school. Ms. Jade had hoped that the girls would have protested something a bit more unfair, such as the sexual harassment they faced, but they wanted to stand up to the administration, so Ms. Jade did not attempt to stop them—this was a step in the right direction in her estimation: the girls working together toward a common goal.

Ms. Jade's students were already experiencing severe trauma in their school because of sexual harassment. When the "dangerous learning" began, the female students caused "a bit of a ruckus" in the main office and the counseling office by eventually reporting sexual harassment—in droves. Instead of the principal and the counselor being pleased that the girls were finding the courage to address these issues in a formal manner, they were upset—and they directed their frustration at Ms. Jade. Ms. Waze, in particular, said to Ms. Jade, "You are making my job harder." Ms. Jade was shocked that Ms. Waze would be angry that the girls were reporting sexual harassment in a proactive manner simply because it made her busier. She got angry too, but said nothing. She felt she had bigger battles to fight.

Many male students were angry with Ms. Jade at all points in time, but particularly during her teaching of the women's studies course. One male student came to her and stated, "What are you doing with this women's studies class? Now all the girls are feminists; they don't let us get away with nothing. They don't play. They think they can do anything, even be a sumo wrestler." Change was occurring, and the changes were reverberating outside of the four protective classroom walls.

Some of the comments that the female students made about the class included the following:

> *At the beginning I didn't like it; I guess I was really negative towards girls in general before the class. But, as it progressed I really liked it and it really opened my eyes a lot and it became my favorite class. I realized it wasn't about whining. You really explained a lot about how sexual harassment is wrong and just there are so many things that have opened my eyes. From the first week, I totally did a 180 on my opinion of the class. You do a really good job explaining why things are degrading toward women or why it was wrong and it made me change and I was all ears. I was ready to listen and see what you had to say.*—Vicky

> *The stuff that we learned I would tell my mom and my sister, like about rape and all that self-defense, I would go home and teach my sister like all the stuff that we did. Before I really didn't trust females. Females need each other; they just don't realize it.*—Alexandra

> *At first I thought it was going to be really bad because it was all girls and girls don't get along very well. But at the end everyone was talking about their experiences so it was actually kind of cool. At the end of the semester I really liked the class. I didn't want it to end. It was fun and different.*—Cynthia[1]

Although the girls entered the class as adversaries, they left as friends, and Ms. Jade considered that a win. Although she experienced resistance from most of her students at one time or another, she worked through that, and the payoffs were enormous. The girls in Ms. Jade's class ultimately bonded to stand up against their harassers in the school. They reported incidents that they experienced, but they also stood up for themselves and for each other in classrooms and hallways when they or their peers experienced sexist comments, degrading remarks, or sexual propositions or leers. They took their learning beyond the classroom and into an imagined future that they created: a school that would not tolerate the harassment of females.

One of the most important lessons Ms. Jade learned from her work was not to shy away from what seems impossible or dangerous, for this is the work that is the most important; in fact, it is the most crucial work one can do. However, she was shocked when the counselor, Ms. Waze, attempted to block her attempts to teach the course in the future.

TEACHING NOTES

Title IX originated as an affirmative thirty-seven-word law, passed in 1972, and states that:

> No person in the United States shall, on the basis of sex, be excluded from participation in, be denied the benefit of, or be subjected to discrimination under any education program or activity receiving federal financial assistance (20 U.S.C. §1681).

It was ostensibly written to prevent sex discrimination in the hiring of female faculty and admission of female students to higher education. Since then, through case law and policy proscriptions, the law has expanded to cover a variety of issues dealing with sex discrimination in its various forms: Title IX protects students of all genders and sexual orientations from sex discrimination in schools.

Students in federally funded institutions, public and private schools, colleges and universities, have a right to an education free from discrimination on the basis of sex, including equitable access to all academic programs, activities, athletics, course offerings, admissions, recruitment, and scholarships, and free from harassment (including assault) based upon sex, gender, gender identity and expression, and sexual orientation. Title IX also protects students from discrimination in academic and non-academic activities because of pregnancy, birth, miscarriage, and abortion. Title IX also protects faculty, staff, and whistleblowers from sexual harassment, sex discrimination, and retaliation.

An educational leader must have knowledge of policies, laws, and regulations enacted by local, state, and federal authorities and possess the capability to respond to and influence the context of schooling (Chouhoud & Zirkel, 2008; Cooper, Fusarelli, & Randall, 2004; Hoy & Miskel, 2004; Leithwood, 2009). In this frame of reference, leaders must stay well informed about the legal rights of teachers and students and aware of current legal issues and their potential impact on schools (Camberon, McCarthy, & Thomas, 2004; Stefkovich, 2006).

Principals play a crucial role in creating school environments that are responsive to heterogeneous student populations and inclusive and responsive to the diverse needs of all students. In a series of articles on schools where traditionally marginalized students thrived, Theoharis (2007, 2008a, 2008b, 2009, 2010) found that principals' advocacy for children was informed by their analyses and realization of the complex causes of marginalization. Theoharis (2010) and other researchers (Riester, Pursch, & Skrla, 2002; Skrla, Scheurich, Garcia, & Nolly, 2004) propose that concern for equity enticed principals to create opportunities for discussions of differences that challenged resistance and barriers to equity-oriented reforms (Shields, 2004; Theoharis, 2008a).

To work for social justice is to take a proactive stance on issues of student marginalization, work to improve the social opportunities of students, and positively influence the learning environment to improve student engagement and academic achievement (McKenzie et al., 2008; Theoharis, 2007; Klingner et al., 2005; Riehl, 2000).

QUESTIONS FOR DISCUSSION

The following questions were written to initiate classroom discussion and help current and future leadership practitioners raise awareness of their beliefs, values, and ethical foundation. The issues of social justice and legal responsibilities that come with the power of leadership are examined.

1. What is the major conflict in this case? Explain your answer.
2. Do you find it ironic that two women, Ms. Jade and Ms. Waze, are embroiled in an unacknowledged conflict, despite the fact that Ms. Jade is committed to feminist principles? Explain. Why do you think these two women are in conflict?

3. Why do you think Ms. Waze is troubled by the class, Ms. Jade, and the heightened reporting of sexual harassment on the part of the students?
4. Does Ms. Jade's commitment to feminism conflict with her pressing students to remain in the class and work through their initial resistance? Explain.
5. The principal is curiously absent in this case. What should the role of the administration be in this case?
6. Describe in detail the requirements of educational leaders under Title IX as well as the rights of students under the law.
7. Describe several strategies you would employ in an attempt to effect a change in current school policy to address school requirements under Title IX.
8. What is the role of a culturally responsive educational leader or a teacher committed to social justice?
9. Should Ms. Jade continue in her endeavor despite staff resistance?
10. Should a similar intervention be created for the males in the school?
11. Should Ms. Jade press for educational interventions that would benefit her students and the school in general, despite the fact that they may cause initial discomfort and resistance?
12. Should Ms. Jade challenge the status quo that has been detrimental to the female student population of the school? Or should she acquiesce to the status quo because it is easier? What are the moral implications of these choices?
13. What is the role of the social justice educator? Is this philosophy in line with national and state expectations of teachers?
14. What are the potential negative implications that Ms. Jade may face because of her work? Does she have recourse in the face of such negative implications?

ADDITIONAL ACTIVITIES

1. As a follow-up to classroom discussion, have students read one of the Dear Colleague Letters on harassment and bullying (Ali, 2010) or sexual violence (Ali, 2011): http://www2.ed.gov/about/offices/list/ocr/letters/colleague-201010.html
2. http://www2.ed.gov/about/offices/list/ocr/letters/colleague-201104.pdf
3. Ask students to write a reaction paper. Have students begin with a summary that demonstrates their understanding of the opinion, main ideas, and supporting ideas in the letters. Then provide an analysis of the letter: What are the strengths and weaknesses of the piece? Is the piece convincing? Why or why not, specifically? Is it

well-researched? Why or why not? Does the piece overlook or leave out anything important? What? Have students provide their reactions: How do you react to the piece on a personal level? How does the piece relate to your experience?

4. Have students work in small groups to discuss how to dismantle the sexual harassment that was so prevalent in this school. What are the requirements under Title IX? Are students' First and Fourteenth Amendment rights being violated? Describe.

REFERENCES

Ali, R. (2010, October 26). Dear colleague letter: Harassment and bullying. US Department of Education, Office for Civil Rights. Retrieved from http://www2.ed.gov/about/offices/list/ocr/letters/colleague-201010.html

Ali, R. (2011, April 4). Dear colleague letter: Sexual violence. US Department of Education, Office for Civil Rights. Retrieved from http://www2.ed.gov/about/offices/list/ocr/letters/colleague-201104.pdf

Camberon, N. H., McCarthy, M. M., & Thomas, S. B. (2004). *School law: Teachers' and students' rights*. Boston, MA: Pearson, Allyn & Bacon.

Chouhoud, Y., & Zirkel, P. (2008). The Goss progeny: An empirical analysis. *San Diego Law Review, 45*(2), 353–382.

Connolly, J., Josephson, W., Schnoll, J., Simkins-Strong, E., Pepler, D., MacPherson, A., Weiser, J., Moran, M., & Jiang, D. (2015). Evaluation of a youth-led program for preventing bullying, sexual harassment, and dating aggression in middle schools. *Journal of Early Adolescence, 35*(3), 403.

Cooper, B. S., Fusarelli, L. D., & Randall, E. V. (2004). *Better policies, better schools: Theories and applications*. Boston, MA: Allyn and Bacon.

De Judicibus, M., & McCabe, M. P. (2001). Blaming the target of sexual harassment: Impact of gender role, sexist attitudes, and work role. *Sex Roles, 44*(7/8), 401–417.

hooks, b. (1994). *Teaching to transgress: Education as the practice of freedom*. New York, NY: Routledge.

Hoy, W. K., & Miskel, C. G. (2004). *Educational administration: Theory, research and practice*. New York, NY: McGraw-Hill.

Jordan, T. R., Price, J. H., & Telljohann, S. K. (1998). Junior high school students' perceptions regarding nonconsensual sexual behavior. *The Journal of School Health, 68*(7), 289–296.

Klingner, J., Artiles, A. J., Kozleski, E., Harry, B., Zion, S., Tate, W, Durán, G. Z., & Riley, D. (2005). Addressing the disproportionate representation of culturally and linguistically diverse students in special education through culturally responsive educational systems. *Education Policy Analysis Archives, 13*(38). Retrieved from http://epaa.asu.edu/ojs/article/view/143

Leithwood, K., & Sun, J. P. (2009). Transformational school leadership effects on schools, teachers, and students. In W. K. Hoy & M. DiPaola (Eds.), *Studies in school improvement: A volume in research and theory in educational administration* (pp. 1–22). Charlotte, NC: Information Age Publishing.

Ochoa, A., & Pershing, L. (2011). Team teaching with undergraduate students: Feminist pedagogy in a peer education project. *Feminist Teacher, 22*(1), 23–42.

McKenzie, K. B., Christman, D. E., Hernandez, F., Fierro, E., Capper, C., & Dantley, M. (2008). From the field: A proposal for education leaders for social justice. *Educational Administration Quarterly, 40*(5), 601–632.

Riehl, C. J. (2000). The principal's role in creating inclusive schools for diverse students: A review of normative, empirical, and critical literature on the practice of educational administration. *Review of Educational Research, 70*(1), 55–81.

Riester, A. F., Pursch, V., & Skrla, L. (2002). Principals for social justice: Leaders of school success for children from low-income homes. *Journal of School Leadership, 12*(3), 281–304.

Schwartz, W. (2000). *Preventing student sexual harassment* (Report No. EDO-UD-00-9). Washington, DC: Office of Educational Research and Improvement. (ERIC Document Reproduction Service No. ED448248).

Shields, C. M. (2004). Dialogic leadership for social justice: Overcoming pathologies of silence. *Educational Administration Quarterly, 40* (1), 111–134.

Skrla, L., Scheurich, J. J., Garcia, J., & Nolly, G. (2004). Equity audits: A practical leadership tool for developing equitable and excellent schools. *Educational Administration Quarterly, 40*(1), 135–163.

Stefkovich, J. A. (2006). *Best interests of the students: Applying ethical constructs to legal cases in education.* Mahwah, NJ: Lawrence Erlbaum Associates, Inc.

Telljohann, S. K., Price, J. H., Summers, J., Everett, S. A., & Casler, S. (1995). High school students' perceptions of nonconsensual sexual activity. *Journal of School Health, 65*(3), 107–112.

Theoharis, G. (2007). Social justice educational leaders and resistance: Toward a theory of social justice leadership. *Educational Administration Quarterly, 43*(2), 221–251.

Theoharis, G. (2008a). "At every turn": The resistance public school principals face in their pursuit of equity and justice. *Journal of School Leadership, 18*(3), 303–343.

Theoharis, G. (2008b). Woven in deeply: Identity and leadership of urban social justice principals. *Education and Urban Society, 41*(1), 3–25.

Theoharis, G. (2009). *The leadership our children deserve: Seven keys to equity, social justice, and school reform.* New York: Teachers College Press.

Theoharis, G. (2010). Disrupting injustice: Principals narrate the strategies they use to improve their schools and advance social justice. *Teachers College Record, 112*(1), 331–373.

NOTE

1. All quotations from Martin, J. L., Nickels, A., & Grier, M. L. S. (Eds.). (In press). *Feminist pedagogy, practice, and activism: Improving lives for girls and women.* New York, NY: Routledge.

THREE

Bus 57: LGBTQ+ Hate Crime, or an Ill-Fated Prank?

Intimidation, bullying, and harassment that take place in schools greatly impact lesbian, gay, bisexual, transgender, and queer (LGBTQ) youth. LGBTQ students who experience school-based discrimination and harassment experience more negative academic outcomes and psychological struggles than their non-LGBTQ peers (Martin & Beese, 2016).

The Gay, Lesbian and Straight Education Network (GLSEN) conducted the National School Climate Survey in 2013 and identified schools as hostile environments for LGBTQ students, the majority of whom experience sexual harassment and discrimination at school because they do not conform to traditional gender roles. Although the rates of school-based discrimination and harassment for LGBTQ students have improved over the years, the overall school climate remains hostile for many (Martin & Beese, 2016).

This case is based on real incidents occurring in Oakland, California, in the fall of 2013. The case was adapted to occur within a school setting, and the schools and district noted within are entirely contrived for the purposes of this case. However, the original bus number, 57, was retained to pay homage to the real victims.

Oakland is considered to be one of the most diverse cities in the United States. In fact, many residents pride themselves on multiculturalism and their tolerance for diversity. However, despite this sense of pride, there is much disparity: there are very wealthy areas with effective schools, low crime rates, and scenic views; on the other hand, East Oakland is rife with poverty, crime, and violence (Slater, 2015).

THE CASE

The Oak Ridge School District, covering a portion of Oakland proper and all of East Oakland, comprises many schools, including two large traditional high schools and two new high schools, opened within the last year: a smaller alternative school for students removed from the traditional schools for truancy, multiple suspensions, and academic distress, and an intervention school. The latter is a federally funded program to assist juveniles who previously have been adjudicated in an attempt at rehabilitation and to prevent continued recidivism.

Statistical findings for the state include the following: Youth ages ten to nineteen comprise 14.5% of the total residents in the state with a total of 15.4% of youth living in poverty. Out of the families that are living below the poverty level, almost 53% are single-female-parent households. Out of the households below the poverty level who have had a child in the last twelve months, 40.1% of those parents are widowed, divorced, or never married, with 46.9% of children raised by a grandparent.

The Alternative School

The Alternative School currently educates 138 students, providing academic and treatment services to nonadjudicated students who struggle academically or socially, behaviorally challenged students, and other at-risk youth ages fourteen to eighteen within the district. The daily operational programing of the school is designed with a therapeutic emphasis and is driven by a personalized Individual Service Plan (ISP) designed to encompass the specific mental, medical, and academic needs of each student.

The development of the ISP is the responsibility of the ISP team, made up of the parent, at least one of the student's general education teachers, at least one of the student's special education teachers, a school district representative, and in some cases a school psychologist. The team is responsible for the ongoing review and revision of the plan. The ISP is developed in consultation with the parents or caregivers of the student.

In order to offer services, the school must maintain state licensure and certification, which are governed through legislative approval, granted through application with the state, and monitored by a state licensing agent. Caseworkers are assigned from the Department of Jobs and Family Services (DJFS) to oversee student placement and to ensure that all services are compliant with the student's ISP.

The Intervention School

The Intervention School provides academic and social services to adjudicated offenders, per district policy. The daily operational programing of the school is designed with an emphasis on academics, job preparation, and service to the community, and maintains a restorative justice discipline policy model. For example, if a student is sanctioned for a behavioral infraction, such as a physical conflict with another student, the students are required to sit together and resolve the conflict, along with staff and expert community members, in order to take responsibility for their part in the conflict, make apologies if necessary, work through positive conflict resolutions strategies, and effectively make the situation right.

All staff and community members involved in the restorative justice model are required to be trained in nonviolent conflict resolution and the restorative justice model in general. This year, the administration is piloting a program in which a select group of students will be trained in this model so that a peer component can be added.

Additionally, students are often assigned a probation officer who acts as a legal representative of the court and subsequent joint decision maker for the county.

School Reform

State school reform officials appointed Dr. Michael O'Donnell, superintendent, to oversee the low-performing schools in the Oak Ridge School District. He was hired two years previously when the district was found to be in "academic distress" by the state board of education. When a district fails to make adequate yearly progress for four or more years, it is placed in Academic Emergency and a state commission becomes the governing board. O'Donnell was given full control over every district decision, and had the authority to limit the rights and roles of the board of education.

O'Donnell was given full authority over personnel and curriculum, with the expectation for him to show rapid turnaround in the schools, with student achievement reports due to the state office every eight weeks. It was O'Donnell's idea to create the two new high schools, and to revise the missions and curricula of the two traditional high schools: one became a performing arts school, the other, a STEM (science, technology, engineering, and math) school.

After the "incident" on Bus 57 (described in the following section), a reporter from a prestigious national newspaper, Mei Chen, traveled to Oakland to investigate. Chen found that the two new schools were disproportionately populated with Black and Brown students when compared to the traditional two high schools in the district.

Additionally, she learned that there had been racial unrest and issues with bullying within the schools. Students informed her that some of the unrest was caused because students from different schools rode the same buses; for although they attended different schools, they lived in the same neighborhoods or in neighboring areas. Chen could find no evidence of diversity training for students or staff, or any interventions devised by O'Donnell. Additionally, after interviewing the actors in this case, Chen also interviewed several teachers and students and found little commitment to diversity within the curriculum, and no attention to multicultural education, despite a diverse student population in terms of race, class, culture, and sexuality.

The Incident on Bus 57

At the end of a long week, a mix of students from the performing arts school and alternative school in the Oak Ridge School District rode Bus 57 home. These two schools were in close proximity to one another. Stacy Stern, a senior who self-identified as "agender" (neither female nor male), wore a T-shirt and a skirt, and dozed as the bus made its various stops.

As Stacy slept, three teen boys watched and snickered nearby. One boy, Leon, flicked a disposable lighter. Before anyone could think, Stacy's gauzy skirt went up in flames. Stacy stood and screamed, and two bystanders pushed Stacy to the ground and beat out the flames. The bus driver stopped the bus and called 911. The ambulance took Stacy to the nearby burn unit, where Stacy would spend nearly a month recovering from second- and third-degree burns over much of both legs—thighs to calves.

Leon, a sixteen-year-old African American male resident of East Oakland, was arrested the next day. There was much contention over whether Leon should be tried as an adult, but ultimately, he was charged with two felonies, both of which included a hate-crime clause. If convicted, Leon was faced with potentially serving life in prison.

Background

Stacy attended the performing arts school. Stacy was interested in art and exploring various aspects of gender identity and expression. Stacy also was attracted to the concept of "genderqueer," which to Stacy meant to question the concept of gender itself. Stacy self-identified as genderqueer because of its perceived gender neutrality, and preferred the pronoun *they* or the gender-neutral pronoun *xe*.

Stacy's parents were aware of "trans kids" after watching a *20/20* special when Stacy was young. Because of Stacy's nontraditional gender expression, they were worried that Stacy would experience isolation and bullying in school. Thus, they opted to send Stacy to small alternative schools: at first a Montessori school from kindergarten to middle school, and later to the performing arts high school. Although she was a shy and introverted child, Stacy's parents were surprised at how publicly Stacy eventually expressed gender in high school. Through Stacy's gender expression, they saw a profound confidence in their child that they had never previously witnessed.

Although supportive, Stacy's parents were worried about the potential violence that Stacy might encounter for openly transgressing gender norms. However, Stacy's parents only ever heard of or personally witnessed one negative comment about their child's gender presentation. While collectively riding public transportation, an elderly man looked at Stacy with a confused expression and then loudly proclaimed, "You're a boy in a skirt!"

Leon attended the alternative school in East Oakland for students labeled "at-risk" for school failure, and for those who school officials feared would drop out. Leon was a junior at the alternative school, his third school in three years. The alternative school possessed one of the worst reputations of all the schools in the district, second only to the intervention high school. There were many troubled youths at the alternative school who had experienced traumatic events in their lives, such as gangs and domestic violence, drug-related problems, and poverty.

Leon lived with his mother, Julia; her second husband, Norman; a toddler brother; and three cousins whom his mother had raised since the death of her sister during the birth of her third child.

Julia was aware that Leon had some developmental delays. He began walking and talking later than his peers, and she was worried that he struggled with reading and showed little interest in school. Although his elementary school recommended retention several times through the years, Julia felt that Leon should remain with his peers. Although he was academically delayed, Leon's teachers thought he interacted well socially. However, school counselors worried that the violence within the community left Leon emotionally stunted. For example, two of Leon's best friends during his elementary years were killed separately by stray bullets while walking home from school. The perpetrators were never found. Around this time, Leon expressed to his mother that he was afraid to attend school. Against his mother's express wishes, Leon began walking to a friend's house or to a local park to avoid school. Despite interventions from his parents and teachers, truancy was a problem that would persist throughout Leon's life.

Leon's mother agreed to send him to the alternative school because she was assured that it would provide him with special programming. The policy for student admittance at the alternative school was intentionally vague. Parents who felt their children required special attention could apply for admittance, but the majority of student attendees came straight to the alternative school from behavioral dismissal from the two traditional schools in the district. Leon's mother hoped that he would not only graduate, but also attend college and find a promising career.

According to Slater (2015), "An investigation by the *San Francisco Chronicle* found that of some 600 black male students who start at Oakland high schools as freshmen each year, only about 300 end up graduating and fewer than 100 graduate with the requirements needed to attend a California state college or university. The odds of landing in the back of a police cruiser, on the other hand, are much better. African American boys make up less than 30 percent of Oakland's under-age population but account for nearly 75 percent of all juvenile arrests. And each year, dozens of black men and boys are murdered within the city limits."

Leon had seen the violence that plagued his community from a young age, losing many friends and family members to gun violence. But his mother thought the alternative school could save him. They had summer internships, where Leon excelled, his supervisors reporting his high level of effort. However, when the academic year began, Leon struggled. When he realized he was falling behind his peers, Leon began skipping class. When questioned by the counselor and truancy officer, Mr. Simkins, Leon readily agreed to return to school.

Mr. Simkins, a lifelong resident of East Oakland, was a self-proclaimed "reformed troubled youth." Although he came from a stable home, Mr. Simkins was attracted to the youth gangs of the 1970s. Although at first merely "hanging out" and trying to gain acceptance from older peers, he was initiated into a gang after the murder of his father by police who mistook him for a gang leader in a traffic stop. Mr. Simkins acknowledges that he did not channel his anger in the most productive way. Charged for his initiation crime as a juvenile, which he never discussed, he spent several years in a lock-up facility where he met a man who would change his life: Mr. Smith. Mr. Simkins never revealed the true identity of Mr. Smith, just that he had counseled him and helped him to complete his high school education and get into college. When Mr. Simkins was released from the juvenile facility, he vowed that he would for the rest of his life help the youth of East Oakland.

Mr. Simkins, surprised by Leon's amiable demeanor, invited him to be a part of a special program for chronically truant students at the intervention school. Although Mr. Simkins did not know at that time whether Leon would qualify, he knew that he wanted this student in his program, as he saw something in Leon that he saw in his own teenage self: he felt Leon would be a positive influence on other students, as students did not readily volunteer to be a part of such a strict program. Mr. Simkins remembered Leon stating, "I want to be successful. I am just not sure how to do that. If you are offering help, I will take it."

Leon's program included additional counseling and more accountability. If students in the program missed more than ten days in a semester, they were dismissed from the program and sent back to the traditional alternative program sans the additional counseling and other supports, or worse: some attendees of this special program within the intervention high school, depending upon their personal situation, often ended up in juvenile detention centers.

Leon used the office of Mr. Simkins daily. Although Mr. Simkins had many duties around the district, he tried to spend most of his time where he perceived the greatest need existed. For Mr. Simkins, that was at the intervention school. So committed was he, he gave students his cell phone number in case he was not on school grounds when students were in crisis. Leon would visit Mr. Simkins's office before and after school and in between classes. If Mr. Simkins was not there, Leon would leave him notes. Leon offered help and hugs to other students when needed or requested and asked Mr. Simkins to call his mother often to provide her with updates, or suggestions on what she could do at home to better help him succeed. His only desire was to graduate and to make his mother proud.

However, Leon was not without his issues. He was having trouble with his coursework. He and his mother requested that he be tested for special education.

During this time, Leon was faced with further violence. A neighborhood friend was killed, and soon after, Leon and his cousin were robbed at gunpoint. Although Leon never told anyone, he considered one of the assailants a friend. Leon was torn between survival and homework. Betrayed and vulnerable, he knew not whom to trust—except for his mother and Mr. Simkins.

Seemingly counterintuitive, this sense of betrayal caused him to turn away from his one safe place: school. Leon felt vulnerable anywhere he went. In his mind, his safest place was alone in his bedroom, so he again began skipping. After being absent from school for one week, and when he could no longer dodge the multiple daily calls from Mr. Simkins, Leon returned to school to receive welcomes and congratulations from fellow students and teachers. He felt proud, and even happier when he saw his cousin waiting for him outside of the school doors. His cousin George, a student at the STEM school, entered Bus 57 to travel home with Leon.

The Video and Arrest

The bus camera video depicts Leon and his cousin George entering the bus, where they meet another seeming acquaintance, who is later identified as Joe. Joe was an older boy that both Leon and George knew from the neighborhood. Neither knew Joe very well, but both respected him as possessing great personal power and confidence.

Soon into the bus ride, Joe visibly points toward the sleeping Stacy and says something inaudible. Joe then passes a lighter to Leon.

Leon later reveals to authorities that "the incident" was meant to be a prank, and that he had absolutely no intention of harming Stacy.

The video reveals Leon flicking the lighter several times before the clothing worn by Stacy actually ignites. Leon's two cohorts appear to egg him on, although the dialogue is inaudible. The video shows the three laughing between lighter flicks.

When the fire starts, George is seen standing and yelling for the bus driver to stop the bus. The three boys exit from the rear emergency door, with Leon leading the way, as Stacy's skirt disintegrates in flames.

The next day, Leon was alone in the office of Mr. Simkins, waiting for him to arrive, when he was arrested. Mr. Simkins walked into his office to meet Leon in handcuffs. "I tried to call you," Leon stated. Nothing seemed to register with Leon. He neither appeared shaken by the events nor seemed to understand what was about to happen to him.

At the police station, two officers questioned Leon. They were friendly, providing him with lunch. They asked him questions about his life, about friends, school, and family. Leon admitted to being on Bus 57 and witnessing a "man's skirt catch fire."

The officers then asked Leon what he thought about men who wear skirts. Leon indicated that although he is homophobic, he does not hate gay people. After more probing from the officers, Leon stated, "They don't need to make it known to everyone that they are 'like that.'"

The officers repeatedly asked Leon to recall the events that occurred on the bus, and ultimately revealed that they possessed a tape of Leon's actions on Bus 57 and that they knew he had started the fire that ignited Stacy's skirt. They then asked Leon to tell them why he did it.

"I was just being stupid," Leon responded in almost a whisper. "I thought it was a joke. I didn't think anyone would get hurt."

Eventually, Leon was charged with assault with intent to cause great bodily injury, a felony, and a hate-crime clause that could potentially add an additional one to three years to his sentence. If convicted, Leon would face a maximum sentence of life in prison.

Leon would not have faced such a punishment were he charged as a juvenile. Joe, who handed Leon the lighter, was not interviewed, arrested, or charged.

Soon after the arrest and of his own accord, Leon wrote Stacy, his victim, a letter entitled "Dear Victim." Leon apologized to Stacy for his actions and for the pain he had caused. He asked for forgiveness and signed the letter, "Love Leon."

Two days later, Leon wrote a second letter to Stacy, this time even more contrite, and asked to meet face to face so that he could apologize in person. Leon then detailed the allegations against him, conceding all but the hate crime charges. Although he had expressed homophobic statements in the past, he indicated in his letter that he too had faced hurtful treatment in his life, both physical and mental, and expressed sorrow at perpetrating that same hurt upon another individual.

Leon's letters were riddled with misspellings and errors in grammar indicating his level of literacy and his continued need for education.

The prosecutor in the case obtained the letters because they contained admissions of guilt. Stacy did not receive the letters for more than a year after Leon originally penned them.

Stacy's Recovery

Stacy arrived home from the hospital, almost one month after the attack, to a crowded street of well-wishers. Marches had occurred daily along the Bus 57 route since the attack, replete with rainbow flags and representation from local and national LGBTQ+ organizations. Stacy was met with cards and gifts from a national audience, including a medical fund to help with rehabilitation costs upwards of $30,000. All of the high schools in the district sponsored "skirt-wearing days" and at George's school, the football team sported shirts with Stacy's name along with the slogan "no hate" during game play. The alternative and intervention schools did not offer organized sports of any kind.

Stacy's parents, later interviewed, indicated that they desired that Leon be tried as a juvenile. When questioned, Stacy conceded that teenagers do "dumb things," but remained confused as to what should happen to Leon.

The Aftermath

The reporter, Chen, indicated that Leon had a close gay friend and a family member who identified as trans, and that he was not truly homophobic; rather, he was trying to impress older peers who had a certain degree of influence over him. Leon's teachers and Mr. Simkins argued that Leon did not possess the emotional maturity to stand up to his older peers.

However, the district attorney, Marsha Decon, did not agree. Decon felt that this was indeed a hate crime, and that Leon should serve as an example that such behavior would not be abided. She further indicated that members of protected classes are just that, and likened hate crimes to segregation.

According to Slater (2015), "Until the mid-1980s, the law made no distinction between crimes motivated by bigotry and crimes motivated by money, passion or boredom. Murder was murder; vandalism was vandalism. The term 'hate crime' arose in response to what was described at the time as an 'epidemic' of neo-Nazi and skinhead violence, although in retrospect it's unclear whether any such epidemic existed" (n.p.).

Research indicates that many offenders are not necessarily biased toward their victims, but instead were influenced by a more powerful and biased peer (Criminal Justice Research, n.d.).

A national LGBTQ+ rights group went on record to support Leon being tried as a juvenile, and expressed the same sentiment to the office of the district attorney. This organization worried about the implication of imposing adult sanctions on a teen.

The Trial

Prior to the trial, Leon was held at the juvenile hall, where he was in school and getting good grades. His main concern was still pleasing his mother and staying out of trouble. Leon did not seem to understand the seriousness of the situation, or the trouble he was already facing.

Leon agreed, after consulting with his mother and his attorney, Darius Levine, to take a plea bargain, admitting to a charge of mayhem. In so doing, the hate-crime charge would be dropped. This deal meant that Leon would serve a five-year sentence, less with good behavior. If all went well, Leon would be released just prior to his twenty-first birthday, having served all of this time in juvenile facilities.

However, on the day Leon's plea was to be entered, district attorney Decon changed the terms of the plea from five to seven years, effectively solidifying that Leon would serve time in an adult prison. Leon was advised to take the revised deal, or the case would go to trial.

Attorney Levine was distraught. He understood that the seven-year sentence could be commuted to five years, but that was only if Leon met certain conditions, including education and rehabilitation, the terms of which were not indicated at sentencing, and if he stayed out of trouble. Levine understood that one could not be assured of a clean record, despite concerted effort, because there was always conflict in prison, especially with younger and vulnerable inmates: those who could not protect themselves, those who were susceptible to negative influences by peers, those like Leon. Additionally, this longer sentence made it more likely that Leon would be transferred to an adult prison when he turned eighteen. Levine questioned whether justice was truly served in this case, and for whom. Was Leon truly a threat to his community? Levine was in the process of getting Leon tested for intellectual disabilities, hoping that the findings would have an impact on Leon's case. Although the district had been in the process of having Leon tested for special education services, this process was not completed because of Leon's arrest.

Mr. Simkins felt that what was happening to Leon was a travesty. He did not feel that Leon's actions were intended to harm Stacy. In fact, Leon really did not understand the consequences of his actions, or how his life was about to change. Mr. Simkins wished he would have fought harder to have him tested for a learning disability sooner, so the attorney would have had some data to use on Leon's behalf.

TEACHING NOTES

Violence and aggressive behavior are not new issues facing schools. However, researchers continue to explore relational causes and the long-term effects that exposure to violence may have on educational and social outcomes. Psychologist Patricia Sullivan from the Center for the Study of Children's Issues at Creighton University documents school bullying, institutional violence, child abuse, neglect, community violence, and domestic violence in her research. Her main concern is that children with disabilities are often deemed unbelievable, so their reports of violence often go unnoticed or fall on deaf ears (Sullivan, 2009).

Children exposed to violence can impose educational and social challenges for themselves as well as their peers. According to Carrell and Hoekstra (2008), "One more troubled peer in a classroom of 20 students reduces student test scores by 0.67 percentile points and increases the number of student disciplinary infractions committed by students by 16 percent" (p. 17). Additionally, victimization can be significantly associated with depression and substance abuse (Luk, Wang, & Simons-Morton, 2010, figures 1 & 2). Behavioral scientists Juvonen and Graham (2001) acknowledge that there are many misunderstandings about the effects of school violence on schooling, but note that more evaluation is needed to help students with disabilities have positive school experiences.

School safety is a fundamental issue for school leaders. The issue of removing disruptive students because of violent behavioral characteristics can contribute to a dysfunctional cycle in which many children experience dual roles as both victim and bully (Carter & Spencer, 2006). Significant exposure to violence can lead to detrimental factors in educational, emotional, and social competency.

Adverse childhood experiences (ACEs) can dramatically affect the mental, physical, and socio-emotional development of individuals and families for a lifetime (Crawford, 2013; Erikson, 1968; Felitti, 2009; Hughes, Lowey, Quigg, & Bellis, 2016; Schimmenti & Bifulco, 2015; Schore & Schore, 2008). Traumatic events in early childhood include physical, emotional, and sexual abuse to the loss of a parent, community violence, neglect, and maltreatment. In 2009, the United States Government Accountability Office (2001) reported more than 1,770 children died from maltreatment. These events have devastating lifelong implications including social attachment, life satisfaction, and resiliency. Between 75–93% of children involved in the juvenile justice system have had exposure to some type of childhood trauma (Adams, 2010).

In 2009, the Child Welfare Information Gateway produced an issue brief entitled *Understanding the Effects of Maltreatment on Brain Development*. This report provides basic information on the effects of childhood abuse and neglect on brain development and helps professionals "understand the emotional, mental, and behavioral impact of early abuse and neglect in children who come to the attention of the child welfare system" (p. 1). The brief further indicates how an environment with nurturing caregivers and supportive professionals can play a significant role in helping abused and neglected children, through the development of intervention strategies that strengthen families and provide needed services.

This evidence indicates that abuse and neglect during infancy and early childhood result in altered brain function. Early traumatization affects the ability to learn, form healthy relationships, and lead healthy and positive lives. This research provides significant information that will aid in the prevention, treatment, and effective intervention of childhood adversity leading to dysfunction.

Biomedical research has revealed that childhood abuse and emotional trauma adversely alter the structural development of the brain, affecting the neuroregulatory systems that determine behavior and physical illness from early childhood to adolescence and well into adulthood. The long-term effects on the body contribute to the processes of disease and aging, compromising the immune system (Moffitt, 2013).

As neuroscience investigates the development of the brain at a molecular level, the link between early childhood adversity, delinquency, and adult disease can be more readily understood (Felitti & Anda, 2009). Childhood adversity is an inhibiting mechanism in brain development that serves as a neurobiological pathway to dysfunction. Understanding the correlation between childhood adversity, delinquency, and institutionalization further demonstrates the need for institutions to cultivate a greater awareness of the effects of childhood adversity.

The cumulative effects are staggering. In one of the largest research studies with a sample of 17,337 adult HMO members, Anda et al. (2006) assessed for having any of eight adverse childhood experiences, which included physical, sexual, and emotional abuse; physical or emotional neglect; witnessing domestic violence; and household substance abuse or mental illness. Many of the adverse childhood experiences occurred together, having cumulative effects. The findings showed that cumulative exposure of the developing brain to repetitive stress response resulted in impairment in multiple brain structures and functions. The expenditures associated with maltreatment place childhood adversity among the costliest health problems in our country (Putnam, 2006).

The connection between childhood adversity, delinquency, and at-risk students further demonstrates the need for schools to cultivate a greater internal awareness and subsequent development of more effective and appropriate protocol for at-risk students. Children exposed to adverse childhood experiences often function in a constant state of fight or flight and are unable to focus in school. A study by the Area Health Education Center of Washington State University found that students with at least three ACEs are more likely to experience academic failure, chronic absenteeism, or behavioral problems where punishment is often ineffective and better results can be achieved with positive reinforcement (Stevens, 2012).

Students with ACEs are often misdiagnosed with attention deficit hyperactivity disorder because they appear impulsive, acting out with strong emotions or anger. Identifying students with childhood adversity, implementing pathways for them to build relationships with compassionate adults, and providing a caring, safe environment would increase student outcomes.

There are internal and external factors that lead to violent behaviors in children. Current research tackles the complex causes and attempts to provide treatment resolutions leading to further development of safety policies. Educators and classified staff who are unfamiliar with traumatic events that affect their students and families can participate in trauma-informed care training that involves recognizing, understanding, and responding to different types of trauma. The training helps school employees look at student behavior through the lens of trauma, emphasizing physical, psychological, and emotional safety for students. The relationships school employees build with students can make a difference in those students' lives.

QUESTIONS FOR DISCUSSION

1. What are the main issues in this case?
2. What were the unintended consequences of the creation of four separate high schools?
3. Did colorblindness or blindness toward minorities play a role in this case?
4. How might childhood adversity play a role in this case? What are its effects?
5. Early childhood adversity is a widespread dilemma affecting the neurobiological function of youth, causing diverse behavioral issues. How might you bring awareness of the implications of childhood adversity to the community?
6. What partnerships would be available to the school that would provide opportunity for helping at-risk youth?
7. What indicators are there in the case that Leon may have had a disability?

ADDITIONAL ACTIVITIES

1. Watch the following video: http://abcnews.go.com/2020/video/transgender-11-listening-jazz-18260857 (Walters, 2013). Think about the implications for transgender students in classrooms and schools. What obstacles might these students face? What should effective school leaders do in order to protect the safety of transgender children? Divide the class into two teams and have each create a leadership plan and corresponding policies for protecting transgender students in elementary, middle, and high schools. Have each team envision the issues that trans students might face at each level of schooling. After proving ample time for brainstorming, collaboration, and leadership plan and policy creation, have each team present their plans to the class and encouraging the other team to provide thoughtful critique and feedback. (Note: this may take more than one class period.)

2. Have students review *Injustice at Every Turn: A Report of the 2011 National Transgender Discrimination Survey* (Grant et al., 2011) for homework, asking them to bring their insights and questions from the reading to the next class.

Discuss in class the implications of the survey findings. Have each team then apply the findings of this report to their previous leadership plan and related policies. Ask students to analyze and evaluate what gaps were found in their own work after reading the report. What aspects of the realities of transgender students did not occur to the teams during their leadership plan and policy creation? What changes should be made in the leadership plans and related policies creation as a result of this reading? Have each team revise their plans, present their revised plans, and discuss and critique both new plans as a class.

3. Take the ACE quiz at http://www.npr.org/sections/health-shots/2015/03/02/387007941/take-the-ace-quiz-and-learn-what-it-does-and-doesnt-mean. Discuss what it does and does not mean.

REFERENCES

Anda, R. F., Felitti, V. J., Bremner, J. D., Walker, J. D., Whitfield, C. H., Perry, B. D., . . . Giles, W. H. (2006). The enduring effects of abuse and related adverse experiences in childhood. *European Archives of Psychiatry and Clinical Neuroscience, 256*(3), 174–186. http://dx.doi.org/10.1007/s00406-005-0624-4

Carrell, S., & Hoekstra, M. (2008). Externalities in the classroom: How children exposed to domestic violence affect everyone's kids. National Bureau of Economic Research Working Paper No. 14246.

Carter, B., & Spencer, V. (2006). The fear factor: Bullying and students with disabilities. *International Journal of Special Education, 21*(1), 11–23.

Child Welfare Information Gateway. (2009). *Understanding the effects of maltreatment on brain development* (Issue brief). Retrieved from http://www.ocfcpacourts.us/assets/files/list-758/file-938.pdf

Craig, C. D., & Sprang, G. (2007). Trauma exposure and child abuse potential: Investigating the cycle of violence. *American Journal of Orthopsychiatry, 77*(2), 296–305.

Crawford, S. (2013). *Life satisfaction in adulthood among those who experienced trauma in early childhood: A qualitative study* (Doctoral dissertation). Retrieved from http://repository.asu.edu/attachments/125883/content/Crawford_asu_0010E_13499.pdf

Criminal Justice Research. (n.d.). Hate crime perpetrators. Retrieved from http://criminal-justice.iresearchnet.com/crime/hate-crime/4/

Erikson, E. H. (1968). *Identity: Youth and crisis*. New York, NY: Norton.

Felitti, V. J. (2009). Adverse childhood experiences and adult health. *Academic Pediatrics, 9*(3), 131–132. Retrieved from http://dx.doi.org/10.1016/j.acap.2009.03.001

Felitti, V. J., Anda, R. F., Nordenberg, D., Williamson, D. F., Spitz, A. M., Edwards, V., & Marks, J. S. (1998). Relationship of childhood abuse and household dysfunction to many of the leading causes of death in adults: The Adverse Childhood Experiences (ACE) Study. *American Journal of Preventative Medicine, 14*(4), 245–258. Retrieved from http://www.acestudy.org/yahoo_site_admin/assets/docs/RelationshipofACEs.12891741.pdf

Grant, J. M., Mottet, L. A., Tanis, J., Harrison, J., Herman, J. L., & Keisling, M. (2011). *Injustice at every turn: A report of the National Transgender Discrimination Survey*. Retrieved from http://www.thetaskforce.org/static_html/downloads/reports/reports/ntds_full.pdf

Hughes, K., Lowey, H., Quigg, Z., & Bellis, M. A. (2016). Relationships between adverse childhood experiences and adult mental well-being: Results from an English national household survey. *BMC Public Health, 16*(1), 1–11.http://dx.doi.org/10.1186/s12889-016-2906-3

Juvonen, J., & Graham, S. (2001). *Peer harassment in school: The plight of the vulnerable and victimized*. New York, NY: Guilford Press.

Kilpatrick, D. G., Ruggiero, K. J., Acierno, R., Saunders, B. E., Resnick, H. S., & Best, C. L. (2003). Violence and risk of PTSD, major depression, substance abuse/dependence, and comorbidity: Results for the National Survey of Adolescents. *Journal of Consulting and Clinical Psychology, 71*(4), 692–700.

Kilpatrick, D. G., Saunders, B. E., & Smith, D. W. (2003). *Youth victimization: Prevalence and implications*. Retrieved from www.ncjrs.gov/pdffiles1/nij/194972.pdf

Luk, J., Wang, J., & Simons-Morton, B. (2010). Bullying victimization and substance use among U.S. adolescents: Mediation by depression. *Prevention Science, 11*(4), 355–359.

Martin, J., & Beese, J. (2016). *Teaching for social justice: Practical case studies for professional development and principal preparation* (Vol. 1). Lanham, MD: Rowman & Littlefield.

Moffitt, T. E. (2013). Childhood exposure to violence and lifelong health: Clinical intervention science and stress-biology research join forces. *Development and Psychopathology, 25*(4), 1619–1634.

The Public Health Management Corporation. (2013). *Findings from the Philadelphia Urban ACE Study*. Retrieved from http://www.instituteforsafefamilies.org/sites/default/files/isfFiles/Philadelphia%20Urban%20ACE%20Report%202013.pdf

Putnam, F. W. (2006). The impact of trauma on child development. *Juvenile and Family Court Journal, 57*(1), 1–11.

Schimmenti, A., & Bifulco, A. (2015). Linking lack of care in childhood to anxiety disorders in emerging adulthood: The role of attachment styles. *Child and Adolescent Mental Health, 20*(1), 41–48. http://dx.doi.org/10.1111/camh.12051

Schore, J. R., & Schore, A. N. (2008). Modern attachment theory: The central role of affect regulation in development and treatment. *Journal of Clinical Social Work, 36*(1), 9–20. Retrieved from http://dx.doi.org/10.1007/s10615-007-0111-7

Slater, D. (2015, January 29). The fire on the 57 bus in Oakland. *The New York Times Magazine*. Retrieved from http://www.nytimes.com/2015/02/01/magazine/the-fire-on-the-57-bus-in-oakland.html?_r=0

Stevens, J. E. (2012). Lincoln high school in Walla Walla, WA, tries new approach to school discipline—suspensions drop 85%. *ACEs Too High!* Retrieved from https://

acestoohigh.com/2012/02/28/spokane-wa-students-child-trauma-prompts-search-for-prevention/

Sullivan, P. (2009). Violence exposure among children with disabilities. *Clinical Child Family Psychology Review, 12*(2), 196–216.

United States Census Bureau. (2014, September 14). *Community facts.* Retrieved from http://factfinder2.census.gov/faces/nav/jsf/pages/index.xhtml

United States Government Accountability Office. (2011). *Child maltreatment: Strengthening national data on child fatalities could aid in prevention* (GAO-11-599). Washington, DC: Government Printing Office.

Walters, B. (2013, January 19). Transgender at 11: Listening to Jazz. *20/20 Special.* Retrieved from http://abcnews.go.com/2020/video/transgender-11-listening-jazz-18260857

FOUR

Building Relationships to Address Chronic Absenteeism: An Urban Principal Takes a Risk

This case on student attendance was developed for education students specializing in K–12 educational administration. It can be used in a leadership, special education, or policy course for future school administrators or teachers. Attendance problems are common, but many schools fail to systematically address absenteeism for the majority of students who are chronically absent (Sprick, Alabiso, & Yore, 2015).

The issue of student absenteeism is an increasingly serious problem facing schools and society in general. The link between chronic absenteeism in high school and dropping out has been well documented (Gleason & Dynarski, 2002), and dropping out has been associated with an increased likelihood of unemployment, and incarceration (Center on Education Policy & American Youth Policy Forum, 2001; Harlow, 2003; Sum et al., 2003). Because of the impact this problem has on society in both social and economic terms, solutions must be explored.

Research into the issues causing student absenteeism has traditionally examined social, family, and personal variables that place students at risk for such behaviors and has focused on truancy. These studies have identified deficient parental supervision (Baker, Sigmon, & Nugent, 2001; Henry, 2007), poverty, substandard living conditions (Baker et al., 2001; Bethke & Sandefur, 1998), and lack of awareness of attendance laws (Baker et al., 2001) as causes of students' nonattendance, with personal causes overlapping with variables within the school.

Academic difficulties, for example, have been linked to truant behavior (Henry, 2007), as have feelings of isolation and alienation that students experience in the school setting (Finn, 1989; Fordham & Ogbu, 1986).

Causes of individual student absenteeism vary greatly and may include chronic illness; transportation problems; academic, social, or coping deficits; and conflict with staff or students (Gleason & Dynarski, 2002; Sprick, Alabiso, & Yore, 2015). Many schools have attendance policies delineating specific guidelines that students must meet, but do these policies meet the needs of students and families? This case will explore attendance in high-poverty schools. Although this case is set in Detroit, Michigan, the case is entirely fictional.

THE CASE

Ms. Prince is the principal at Jefferson Middle School, which is located in Detroit, Michigan. Jefferson Middle School houses grades 6–8, with a student body of 400 students; the population is 100% free and reduced lunch with a student demographic of 52% female and approximately 15% special needs students, and a student body composed of 97% African American, 1% mixed race, 1% white, .5% Hispanic/Latina/o and .5% Asian.

Jefferson Middle School was designated as a School of Promise. The State Department of Education developed the Schools of Promise program to identify, recognize, and highlight schools that have made substantial gains in ensuring high achievement for all students. Schools of Promise are eligible if they serve 40% or more socio-economically disadvantaged students, earn a letter grade of A or B for two consecutive years, and reach 80% proficiency or higher for every group and subgroup in every subject area on state assessments.

Ms. Prince had always aspired to be a principal. She knew she wanted to influence the lives of students more positively, and she wanted to accomplish this goal by serving as a principal of a high school. As such, she saw teaching as a means to her end goal and thus, she taught for three years primarily in urban school settings in a large metropolis in the Midwest.

Ms. Prince strongly believed that all children have the right to equal access to a high-quality education. Because of her experiences in varied educational environments, she had witnessed inequities: families who felt disenfranchised, and students who felt disconnected from school. Thus, she felt compelled and called to serve this population of students primarily in urban school settings. She continued to see her role in education in high-need urban settings, where she could influence policy and advocate for equity-based practices and resources that would ensure improved education, stellar student achievement, and positive learning outcomes for children.

Ms. Prince, herself an African American woman educated in a high-poverty urban school district, benefited from the magnet school programs of the 1970s. Aimed at desegregating urban centers, magnet schools drew students from surrounding areas by offering high-quality and nontraditional programming, such as the fine arts (Betts, Rice, Zau, Tang, & Koedel, 2006; Gamoran, 1996; Smrekar & Goldring, 1999; Williams, 2010). Although magnet schools are largely a remnant of an idealized past promoting the goal of racial justice and educational equity, they have been replaced in our neoliberal present by market-based for-profit schools that actually serve to perpetuate racial and socioeconomic segregation (Nicholas, 2011; Scott & Quinn, 2014; Sigal, 2012).

When Ms. Prince first began her tenure as principal, she often heard claims from her teachers about how parents just did not seem to care about the education of their children. Ms. Prince felt that instituting home visits would help her teachers, most of whom were white, middle class, and from the suburbs, get to know the students and their families and reduce the marginalization felt by the parents.

However, she also understood that she would have to sell this idea to her parents. She did not want parents to think that they were "on trial" or in the position of being judged by teachers who might not understand the struggles of living in an urban setting. One way of doing this was to increase the personal contact she had with her students' families. Each morning she greeted parents by name as they dropped their children off at the front door and took a personal interest in what was happening in their lives. She really got to know the families in her school. Ms. Prince felt that building relationships was the key to student success within the school, and she was convinced that home visits were the key to building such relationships.

A town hall meeting was held at the end of the school year to discuss ways to increase the connection between home and school, and the idea of home visits was put forth by Ms. Prince. While their response could not be categorized as enthusiastic, most parents met the idea of home visits with acceptance, probably because of the trust and rapport that Ms. Prince had built with them.

It was after the meeting that some of the teachers came forward with their concerns. Mr. Waterman, a white science teacher in the district for fourteen years, asked, "Are we required to be part of the home visits? It just seems like a waste of time. These parents don't care what we do at school! I already have so much work with standards and assessments that I don't have time for this!" Mrs. Landry, a white math teacher in the district for twenty-three years, said, "I would rather not be put in the position of going into unsafe locations to visit families who do not want us there in the first place."

Home visits were conducted at the onset of the next school year for all families in the school. Because some of the teachers were apprehensive about visiting the homes of their students based upon news reports of crime in the area, which included many housing projects, Ms. Prince developed collaborative teams to carry out the visits, consisting of the school counselor, paraprofessionals, teachers, and herself. This initiative was explained to parents at the parent information meeting at the beginning of the school year.

Ms. Prince sent letters to families asking them to attend a parent information session in which school policies and procedures, such as school uniforms, and home visits were explained. When parents enrolled their children in the school, they were asked to sign a parent pledge, and to set up a time with the office for their home visit. At the parent information session, Ms. Prince explained, "In order for your child to be successful, we really need you to work with the teachers to educate them about your child's needs."

In some cases, parents opted to meet on neutral ground, such as a coffee shop or a diner; Ms. Prince understood that some parents were uncomfortable allowing school personnel into their homes because of their previous negative experiences with school officials, or their own negative experiences as students in urban schools. Thus, meeting outside the home was often more convenient and less intrusive.

In an effort to build relationships, and to discuss student academic progress and opportunities, the faculty developed a complimentary new initiative: My Achievement Plan (MAP). Each year, the MAP served as a starting point of discussion for the collaborative team consisting of educators, caregivers, and the student to provide what the student needed to excel. Parents and their children met with teachers to discuss the previous year's academic performance, identify areas for focus, and write academic goals. This was the opening conversation for home visits.

Further, the teams brought school supplies and books and discussed with the children and families their aspirations and goals for their future beyond middle and high school. Some parents would express academic and employment needs. As such, the team would provide academic and employment guidance and resources. They knew that if the parents had more economic resources, they would be better able to assist their children. These visits helped create inclusive schooling environments for students and families from culturally diverse backgrounds (Johnson, 2014), and built strong relationships between home and school.

Ms. Prince promoted and inspired a responsive and collaborative community within her school. For example, she ensured that all of her teachers and staff, from paraprofessionals to bus drivers, were trained in culturally responsive practices, which ultimately meant that no employee was permitted to stereotype children, parents, or community members; make disparaging comments; or blame parents and families for academic or behavioral challenges. Additionally, all educators and other staff members were part of conferences with parents regarding their children.

Together, they would discuss the concerns or challenges the student was experiencing; develop an action, academic, or behavioral plan; and follow up with subsequent meetings to ascertain if they were meeting the goals for each student. All conference members became active participants in solutions for students. The objective was to ensure that each child was positioned to be successful. Because of these practices and by building genuine relationships, Ms. Prince had a history of remaining in touch with former parents many years after their children graduated. Parents knew Ms. Prince had their children's best interest at heart.

Despite all of this, Ms. Prince knew she had an attendance problem at Jefferson Middle School. In the 2015–16 school year, 26% of the students were chronically absent (that is, absent 10% or more of the year), and only 46% had regular attendance (absent 5% or less of the year). In a conversation with district administrators, Ms. Price stated, "Occasionally, a teacher or attendance clerk would raise a red flag, but as a staff, we didn't think we could effectively address what many saw as primarily a home-based problem without involving the parents in the process. But the aha moment came after our teachers roughly tabulated the number of students who were chronically absent in their classrooms. We were blown away by how much school our students were missing."

Missing 10% of the year or more for any reason—including unexcused absences, excused absences, and suspensions—places students at significant risk of negative educational outcomes, including academic difficulty and failure, increased involvement in the juvenile justice system, and dropping out (Gleason & Dynarski, 2002; Sprick et al., 2015). To reduce these adverse consequences, Ms. Prince and her staff worked to address attendance issues for all students who exhibit patterns of chronic absenteeism.

The two most common attendance metrics are average daily attendance (ADA) and truancy. Average daily attendance is the calculated average number of days of attendance for all students during the school year. Even with a relatively good ADA (95% or above), a school may have many individual students with poor attendance.

When ADA is the only metric analyzed, many chronically absent students are not identified. For example, in a school of 500 students, the ADA may be 95% if 475 students have good attendance while 25 students exhibit chronically absent behaviors. In order to get an accurate account of absenteeism in her school, Ms. Prince would need to look at several different types of attendance data.

The number of students with chronic absences compelled Ms. Prince to examine the reasons for these attendance issues. She often communicated a simple philosophy: "We cannot educate children who are not in attendance. Student attendance may be the most important factor influencing academic performance and academic success, and I believe it promotes a high work ethic as well. We need to involve everyone in this problem and find a solution." As such, she sought to raise awareness with her families, children, and staff, impressing upon everyone that attendance was part of educational success. Thus, to maintain a higher attendance rate, initially, she would unite the staff and speak to everyone at a special in-service. This year the in-services and school-wide goals would focus on culturally responsive practices and increasing student attendance.

During the school year, Ms. Prince convened the staff at regularly scheduled staff meetings where, among other agenda items, they would discuss the issue of attendance. Ms. Prince told her staff, "Given the magnitude of the attendance problem at Jefferson Middle School, we know that we have to invest significant support and resources to make truly systemic changes. We also need to make sure we talk to parents regularly about attendance, listen, and respond to what we hear." Ms. Prince felt it imperative that teachers were at the front lines of this issue.

Each month, teachers received updated data listing students in their classes by attendance category: regular, at-risk, and chronic absence. Teachers also received ADA reports for the month and year. The reports provided teachers with the aggregate number of days of attendance for each student divided by the number of days that school was in session for each timeframe. These data clearly identified students struggling with chronic absenteeism.

To determine which students were absent and tardy, Ms. Prince began systematically reviewing reports and instituted practices such as calling parents if children were habitually absent or tardy, arranging car pools if transportation was a factor, and talking with parents to determine what other underlying reasons may have been preventing their children from attending school.

The needs of her students might have been surprising to her teachers, but not to Ms. Prince. If Ms. Prince could pinpoint one critical need, it was not the lack of support in the home, which many teachers perceived it was, but rather the critical needs of the family structure itself. The urban center within which the school was located was rife with unemployment and underemployment; adult family members often had to take on multiple jobs in order to make ends meet, leaving little time to help children with homework or come into the school for conferences. But Ms. Prince understood that this "absence" of parental involvement, as many of her teachers perceived it, did not mean that the parents did not love their children, or care about their education.

Realizing this, she was determined to know all of the resources in the Detroit area that were available to her families. She felt the issues facing the school, and attendance in particular, were more about helping families than assisting individual students.

Parents felt comfortable coming to Ms. Prince and asking her for help. For example, and in the spirit of building relationships, on several occasions Ms. Prince attempted to communicate with the Matthews family, who had three students attending the school who demonstrated chronic absenteeism. Ms. Prince was greatly concerned because this family had a profound impact on the attendance rate, for there were three students simultaneously missing school. Ms. Prince conferred with the parents, often explaining that truancy from school could be considered educational neglect. Ms. Prince explained that if the nonattendance continued, she would be obligated to call Child Protective Services (CPS).

After several more conferences and asking what the parents needed or if there was anything that Ms. Prince could do to help, the students continued to be chronically absent. Unfortunately, Ms. Prince was obligated to call CPS, at which time Mrs. Matthews met with her in tears stating, "I do not want my children taken away." Ms. Prince clarified, "That is not my goal, and this is not something I wanted to do, but I have legal obligations as an administrator." Ms. Prince asked again, "Why aren't the children in school?" Mrs. Matthews replied softly, "I do not have uniforms." Ms. Prince picked up the phone and dialed the United Way resource for citizens, and was able to secure several uniforms for each of the children. From that point, the Matthews children were in school.

Ms. Prince considered the hardship the uniform policy, which was in place prior to her tenure, put on her families. The uniform policy required students to wear white polo shirts, khaki pants, and black, non-athletic shoes with white socks. At first, Ms. Prince thought this was a positive policy, creating "uniformity" among the students that would reduce bullying based upon status symbols such as designer-label clothing and shoes. And, as educational reformers would put it, uniforms would reduce gang affiliations through clothing. However, upon reflection, she wondered, "How many suburban public school children are required to wear uniforms?" "Discipline and punish," she thought.

Her position as administrator was radicalizing her. She soon realized that uniform policies were simply Band-Aids on a larger problem that policy makers often refused to acknowledge: systemic poverty, the marginalization of children of color and of poverty, or both. She subsequently revoked the uniform requirement of the school.

Although Ms. Prince thought she had a handle on how best to meet her greatest challenge, student attendance, through home visits and speaking to parents, she was inspired to change her position after watching *60 Minutes* (Campanile, 2016) one evening. While returning e-mails one Sunday night, the television on in the background, she stopped dead when she heard the beginning of a story about a Catholic school in Newark, New Jersey: St. Benedict's. At St. Benedict's, the students are largely responsible for running the school, and they are empowered to self-govern.

After the white flight of the 1960s and 70s, St. Benedict's was in danger of closing, and did so for one year. However, Benedictine monk Edwin Leahy devised a plan to reopen the school and keep it open within the inner city, despite a faction hell-bent on moving the school to a "safer" area. The school motto is "Whatever hurts my brother hurts me." Despite the fact that St. Benedict's was an all-boys Catholic school, Ms. Prince thought she could adopt some of empowerment principles and adapt them for her school, as her students were accustomed to being highly regulated. As Leahy stated, "It's a population that never gets to have control." Ms. Prince could not have agreed more.

Ms. Prince knew that not only was St. Benedict's an all-boys school, it was also private: a tuition of $12,000 per year; with scholarships, parents paid half that amount. But Ms. Prince thought she could take much from the story: the self-governing aspect of the school; the empowerment; the fact that students, if in charge of governing the school, would have a vested interest in, and be responsible for, one another, and subsequently be rewarded through grades, attendance, and personal success.

When the reporter questioned Leahy about the potential repercussions of placing students in charge of potentially dangerous situations, he stated, "That's a better learning experience for them." Ms. Prince well knew that much could be learned from making mistakes. She was moved by this interview, as she witnessed students, responsible for each other, going to find missing students and getting them back to school. The next day, she had a new plan for her staff. Her first order of business would be to show the *60 Minutes* broadcast, and to gauge the perceptions of her staff.

With collaborative teams in place, representative of students, parents, teachers, staff, administrators, and community members, Jefferson Middle School adopted a democratic process where the freedom and rights of the individual students do not encroach upon others in the school; where an interactive process is used to devise better solutions than any one individual could; and where a learner-centered process is embraced. Democracy in the school was operationalized as the empowerment of a group of students to self-govern, to make real decisions about their own education, including what they want to learn and, ultimately, what is decided by the students actually happens. In this way, students take true responsibility for their own education.

In a democratic school there is structure and discipline to decisions. At Jefferson Middle School, all important decisions were subsequently made in school meetings, with all students participating. Monday mornings were set aside for school meetings in which decisions on school operations were decided by straight majority. Oftentimes, these meetings were long and emotional because of the issues being discussed, such as attendance, dress code, discipline policies, and curriculum. Daily morning meetings were held in which student leaders reported the day's attendance and upcoming activities, with everyone being provided an opportunity to share.

Jefferson Middle School was a place where students made decisions about their own education and, therefore, students felt valued and demonstrated an interest in school and became self-motivated to learn. The attendance problems were greatly reduced, and academic achievement increased.

But more important, it was the comments expressed by students and their families that moved Ms. Prince the most. Mrs. Martinez, mother of a sixth grade girl and an eighth grade boy, said this about the change in relationship between teachers and students: "I like the way teachers talk to my children now, and the way that they treat them. They give them a real sense of community and a sense of hope." What had manifested itself outwardly as poor attendance had very little to do with lack of parental support, and had more to do with the emotional distress families faced but could overcome with assistance from the school.

Ms. Prince reflected on her time at Jefferson Middle School. During her tenure as principal she had instituted many changes; some worked and some did not, but the one constant was the time invested in building a sense of community in and around the school. It was through these relationships that people trusted her to make the best decisions for the students, and that was why the democratic school experiment was met with such enthusiasm and acceptance from students, parents, and teachers at the time it was proposed. She felt this change was the greatest of her career, for it benefited students the most.

TEACHING NOTES

Over the past forty years, income inequality for children has risen in the United States, which is a strong contributor to the increasing achievement gap for US children (Duncan & Murname, 2014). Students from low-income families often begin their academic careers already behind developmentally and cognitively. According to Jensen (2013), there are seven factors as to why impoverished students struggle with engagement in the classroom. The factors are as follows: health and nutrition, vocabulary, effort, hope and the growth mindset, cognition, relationships, and distress. To combat these factors, Jensen recommends that teachers be willing to get to know their students, make connections, and establish relationships. Strong teachers can help low-income students build bridges to success.

Culturally responsive pedagogy (CRP) compels educators to facilitate student engagement and academic success with their own experiences and identities to become cocreators of classroom knowledge (Martin & Beese, 2016). According to Ladson-Billings (2009), CRP involves academic achievement, sociopolitical consciousness, and cultural competence. Because CRP seeks, through education, to identify, problematize, and ultimately transform institutions and society with the goal of ending all forms of oppression, culturally responsive teachers must not only possess the will to end oppression but the *knowledge* to inform their choices and actions (Griner & Stewart, 2012).

Howard (2013) defines "responsiveness" as dealing with "our capacity as teachers to know and connect with the actual lived experience, personhood, and learning modalities of the students who are in our classroom" (p. 131). Thus, culturally responsive educators take the time necessary to research the experiences, individuality, and learning styles of all of their students in order to better reach/teach them by meeting them where they live (Goldenberg, 2014). CRP is a strategy that promotes the examination of social, educational, and political issues by giving students a voice (Chapman, 2007).

QUESTIONS FOR DISCUSSION

1. What do the parent, teacher, school, and community partnerships look like in your school community?
2. Take a minute and think about the schools you attended as a student. Did your teachers and the staff form a community committed to your growth?
3. In schools "one voice [continues to be] eerily silent—the voice of the child" (Sands, Guzman, Stephens, & Boggs, 2007, p. 341). Some educators believe that students and their families should be involved in decisions that impact their participation in school (Gunter & Thomson, 2007). Discuss the voice of the child and their parents in shaping school climate and its impact.
4. How might you create conditions that will enable students labeled at-risk, many of whom are also nondominant students, to find school success and extricate themselves from the prison pipeline to which they are vulnerable?

ADDITIONAL ACTIVITIES

1. Do you believe that more money and resources for schools with high rates of low-income students will help close the achievement gap? Why or why not?
2. Watch the *60 Minutes* episode referred to in this case, and brainstorm ideas from the episode that you could utilize in your own school: http://www.cbsnews.com/news/60-minutes-newark-school-st-benedicts-scott-pelley/ (Campanile, 2016).

3. Develop a multitiered system of support that effectively allocates resources and personnel who will collect and analyze attendance data. What does robust and accurate attendance data look like? What data does your current data system provide? You might consider the percentage of students attending school regularly; the percentage of students with chronic absences; individual students who have regular attendance, are at risk of chronic absenteeism, or are chronically absent; attendance rates by month and day of the week; and attendance rates by grade level. Who will be involved in examining the data? What steps will you take to identify and address chronic absenteeism?
4. List action steps that would help engage all stakeholders in the new approach to a democratic school.
5. Examine the income gap among families in your school district. What are the differences in student achievement between groups? What programs are in place to facilitate a closing of the gap?
6. Educators need to consider the specific needs of the school and community when working to prevent low attendance. Tailored strategies typically require data collection through surveys, focus groups, discussions with students and families, etc. Use the data to identify and then address factors that contribute to large numbers of student absences. What common themes can be found in your data collection efforts, and how will you tailor strategies to meet the specific needs of your students?

REFERENCES

American Academy of Pediatrics. (2003). Out-of-school suspension and expulsion. *Pediatrics, 112*(5), 1–6.

American Bar Association. (2001). Zero tolerance policy. Retrieved from http://www.abanet.org/crimjust/juvjus/zerotolreport.html

Baker, M. L., Sigmon, J. N., & Nugent, E. (2001). Truancy reduction: Keeping students in school. *Juvenile Justice Bulletin*. US Department of Justice.

Bethke, L., & Sandefur, G. (1998). *Disruptive events during the high school years and educational attainment* (No. 1168-98). Institute for Research on Poverty.

Betts, J., Rice, L., Zau, A., Tang, E., & Koedel, C. (2006). *Does school choice work? Effects on student integration and academic achievement*. San Francisco, CA: Public Policy Institute of California.

Campanile, G. (Producer). (2016, March 20). The resurrection of St. Benedict's. *60 Minutes*. Retrieved from http://www.cbsnews.com/news/60-minutes-newark-school-st-benedicts-scott-pelley/

Center on Education Policy and American Youth Policy Forum. (2001). *Higher learning = higher earnings*. Washington, DC: Center on Education Policy and American Youth Policy Forum.

Chapman, T. K. (2007). Interrogating classroom relationships and events: Using portraiture and critical race theory in education research. *Educational Researcher, 36*(3), 156–162.

Christenson, S. L., Sinclair, M. F., Lehr, C. A., & Godber, Y. (2001). Promoting successful school completion: Critical conceptual and methodological guidelines. *School Psychology Quarterly, 16*(4), 468–484.

Duncan, G. J., & Murname, R. J. (2014, March). Growing income inequality threatens American education. *Phi Beta Kappa*, 8–15.

Evenson, A., Justinger, B., Pelischek, E., & Schulz, S. (2009). Zero tolerance policies and the public schools: When suspension is no longer effective. *Communique, 37*(5), 1, 6–7.

Finn, J. D. (1989). Withdrawing from school. *Review of Educational Research, 59*(2), 117–142.

Fordham, S., & Ogbu, J. (1986). Black students' school success: Coping with the burden of acting white. *Urban Review, 18*(3), 176–206.

Gamoran, A. (1996). Student achievement in public magnet, public comprehensive, and private city high schools. *Educational Evaluation and Policy Analysis, 18*(1), 1–18.

Gleason, P., & Dynarski, M. (2002). Do we know whom to serve? Issues in using risk factors to identify dropouts. *Journal of Education for Students Placed at Risk, 7*(1), 25–41.

Goldenberg, B. (2014). White teachers in urban classrooms embracing non-white students' cultural capital for better teaching and learning. *Urban Education, 49*(1), 111–144.

Griner, A. C., & Stewart, M. L. (2012). Addressing the achievement gap and disproportionality through the use of culturally responsive teaching practices. *Urban Education, 48*(4), 585–621.

Gunter, H., & Thomson, P. (2007). Learning about student voice. *Support for Learning, 22*(4), 181–188.

Harlow, C. W. (2003). Education and correctional populations, Bureau of Justice Statistics special report. Washington, DC: U.S. Department of Justice.

Henry, K. (2007). Who's skipping school: Characteristics of truants in 8th and 10th grade. *Journal of School Health, 77*(1), 29–35.

Howard, T. C. (2013). How does it feel to be a problem? Black male students, schools, and learning in enhancing the knowledge base to disrupt deficit frameworks. *Review of Research in Education, 37*(1), 54–86.

Jensen, E. (2013). How poverty affects classroom engagement. *Educational Leadership, 70*(8), 24–30.

Johnson, L. (2014). Culturally responsive leadership for community empowerment. *Multicultural Education Review, 6*(2), 145–170.

Ladson-Billings, G. (2009). *The dreamkeepers: Successful teachers of African American children* (2nd ed.). San Francisco, CA: Jossey-Bass.

Martin, J., & Beese, J. (2016). *Teaching for social justice: Practical case studies for professional development and principal preparation* (Vol. 1). Lanham, MD: Rowman & Littlefield.

Nicholas, J. (2011). Understanding school choice: Location as a determinant of charter school racial, economic, and linguistic segregation. *Education and Urban Society, 45*(4), 459–482.

Rumberger, R. W. (1995). Dropping out of middle school: A multilevel analysis of students and schools. *American Educational Research Journal, 32*(3), 583–625.

Sands, D. I., Guzman, L., Stephens, L., & Boggs, A. (2007). Including student voices in school reform: Students speak out. *Journal of Latinos and Education, 6*(4), 323–345.

Scott, J., & Quinn, R. (2014). The politics of education in the post-Brown era: Race, markets and the struggle for equitable schooling. *Education Administration Quarterly, 50*(5), 749–763.

Sigal, B. P. (2012). School choice and educational opportunity: Rationales, outcomes and racial disparities. *Theory and Research in Education, 10*(2), 171–189.

Smrekar, C., & Goldring, E. (1999). *School choice in urban America: Magnet schools and the pursuit of equity. Critical issues in educational leadership series*. New York, NY: Teachers College Press.

Sprick, J., Alabiso, J., & Yore, K. (2015, November). Dramatically improving attendance: A data-driven multitiered approach helped this district tackle chronic absenteeism. *Educational Leadership, 73*(3), 50–54.

Sudius, J., & Farmer, M. (2008). Putting kids out of school: What's causing high suspension rates and why they are detrimental to students, schools, and communities. *Open Society Institute, Baltimore.* Retrieved from https://www.opensocietyfoundations.org/sites/default/files/whitepaper2_20080919.pdf

Sum, A., Khatiwada, I., Pond, N., Trub 'skyy, M., Fogg, N., & Palma, S. (2003). *Left behind in the labor market: Labor market problems of the nation's out-of-school, young adult populations.* Northeastern University, Center for Labor Market Studies. Prepared for Alternative Schools Network, Chicago, Illinois.

Taulbert, C. L. (2006). *Eight habits of the heart for educators. Building strong school communities through timeless values.* Thousand Oaks, CA: Corwin Press.

Wilkins, J. (2008, February/March). School characteristics that influence student attendance: Experiences of students in a school avoidia. *High School Journal.*

Williams, S. M. (2010). Through the eyes of friends: An investigation of school context and cross-racial friendships in racially mixed schools. *Urban Education, 45*(4), 480–505.

FIVE

The Turnaround Leader: Complex Solutions for Urban School Reform

Research over the past thirty years has found that effective principals can significantly impact student achievement and learning (Marzano, Waters, & McNulty, 2005; Steiner, Hassel, & Hassel, 2008). The school turnaround process must be systematic and comprehensive to ensure sustainability (Chrisman, 2005). The turnaround principal is an individual possessing a complexity of competencies. Turnaround principals bring formal training and perceptiveness to their jobs to not just improve but also reinvent schools so that students will excel.

In this context, the word *turnaround* is defined "as a documented, quick, dramatic, and sustained change in the performance of an organization" (Rhim, Kowal, Hassel, & Ayscue, 2007, p. 4). In the context of schools, "turnaround" status involves dramatically improving a prior pattern of low student achievement, discipline problems, low levels of parental involvement, and low staff morale (Duke, 2006). Turnaround schools to maintain the improvement gains they have made in student achievement for a minimum of two years (Chrisman, 2005).

Above all, a turnaround principal must have the underlying competencies, skills, and strategies—such as the ability to analyze data to drive student success, develop systems of public support, and research and select the best educational practices necessary—in order to affect desired changes within a school, which can include a complete overhaul of instruction and evaluation systems as well as school operations.

Successful turnaround leaders who bring about significant change in school performance have consistently demonstrated some combination of actions within four general categories: analysis and problem-solving ability, striving for results, influence both inside and outside the organization, and the ability to measure, report, and improve (Rhim et al., 2007).

These actions lead to a continuous cycle of data-driven planning, visionary leadership, effective communication, monitoring and evaluation of initiatives, and modification of plans when necessary.

One of the actions most consistently related to successful turnaround schools is breaking organizational norms or discarding rules and routines that hinder progress. Effective turnaround principals focus on a few crucial initiatives that will achieve dramatic, early results that demonstrate success, initiatives that are possible and that will build momentum for future improvements and reform (Reform Support Network, n.d.).

This case is about such a turnaround principal, Mr. Oberton. Not only did Mr. Oberton face many academic challenges, but also he faced difficulties because of his unique student population.

THE CASE

Elm Community Learning Center is a K–5 building that is part of the Arcadia Public Schools inner-city cluster in the state of Texas. School clusters are groups of geographically defined attendance areas such as specific elementary and middle schools that feed into a particular high school.

The school was built in 1906 and was named after former superintendent Roger Elm, who served from 1868 to 1883. The school was rebuilt in 2009 during the Community Learning Center (CLC) initiative and is one of eight schools considered part of the Impact Network.

According to Arcadia Public Schools, the goal of the Impact Network is to turn around underperforming schools by implementing dramatic and comprehensive interventions. Schools affiliated with the Impact Network operate as pilots for new initiatives. Administrators are responsible to collecting data on new initiatives and determining their effectiveness. Initiatives must show a significant positive effect on student progress before being implemented in other schools within the district. Because of their training, these principals are considered turnaround specialists.

There are 499 students at Elm CLC with a demographic makeup of 35.8% Asian or Pacific Islander, 35.2% African American, 14.6% Hispanic/Latina/o, 11.4% white, and 2.8% multiracial. One hundred percent of the student population qualifies for free or reduced lunch, and there is a 7.3% mobility rate. The phenomenon of student mobility is associated with student who change schools for other reasons that academic promotion. Student mobility is positively correlated with academic and behavioral problems (Hartman, 2006).

Elm CLC is located in the North Hill Community of Arcadia, Texas, which has always been known for its diversity. The area has seen a shift in demographics over the past twenty years because of refugee relocation.

The International Institute has relocated refugees from Burma, Afghanistan, Iraq, and Bhutan to this area because of the resettlement services it provides. These services include English as a Second Language classes, interpreting and counseling services, employment assistance, and services that assist in the naturalization process. The International Institute is a place where immigrants and refugees can find answers to their questions and the support they need to rebuild their lives in the United States.

The institute is located in the heart of the Arcadia Public Schools North cluster, which is why many immigrant children attend Elm CLC. The school was recently featured on National Public Radio (NPR) as the most diverse school in Texas because of the influx of refugees from the political hotspots around the world (Schultze, 2015). Elm CLC has seen its student population drastically change in comparison to the rest of the district outside of the North cluster.

Elm CLC students, mostly refugees, must overcome many barriers, including poverty; all of the students are identified as economically disadvantaged. Students struggle with more than academics when they come to the United States, and Elm CLC is touted as not just a place to learn, but also a place to eat, be warm, and feel safe. Because of war and resulting political and social unrest, Elm CLC is a place where many students are attending formal schooling for the very first time in their lives. Many of the students come to Elm CLC from refugee camps, and some families have a difficult time adapting to the community and school.

Most of the refugees who enroll at Elm CLC are from Nepali refugee camps, but there are over twenty countries represented in the school. The International Institute helps families transition to life in the United States, but services are only provided for three months; then families are on their own to find other means of support, if necessary. Consequently, families typically go to the school for support. The school helps with anything it can, including sending Arcadia Public School interpreters to family homes in order to speak with landlords who more often than not do not speak the native language of the family.

David Oberton was a fifth-year administrator at Elm CLC. Oberton believed in leading with the heart. To motivate people, he took the time to build relationships and to understand each one of his team members (faculty, staff, and other administrators) as individuals. Having coached baseball for twenty years, he looked at leading a school and coaching a team as the same thing. He perceived low-performing inner-city schools as getting a "bad rap" because many assume that they do not have qualified administrators or teachers because the test scores are low, but he preferred and even chose to work in these types of schools because he felt that urban children also deserved a high-quality education with great teachers and leaders who believed in their potential.

Mr. Oberton had seen children come to school hungry and in need of clothing. In his first year as principal, a young student asked if he could take a bag of apples left over from lunch home to his brother because there was little food there. This small incident stuck with Mr. Oberton, and he often used it as an example of responsive practices when orienting new staff. He would share this with his team:

> You can follow the district policy, you can do the right thing, or you can do both. Our district policy indicated that no food is permitted leave the cafeteria. But was that the *right* thing to do? I thought not. I simply zipped the apples into the student's backpack.
>
> But I also learned a lesson. I learned that if this student, whose family was recently relocated from a refugee camp and still looking for work, was hungry, many others were too. I then began collecting unopened and extra food at lunch. Students placed the food items in a bin and the staff went around the lunchroom with the extras. This was to ensure that everyone had something to eat.
>
> This turned into a food pantry, where members of our team as well as community members collected and donated food to our pantry. My philosophy is this: no problem is unsolvable. You see a need? Fill it. But if you can involve the students and the community in the solution, even better. We cannot view our families as the problem.

Mr. Oberton inspired many with his speeches and motivated his team to devise creative solutions to problems faced by the school, which in his estimation included students, their families, and the community. And there were always problems to be solved, usually systemic problems resulting from families' former refugee status. However, Mr. Oberton did not wash his hands of these issues.

Another major struggle for many of his families was health care. Mr. Oberton once took his son to the emergency room for a sports injury and upon their arrival noticed there were many children from Elm CLC. He thought, "It looks like a doctor's office waiting room." He realized that the emergency room was the only way his families could get the medical care they needed. Most of his students did not have social security numbers when they arrived at the school and did not have their shots or medical records available. Mr. Oberton thus deemed it imperative for the school to provide access to medical care.

The state of his students' overall health evidenced the need for both prevention and treatment. Mr. Oberton was well aware that students' academic performance suffers when they have unmet health needs (Jensen, 2009). Chronic health conditions result in multiple absences and decreased focus in the classroom. Children who missed too many days of school were often held back for remediation the following school year (Mims, Stock, & Phinizy, 2001).

A clear need for this community was access to consistent health care. As Mr. Oberton explained in a faculty meeting, "Our children are struggling to get the health care they need, and this urgent need affects the number of days they miss, and their ability to learn." Mr. Oberton was inspired by Amy Manning, who wrote, "Efforts need to be made to ensure that quality health care, aimed at taking care of the whole child, is available to all children and must include physical and mental health services, as disease knows no boundaries" (2009, p. 9).

Mr. Oberton often asked himself, "What can be done?" His response was physical access to services through a school-based health clinic (SBHC) that offered both physical and mental health services. The SBHC was a collaborative partnership between the local hospital outreach program and the school, with primary services being provided by a nurse practitioner onsite. In the first year of the SBHC's inception, more than 72% of students used the center and received services in both physical and mental health care.

However, the greatest challenge Mr. Oberton and his staff had to overcome was to understand the cultures of the students. There were many instances of cultural differences that affected daily life at Elm Elementary, such as the Buddhist practices of the Bhutanese students, including dietary restrictions, which required the school to provide vegan options for the students.

Principal Oberton felt the strong need to provide cultural and diversity sensitivity training to his staff. He applied for and was awarded a grant from the local Rotary Club in order to bring in a team of international experts to observe the classrooms and devise a personalized training for the staff. He planned to continue the trainings in subsequent years with refreshers at staff meetings and to bring the trainings to the student level. However, this training would occur the following year when grant funding would be awarded.

In the meantime, Principal Oberton had to do his best to be culturally responsive, and to encourage his staff to do the same. In the spirit of being culturally responsive, he lined the hallways with flags from every country represented in the school and made interpreters available to all students and families. However, some teachers argued that it was the efforts to assist refugees that created dissent from the African American families—Mrs. Strong was one of those teachers. Principal Oberton would soon realize that his greatest obstacle was the perceptions of his staff.

Mrs. Strong, a veteran teacher in the district but new to the Elm Community Learning Center, had concerns about one family in particular, an African American family: the Joneses. Mrs. Strong had Twyla and Tina Jones as students in her third grade classroom. Mrs. Strong perceived Ms. Jones to be overprotective and overinvolved in her girls' schooling. She always hesitated to contact Ms. Jones when there was a problem, or even if there was good news, for she felt Ms. Jones asked too many questions, and often questioned her methods. Mrs. Strong did not appreciate this type of parent. She had been teaching for over twenty years, and felt she had surpassed the time to be questioned by parents, especially by a parent of children who were often, in Mrs. Strong's estimation, ill-behaved. She thought it was odd that the twins were not split up and put into different classes, but she did not question it.

On a Tuesday on the first spring day where it was warm enough to play outside, Mrs. Strong received a phone call from the office, indicating that the twins would be leaving early that day. Mrs. Strong pulled the twins aside to inform them that they would be leaving early. Twyla asked if she could use the bathroom before being called down to the office. Mrs. Strong nodded and continued with the lesson.

Vanessa Jones was on her way to pick up the twins when she rounded the corner from the parking lot and noticed Twyla alone on the playground, swinging on a swing. Ms. Jones could not get into the playground for the twelve-foot-high fence surrounding it, so she called her daughter to where she stood. As Twyla ran to her mother, Ms. Jones asked, "Twyla, honey, why are you out here in the playground by yourself?" She was barely able to the keep the alarm out of her voice. "I needed to go to the bathroom before you got here. After I went, I saw the door open, and the swing was just calling me." Ms. Jones nodded and replied, "Please go back into the school and meet me in the office."

Ms. Jones entered the office and as she did so, the secretary, Mr. Sams, who knew her by sight, called to Mrs. Strong's room to ask to send the twins down. Ms. Jones interjected, "Oh, she only needs to send down Tina; Twyla isn't in the classroom." Mr. Sams looked confused. At that moment, Twyla entered the office. "Did you want to see Mr. Oberton, Ms. Jones?" Mr. Sams inquired. "You know I do," Ms. Jones replied firmly, as she hugged her child to her side.

Mr. Oberton entered the main office from the interior principal's office, greeted Ms. Jones by name, and invited her into his office just as Tina entered. Ms. Jones asked the twins to wait for her outside the principal's office, and pointed to some chairs for them to sit. Mr. Oberton and Ms. Jones then entered Mr. Oberton's office and closed the door.

As the two sat down in adjacent chairs on the same side of the principal's large and imposing desk, Mr. Oberton began the conversation by complimenting the girls on their performance this year. "I know it has been difficult for everyone." He nodded at Ms. Jones.

"I thank you for your concern, Mr. Oberton, and today I am not angry. I am scared. When I walked up from the parking lot, Twyla was *outside. By herself.* Swinging on a swing! I am very upset. I mean, what is her teacher thinking? Why is there an unlocked door where students can leave the building, and where someone could easily take them?"

Ms. Jones's concerns were not unfounded. Her other daughter, Hailey, in the fifth grade at the time, was taken from another schoolyard during recess. Her body was found one week later. Ms. Jones's husband was still struggling with grief, and the family had moved to a new home, neighborhood, and school, thinking the move would help with the grieving process.

Mr. Oberton did not hide his shock. "I am so sorry. Let me see what I can find out. Take your girls to their appointment, and I will give you a call this evening."

After school, Mr. Oberton went to Mrs. Strong's classroom and inquired about the events of the day. He asked why Mrs. Strong had never checked on Twyla, who had been missing from the classroom for at least ten to fifteen minutes prior to her mother arriving at the school. Mrs. Strong looked stunned. "You know," she replied, "the thought never occurred to me that Twyla never returned to the room. They are identical. I guess I saw one, and thought it was the other. I really do apologize."

"I think it is Ms. Jones that you need to apologize to," suggested Mr. Oberton. "This family has been through a lot, and the last thing they need is to be worried about another child."

Mrs. Strong's face went from initial shock, at the thought of apologizing to a mother whom she did not respect, quickly to confusion. "First, I do not understand why I need to apologize to that woman. She is constantly complaining, questioning, and looking for handouts. I think she is jealous about the special services we provide for the refugee children here. Second, what have they been through that entitles them to some type of special treatment?"

Mr. Oberton looked sad. "Do you really not know what happened to the Jones family last year?" Although Mr. Oberton had sent memos, with permission from the parents, about the Jones family tragedy prior to their children's arrival at Elm Community Learning Center, Mrs. Strong had never read them. "Please review all of your e-mails from the beginning of the year, and let's meet tomorrow to discuss this more."

Mr. Oberton then went to review the hallway security tapes and learned that a custodian had left a door propped open while taking trash to the dumpster, and failed to close the door when finishing. Mr. Oberton then picked up the phone to call Ms. Jones to explain what had happened. He suggested that both meet with Mrs. Strong the following Monday.

PEDAGOGY, PRAXIS, AND DISCOURSE ANALYSIS

Successful turnaround leaders take bold actions, enabling them to set high expectations for their staff and students that lead to dramatic gains. Despite the barriers posed by his student population, Mr. Oberton set challenging goals, and his staff and students were able to reach a high standard of performance with quite a turnaround in math and literacy scores. By problem solving and conceptual thinking, seeing patterns among seemingly unrelated things, he was able to put in place several initiatives such as the food bank, SBHC, and cultural competency training to meet the needs of his students; he was able to go beyond what was expected of his school.

According to Blankstein and Noguera (2015), "As we have seen inequities widen and despair grow in communities where poverty has become deeply entrenched, more and more people have come to the conclusion that they have no possibility of improving their lives. When hope disappears, some become despondent and turn to substance abuse while others come to the conclusion that they want change now and that they have nothing to lose" (p. 10). Blankstein and Noguera have developed a new paradigm in order to interrupt this inequity and despair, and to achieve "excellence through equity," which is informed by the intersection of three pillars: child development, neuroscience, and environmental influences on how children learn and develop (p. 14).

Blankstein and Noguera understand that not all children learn in the same ways or at the same pace, and that these facts do not imply any deficiencies on the part of students per se; however, the facts presuppose, as the authors argue, that schools should devise creative and individualized solutions for all of their students' learning needs. In order to do this, the examination of neuroscience research is crucial. The idea of neuroplasticity, that the brain can in fact change and grow, is a mindset in direct opposition to the philosophy of tracking.

According to Oakes (2005), tracking students by test scores, previously perceived as determining fixed learning abilities, more often than not results in a system that is segregated by race and class, with low-income students and/or students of color being disproportionally represented in the lower tracks, and privileged students in the advanced classes. As Blankstein and Noguera (2015) argue, ". . . when students are encouraged to view academic success as a product of hard work rather than an outgrowth of natural intelligence, they are more likely to perform at higher levels" (p. 17).

Finally, Blankstein and Noguera (2015) suggest interacting with the environmental factors influencing a student's life and learning, such as family, peers, and neighborhood, i.e., food insecurity and housing. When schools can address the environmental factors that may influence a student's performance in school, they are helping to improve the lives of students and make educational success more viable. To do this, leaders must be able to collaborate with all stakeholders by utilizing community resources and engaging parents in all aspects and stages of educational interventions.

Finally, Blankstein and Noguera (2015) argue that *courageous leadership* "is the engine that drives the paradigm shift" (p. 22). Leaders must take creative risks in order to meet the needs of all of their students.

TEACHING NOTES

Educators should be aware that the expectations they hold of their students can be influenced by their own racial bias (Kirwin Institute, 2012; Steele & Cohn-Vargas, 2013). Aversive racist and stereotypical attitudes activated unconsciously or involuntarily are also known as implicit bias (Cohn-Vargas, 2015). Implicit racial bias "can affect a student's self-esteem, motivation, and academic performance" (Kirwin Institute, 2012, p. 15).

Implicit biases are pervasive in that they are widely held by persons in our society, often without their knowledge. Persons who see themselves as unprejudiced and nondiscriminatory are oftentimes guided in their interactions by these implicit biases—even as they generally believe themselves to be just and fair in their dealings with others. This is especially problematic behavior in persons who hold positions of authority and/or power.

Implicit and explicit biases are related to each other, in that what we actively think about and how we actively interact with others is rooted in deep-seated notions of stereotypes and feelings about them. Explicit biases are those deep-seated notions that we actively acknowledge, and implicit biases are those that we either do not acknowledge or do not understand that we hold. Because we are unaware of our beliefs, we sometimes take action based on them without realizing it. A teacher may state and believe that he or she holds equal expectations for all students, but in truth, "implicit bias lowers expectations for students of color and stimulates subtle differences in the way the teacher behaves toward these students—less praise and recognition and more discipline, for example" (Kirwin Institute, 2012, p. 15).

Implicit racial bias fuels racial stereotypes. Stereotype threat is an unconscious response to a prevailing negative stereotype about an identifiable group by a member of that group (Rudd, 2012). There is evidence of systematic bias in the use of exclusionary discipline. Black students are disproportionately represented in office referrals, suspensions, and expulsions and for less serious and more subjective reasons than white students who commit the same offenses (Skiba, Michael, Nardo, and Peterson, 2000; Lewin, 2012).

Implicit biases actually may be entirely different than our stated positions. We may *say* that we believe that certain persons are "good" or "equal"; however, our internalized understandings of them and subsequent internalized belief systems about them (implicit bias) do not reinforce our stated beliefs. Once we are able to analyze and reflect on our own beliefs, we can understand the truly negative impact they have on others and take steps to change those beliefs into something more constructive.

QUESTIONS FOR DISCUSSION

1. How would you characterize Mr. Oberton's leadership style?
2. Do Mr. Oberton's actions and practices fall into the realm of the "white savior complex"? Explain your answer.
3. Which initiatives of Mr. Oberton's should be institutionalized throughout the district?
4. Was Mr. Oberton able to set clear expectations and hold others accountable in the situation with Ms. Jones and Mrs. Strong? What should happen next in the case? What other examples of holding individuals accountable can you find in the case?
5. To drastically turn around a failing school, leaders may have to change structures such as the length of the school day. What structures were changed in this case? Where these directly related to academic achievement? Explain your response.

ADDITIONAL ACTIVITIES

Read the following two articles based on the work of Malcolm Gladwell: Marinov, A. (2009). The ethnic theory of plane crashes. Retrieved from http://www.publicspeakingtoolkit.com/ethnic-theory-of-plane-crashes.html. Abraham, M. (2012). The curious case of 'Outliers' & the pursuit of excellence—I. Retrieved from https://monceabraham.wordpress.com/tag/power-distance-index/

Discuss how the Power Distance Index (PDI) can lead to cultural mismatch. Then answer the following questions:

- What are the consequences of cultural mismatch for students? Teachers, families?
- How can a principal minimize the risks of cultural mismatch?
- How can a principal create and sustain a culturally responsive school culture?
- Have students take a few of the Harvard Implicit Bias tests from Project Implicit: https://implicit.harvard.edu/implicit/. Next, encourage students to develop a sense of reflection. Ask, "Does the way I approach students affect outcomes?"

REFERENCES

Abraham, M. (2012). The curious case of 'Outliers' & the pursuit of excellence—I. Retrieved from https://monceabraham.wordpress.com/tag/power-distance-index/

Aris, M. (1980). *Bhutan: The early history of the Himalayan kingdom.* New Delhi, India: Manjushri Publishing House.

Blankstein, A. M., & Noguera, P. (2015). *Excellence through equity: Five principles of courageous leadership to guide achievement for every student.* Alexandra, VA: Association for Supervision and Curriculum Development.

Chrisman, V. (2005). How schools sustain success. *Educational Leadership*, 62(5), 16–20.
Cohn-Vargas, B. E. (2015). Tackling implicit bias. *Teaching Tolerance*. Retrieved from http://www.tolerance.org/blog/tackling-implicit-bias
Datnow, A., & Castellano, M. E. (2001, April). Managing and guiding school reform: Leadership in success for all schools. *Educational Administration Quarterly, 37*(2), 219–249.
Duke, D. L. (2006). Keys to sustaining successful school turnarounds. *ERS Spectrum, 24*(4), 21–35.
Hallinger, P. (2005). Instructional leadership and the school principal: A passing fancy that refuses to fade away. *Leadership and Policy in Schools, 4*(2), 1–20.
Hallinger, P. (2003). Leading educational change: Reflections on the practice of instructional and transformational leadership. *Cambridge Journal of Education, 33*(3), 329–352.
Hallinger, P., & Heck, R. H. (1998). Exploring the principal's contribution to school effectiveness: 1980–1995. *School Effectiveness and School Improvement, 9*(2), 157–191.
Hallinger, P., & Anast, L. (1992). The Indiana principal leadership academy: Assessing school reform for principals. *Education and Urban Society, 24*(3), 410–430.
Hartman, C. (2006). Students on the move. *Educational Leadership, 63*(5), 20–24.
Jensen, E. (2009). *Teaching with poverty in mind*. Alexandria, VA: Association for Supervision and Curriculum Development.
Joseph, M. C. (1999). *Ethnic conflict in Bhutan*. Daryaganj, New Delhi, India: Nirala Publications.
Kirwin Institute for the Study of Race and Ethnicity. (2012, August 11). Implicit racial bias: Implications for education and other critical opportunity domains. Retrieved from http://kirwaninstitute.osu.ed/docs/AACLD_implicit_bias_and_education. pdf
Leithwood, K. A., & Riehl, C. (2003) *What we know about successful school leadership*. Philadelphia, PA: Laboratory for Student Success, Temple University.
Lewin, T. (2012, March 6). Black students face more discipline, data suggest. *The New York Times*. Retrieved from http://www.nytimes.com/2012/03/06/education/black-students-face-more-harsh-discipline-data-shows.html
Lezotte, L. (1991). *Correlates of effective schools: The first and second generation*. Okemas, MI: Effective Schools Products Ltd.
Manning, A. R. (2009). Bridging the gap from availability to accessibility: Providing health and mental health services in schools. *Journal of Evidence-Based Social Work, 6*(1), 40–57.
Marinov, A. (2009). The ethnic theory of plane crashes. Retrieved from http://www.publicspeakingtoolkit.com/ethnic-theory-of-plane-crashes.html
Marzano, R. J., Waters, T., & McNulty, B. A. (2005). *School leadership that works: From research to results*. Alexandria, VA: Association for Supervision and Curriculum Development.
Mims, K., Stock, R., & Phinizy, C. (2001). Beyond grade retention. *eJournal of education policy*. Retrieved from https://nau.edu/uploadedFiles/Academic/COE/About/Projects/Beyond%20Grade%20Retention.pdf
Oakes, L. (2005). *Keeping track*. New Haven, CT: Yale University Press.
Reform Support Network (n.d.). *Turnaround leadership: How to identify successful school leaders*. Retrieved from https://www2.ed.gov/about/inits/ed/implementation-support-unit/tech-assist/turnaround-leadership.pdf
Rhim, L. M., Kowal, J. M., Hassel, B. C., & Ayscue, E. (2007). *School turnarounds: A review of the cross-sector evidence on dramatic organizational improvement*. Chapel Hill, NC: Public Impact for the Center on Innovation & Improvement. Retrieved from http://www.centerii.org/survey/downloads/Turnarounds-Color.pdf
Rudd, T. (2012). *A quick look at standardized testing and stereotype threat*. Columbus, Ohio: Kirwan Institute for the Study of Race and Ethnicity.
Schultze, M. L. W. (Narrator). (2015, September 9). Ohio town welcomes refugees, puts together a good soccer team (Radio broadcast episode). *Morning Edition*. Washington, DC: National Public Radio.

Skiba, R. J., Michael, R., S., Nardo, A. C., & Peterson, R (2000). *The color of discipline: Sources of racial and gender disproportionality in school punishment*. Bloomington, IN: Indiana University, Indiana Education Policy Center. Retrieved from https://link.springer.com/article/10.1023%2FA%3A1021320817372

Steele, D. M., & Cohn-Vargas, B. E. (2013). *Identity safe classrooms: Places to belong and learn*. Thousand Oaks, CA: Corwin.

Steiner, L. M., Hassel, E. A., & Hassel, B. (2008, June). *School turnaround leaders: Competencies for success* (Part of the School Turnaround collection from Public Impact). Chapel Hill, NC: Public Impact. Retrieved from http://www.publicimpact.com/publications/Turnaround_Leader_Competencies.pdf

Waters, T., Marzano, R., & McNulty, B. (2003). *Balanced leadership: What 30 years of research tells us about the effect of leadership on student achievement*. Aurora, CO: Mid-Continent Research for Education and Learning.

SIX

"But I Don't See Color!": Colorblindness and Implicit Bias in a Predominantly White Institution

As Carol Dweck describes in her book, *Self-Theories* (2013), the difference between entity theory and incremental theory can be encapsulated in the context of a first impression. Incremental theory is highly adaptable and entity theory is maladaptive, with individuals seeing things as fixed or in black and white. Individuals with an incremental self-theory tend to have a growth mindset, whereas entity theorists generally have a fixed mindset. Individuals with an entity mindset require quick or easy success; they often have low self-esteem, and they find themselves with clouded judgment as it relates to their perceptions of the abilities of others. These individuals tend to place blame elsewhere, rarely look for opportunities to grow, and, in fact, try to hold on to past practices even when they are failing. Fear drives a lot of the thought processes of individuals possessing entity mindsets.

On the other hand, a growth mindset allows for individuals to see possibilities and look for solutions. The growth mindset, also known as incremental theory, presupposes that all can continue to grow and learn, and that, with effort and guidance, people can become better. People possessing growth mindsets do not judge others only by first impressions; rather, they allow others to recover from mistakes within each setting. Those possessing growth mindsets are less likely to operate by stereotyping others, believing that people can change, situations might drive behavior, and people deserve more than one chance before a "first impression" should be formed. Conversely, individuals possessing entity mindsets believe one has little potential for change; one situation can define a person forever, and these individuals will avoid information that might change their initial reaction to a person.

Bias is best addressed through education or exposure to difference. If individuals possess entity mindsets, it is likely that they will seek validation of their initial, singular impression of others. As educators, we need to recognize mindsets—within ourselves, our colleagues, and our students—and interact in deliberate ways to help each other "unlearn" our biases.

BACKGROUND OF THE CASE

Dr. Vivian Vasquez, a native of Chicago, was thrilled when she was offered a tenure-track position just after completing her doctorate in education at a prestigious university in Chicago. Although she would be moving to a rural area, to which she was unaccustomed, she welcomed the change.

Dr. Vasquez was hired in the education department of a small liberal arts school in the South to teach undergraduate courses in multicultural education and literacy, and graduate courses in curriculum theory. Her areas of expertise included English education, multicultural education, and curriculum theory.

When she arrived at her new institutional home, she became conscious that she was one of only a few minority faculty members, and the only Latina on campus. The faculty in general was made up of approximately 150 members, and the Education Department consisted of eight tenure-track faculty and several adjuncts (all white). But she was confident that she was hired for her expertise, and was not simply a "diversity hire." She was determined not to compromise her beliefs, but to give her all to this job and to her students. Dr. Vasquez saw herself as an antiracist teacher for social justice, and she had no qualms about making this public.

Upon accepting the position, she was informed that she was hired for her leadership capabilities. Many faculty members in other departments confided in her privately that they hoped she would "heighten the expectations in the education department." She quickly learned that the education courses were neither rigorous nor scholarly; most professors did not even require students purchase course texts, and most students received As in their education courses.

Dr. Vasquez had vast experience teaching high school (ten years) and university courses (five years), and was known for her high expectations. Prior to leaving public education to pursue her doctorate, she had also been a middle school principal in an urban school for five years. Despite her level of rigor, Dr. Vasquez was always well liked by students and received stellar course evaluations, but for the few outliers who resented difficult coursework and material that challenged their points of view, such as courses in multicultural education.

While teaching a graduate seminar for current and aspiring principals in Chicago, Dr. Vasquez began her class by discussing the concepts of benign racism, the dehumanization of minority students, and implicit bias.

Benign racism occurs when the struggles of people of color are made invisible to whites through the mask of colorblindness. Benign racism involves the history and legacies of slavery, Jim Crow, and radical resistance movements being removed from the curriculum, which leads to the perpetuation of stereotypes of people of color. The continued stereotypes of people of color exonerate whites from complicity in white supremacy. Whites benefit from the continued stereotypes of people of color to relieve them from complicity in a system from which they unfairly benefit; for if all people are created equal, then whites are allowed to believe they have earned their places in society (Lensmire & Snaza, 2010).

Dr. Vasquez informed her class that African Americans have been labeled as violent, unintelligent, quick to anger, and dangerous (Goff, Jackson, Di Leone, Culotta, & DiTomasso, 2014; Penner & Saperstein, 2013). Citing various research, she taught her students that Black children have been labeled as culturally deprived and ascribed a lower status within classroom settings, including being disproportionately referred for special education services (Spencer, 2012).

Dr. Vasquez shared a recent study with her students authored by Goff et al. (2014), which found that Black youth were more likely to be perceived as older as thus more culpable for their actions than their same aged white counterparts, both in schools and within their communities. She indicated that Goff et al. found that Black children are thus eighteen times more likely to be sentenced as adults within the criminal justice system. The researchers also argued that it is the dehumanization of Black children that contributes to this attribution of "adult severity" (p. 527). Essentially, all children are not thought to be deserving of the privilege of innocence. Black children are more likely to be seen as being more similar to adults than are their white peers, and thus less worthy of societal protections.

As Dr. Vasquez argued, "We are all influenced by media and societal messages. Implicit bias occurs when we treat others differently because of the unconscious biases we hold, which stem from stereotypes that we consciously or unconsciously have learned."

When she first introduced such topics, Dr. Vasquez's white students typically began to protest, and her students of color remained silent. The common refrains from white students repeated over the years included, "But I am not racist!" "I don't see color." "I treat everyone the same!" "I love all of my students—how can this be true?"

Dr. Vasquez always attempted to be reassuring. "I know you feel this way, but implicit bias is something we cannot control if we simply refuse to acknowledge its existence. There is no way we are all not impacted by the stereotypes placed on nondominant cultures, sexes, and sexualities in our culture. We all hold stereotypes, and we bring these into our classrooms—they alter how we treat our students, even if we do not know it. We have to actively fight our biases." Dr. Vasquez then directed her students to open their browsers and go to Harvard's Project Implicit website. As students were following the directions, an older student, David, raised his hand.

Dr. Vasquez acknowledged David, and he began, "I just realized something as you were talking," he began tentatively. "I teach in the suburbs. I grew up in the suburbs. Believe it or not, I only have two Black students in my school. They are brothers and they live in foster care. I have always avoid talking to them. I did not even realize why until just now. When I do have to talk to them, which is only when one or both are sent to my office for a discipline referral, my heart begins to flutter." At this point, David's voice began to crack. "I just now realized that I am afraid of them."

At David's admission, the class took a collective pause. Dr. Vasquez could feel her students of color tighten in their seats. She saw looks of shock and surprise on the faces of her white students, especially when they took in David's outward appearance: a large, hulking white man in his late forties.

"David," Dr. Vasquez began, "I want to thank you for sharing that. That was very brave. But I want to challenge you. I want you to try to speak to these two students more, and not less, and not just when they are in 'trouble.' And I want you all to think about this: is the implicit bias of the teachers in David's school leading these two Black students to be referred more than their white counterparts? And how does implicit bias operate in your own school?"

Dr. Vasquez then led the students in taking the Harvard Implicit Bias test on Race, which requires participants to pair faces of European origin with positive adjectives, and faces of African origin with negative adjectives. Then the test reverses and participants are directly to do the opposite: pair positive adjectives with faces of African origin, and negative adjectives with faces of European origin, effectively testing the speed of participants and indicating implicit bias. According to Project Implicit (n.d.), "It [the test] indicates that most Americans have an automatic preference for white over black" (n.p.).

As her students took the test, many of her white students complained aloud that they were uncomfortable, and that they did not like the simulation. Upon gaining their results at the end of the test, three white women in the class burst into tears.

Dr. Vasquez led a fruitful debrief, and indicated it was crucial for educators to acknowledge and actively unlearn their biases and related stereotypes. Dr. Vasquez continued her semester-long seminar by seeking to always challenge her students, and to support them when they felt uncomfortable in doing this work. Although no student seemed overtly angry with her for the content of the course, on her final course evaluations there were a few students who indicted her for "delving into content that made students feel they were not good educators" and said that she "expected too much."

THE CASE

When Dr. Vasquez began working in her new institutional home, a predominantly white institution (PWI), she quickly learned that her undergraduate students had come from small towns and villages that were even less diverse than this PWI. Dr. Vasquez had vast experience teaching multicultural education, to both undergraduate and graduate students, with great success, so she created her courses and began to teach as she always had.

Things began swimmingly. As a native of an urban metropolis, Dr. Vasquez was shocked by how nice everyone was everywhere she went, not only at the university, but also in the small town to which she had moved. Strangers seemed to know that she was a newcomer and greeted her with helpful information and well wishes. Her university projected the same overwhelming sense of "niceness" as well. During her first week at the university, her department chair, Dr. Joseph Keane, greeted her by bringing her a daily cup of coffee to her office. She thought, "I could get used to this." But this feeling did not last for long.

Dr. Vasquez taught two sections of the required sophomore-level multicultural course, in the first year of its inception. Dr. Vasquez was not aware that this was a new course upon her hire. Almost immediately, she noticed something amiss when she entered her multicultural classes of all white students, every Monday, Wednesday, and Friday: she felt a visceral resistance to her, to the content, and to the idea that the course was even relevant to the students. Although teaching this content was always challenging, she had never quite felt this way. It was as if students resented having to take the course at all, and they blamed her for it. She learned later that most of her students felt they would return to their hometowns to teach at their former schools, teaching students who looked exactly like them.

In the second week of class, during her unit on privilege, which was reinforced by scholarly articles and data, a white male student proclaimed, "Every race has privileges. I may have some, but other races have privileges that I do not have." Dr. Vasquez attempted to reinforce the notion of privilege, as she suspected this student had not done the reading, but he simply shut down, giving her angry stares for the rest of the class. She never saw him again, as he dropped the class that day. She later learned that he took the course the following semester with another professor.

Dr. Vasquez attempted to contextualize for her white students, who had never experienced racism or discrimination, the experiences of those who did. Her students were under the assumption that if they had not experienced it, then it did not exist. She thought she was living in the twilight zone. She recollected to her students about a former student of hers—a new female administrator of color working in a predominantly white school. When this new administrator, whom she referred to as Ms. Haynes, broached the idea of teaching diversity and multiculturalism within the school, she was met with resistance from the parents.

Not only was she called the "N word" in person and over the phone, but also parents and teachers in the school communicated to her, "We do not have any diversity here, so this programming is irrelevant." Ms. Haynes knew that her white students would only benefit from learning about diversity, and that they would be at a disadvantage when they eventually left their all-white insulated communities, but her protests fell on deaf ears.

It was these types of stories and this perspective, that her students would be at a disadvantage if they were not well-versed in issues of diversity when they eventually left their all-white insulated communities, that Dr. Vasquez brought to her PWI. As previously stated, the year that Dr. Vasquez started at the institution, 2013, was also the inaugural year of the multicultural education course requirement in the department of education, although Dr. Vasquez was not informed of this until after she began the semester. When she was made aware of this fact, she was shocked. Multicultural education and diversity were not priorities at her current institution, as they had been at every other institution she had ever attended, despite the fact that state and local teaching standards required a commitment to and evidence of diversity programming.

Although the reader might consider this a setup, as most of the education department resisted the introduction of the new multicultural course, Dr. Vasquez did not think anything of sabotage. Instead, she tried even harder to convince her students of the importance of this content.

Perhaps the most interesting exchanges Dr. Vasquez experienced in that first semester were with a student named Drew. Drew also resisted the content; he would state, "We have a Black president now, so what's the problem? I do not see racism. I see everyone as the same. Everyone should see everyone else as equals. I am not sure why we need this class. I do not have a problem with anyone else, so I am good." But then, in the next breath, he revealed a story from his senior year of high school, when a group of white students hung nooses in the locker of the lone Black student in the school; this had occurred only two years prior, as Multicultural Education was a sophomore-level course. Dr. Vasquez was incredulous at the cognitive dissonance occurring in the minds of Drew and many of her other students.

To make matters worse, the few faculty of color working in the institution revealed to her that there were many "sundown towns" in the surrounding areas, where people of color were not welcomed ever, but especially not after sundown.

To her great surprise, on a day that Dr. Vasquez spoke of the historical dehumanization of African Americans through various cultural symbols such as lawn jockeys, or racially caricatured lawn ornaments, she saw one of her female students visibly upset. Dr. Vasquez asked her student, Julia, if she was okay, but Julia was hesitant. Dr. Vasquez paused, but Julia offered, "I am just really upset right now. I was taught in elementary school by one of my teachers that lawn jockeys were beacons, safe zones, signposts for the Underground Railroad."

Dr. Vasquez was more than a little surprised by this exchange, but it simply fueled her passion to provide more evidence to her students so that they could realize and understand the importance of diversity, current and historical racism, and the dehumanization of people of color. Despite her continued efforts, overwhelmingly, her students continued to project the philosophy of colorblindness: "I don't see color; I see everyone as the same." They thought this was enough. In their minds, if they believed this, they were doing enough. In some way, colorblindness got them "off the hook" and alleviated them from doing any of the hard work that made them feel guilty or uncomfortable.

After a few years, Dr. Vasquez became acclimated with her students and her institution, and she figured out how to more effectively teach this "unsafe content." She found that if she had other students reinforce the content, it was better received. To that end, she trained several trusted students in the famous cross-cultural simulation BaFa BaFa.

BaFa BaFa was invented in the early 1970s and involves dividing a group of people into two, and then isolating them from each other. Once separated, the two groups, now Alphas and Betas, are taught the norms, values, and language patterns of their two distinct cultures. Eventually, the two cultures intermingle and much can be learned about culture shock, and the difficulty of seeing beyond one's cultural lens.

Dr. Vasquez and her traveling band of BaFa BaFa-ians traveled about four times per year to deliver the simulation: to doctoral students, master's students, undergraduate students, and a group of professors, all to great success. Participants always gained much from the simulation, and reported feeling transformed at the end. This all changed when they facilitated BaFa BaFa with a group of high school teachers in an urban district near the university.

Dr. Vasquez had been working with this particular district all year on its diversity initiatives. Trene Mars, a former graduate student of Dr. Vasquez who had recently been promoted in her district to a teacher trainer, reached out to Dr. Vasquez when problems arose in the district's diversity and inclusion initiatives. Dr. Vasquez provided Trene with guidance and materials to assist her, and she, along with another colleague, facilitated several "train the trainers" workshops to those who would be providing the diversity material to district teachers.

The majority of teachers in this urban district were white; the majority of students were Black and Brown. Most of the teachers had not been previously trained in culturally responsive practices, and most were also openly hostile to the diversity and inclusion programming. Most important, Dr. Vasquez served as a support system for Trene, who, as one of the few African American teachers in the district, was struggling with being "frozen out" by resistant teachers. The teachers, again, most of whom were white, would complain and vent to the other white trainers, but they said nothing overtly to Trene.

When Dr. Vasquez visited the school with a colleague from a neighboring university, she asked to sit in the discipline room. She noticed only Black and Brown students there. In the hallways they walked, she did not see anything amiss; she did not witness overt disrespect or chaos. She wondered if cultural mismatch and implicit bias were at play in the district.

BaFa BaFa would be the culminating diversity experience for 200 district high school teachers at the end of a difficult year. Dr. Vasquez met with her four undergraduate facilitators (two of whom had facilitated the simulation several times before, and two new recruits who would be facilitating the simulation for the first time—and assisting the senior facilitators), Trene, and another white facilitator from the school district, Tricia. Confident that her students would do well, as they had facilitated this simulation many times with great success to various populations, Dr. Vasquez regrettably reminded the group that she was unable to attend the session, as she would be presenting that same day at a national conference, but asked what additional supports were needed. The student facilitators assured the group that they were ready, and everyone left the meeting feeling confident.

Driving through two states toward her conference destination, Dr. Vasquez worried about her students. At a rest stop, she texted her students good luck, and asked them to call her when they finished for a phone debrief on the experience.

A few hours later, while sitting at lunch with her co-presenter and traveling companion, Dr. Vasquez heard from the facilitators. They informed her that the participants, all high school teachers working in an inner-city school district, were not only openly resistant to them and to the content, but also blatantly disrespectful.

The students had been warned that this was a tough group, but they felt they were prepared.

WHAT HAPPENED: BAFA BAFA

The student facilitators passed out ribbons randomly by color in order to separate friends and cliques, and to break the one large group into two smaller groups.

The student facilitators faced resistance from this initial stage of the simulation. The teachers argued with the facilitators, rolled their eyes, gave nasty looks, or complained about being separated from their friends. A couple teachers flat out refused to take the ribbon assigned to them, and proceeded to yell at the facilitators, demanding a different color ribbon.

One teacher in particular cursed at one of the facilitators because she did not receive her preferred color, which her friend had received. Another teacher declared that this separation into groups was "segregation at its finest" after being handed a ribbon.

As the simulation continued, some teachers completely dropped out and instead chose to sit down, talk with their friends, or become immersed in their cell phones. At one point, a teacher gave one of the facilitators the middle finger when he asked the teacher to rejoin the simulation.

The two senior facilitators, who had facilitated BaFa BaFa several times before, decided to end the simulation early, because of the poor engagement levels of the participants and their complete disregard for the rules of the game, in favor of a longer debrief session.

THE DEBRIEF

In this type of simulation, the debrief generally occurs in two parts. First, the Alphas and the Betas meet separately to debrief their experiences. Then, the entire group sits together and debriefs their experiences as a whole.

The Alphas

When the Alpha facilitators gathered the Alphas for the debrief, the teachers' true feelings were revealed: they made excuses for why they felt the simulation was unsuccessful; they blamed the administration for asking them to participate in such a "useless exercise," and they bemoaned the fact that they were being asked to change their classroom practices despite being successful in the past. The teachers were resistant to being asked to change. The student facilitators felt that these excuses were unbecoming of professionals and educators.

The Betas

The Beta debrief was much different. The teachers were very open to talking. They began drawing connections between the simulation and their classrooms, and seemed to actually understand the behaviors they witnessed in themselves and their peers. One lesson from the simulation that a teacher pointed out was her difficulty in communicating across language barriers, such as foreign languages or verbal disabilities.

During the simulation, Alpha and Beta observers were sent to the opposite culture and asked to interact, despite not knowing "the rules" of the "opposite" culture. Because of this, one teacher stated that she finally saw how her students with autism felt, trying to operate in a world where "the rules and norms of society are unclear to them."

Another teacher pointed out the connection to students of different races. She stated, "Each race possesses a different set of experiences due to tradition and level of privilege. This means that norms can be unclear to students of different backgrounds, so teachers should be understanding and cooperative in dealing with these issues. It is not the students' fault." The student facilitators felt that the Beta debrief was positive and enlightening.

Full Group Debrief

Although the Betas were slightly more open to conversation during their individual debrief, and some understood the purpose of the simulation, during the large group debrief, those voices did not speak out.

In fact, the debriefing with the full group was completely different than the debrief with the Betas by themselves. Teachers were combative and resistant to constructive criticism. The student facilitators felt forced to show the teachers the error of their ways.

One teacher indicated that she felt it difficult to listen to constructive criticism from her peers in the debrief about her methods of teaching because she, as a teacher, had already been successful, and she had been teaching the same way for years. Many teachers began nodding along with her, and some clapped.

Other teachers seemed not to care at all. One declared that she wished all of her students were like "you" (indicating the student facilitators). The student facilitators were troubled by this statement. They felt that this teacher did have students "just like them"; she simply did not perceive them to be worthy of teaching or capable of learning. The student facilitators felt that with a positive environment, students would be more eager and apt to learn. They felt that this teacher could not see the strength and potential in all of her students.

After much open dissention, the two senior facilitators communicated their disappointments and criticisms to the audience. One, a junior undergraduate biracial woman, indicated that she would not feel comfortable having her future children in that school system. Her cofacilitator, an openly gay white male, stated to the audience that students are very perceptive about the attitudes that teachers hold toward them, and will respond in kind. He stated that if teachers are disrespectful, the students in turn will be disrespectful; if teachers demand respect and order in their classrooms without offering students any stability in return, the result will be disastrous.

In general, the majority of the teachers did not hear what any of the student facilitators had to say, and instead shrugged them off. However, some teachers in that room did understand the purpose of the simulation, and stated that they would try to improve their teaching styles because of it.

The student facilitators later indicated to Dr. Vasquez that if even one teacher was impacted by the simulation or could better understand students, then they would deem the experience a success. Despite the astounding negativity the student facilitators experienced, they gained much from the experience. Although Dr. Vasquez was horrified by the behavior of the teachers and was worried about her own students, she was ultimately grateful that her students were able to frame the experience in a positive manner. The school administrators, as well as Trene and Tricia, all expressed to the student facilitators in the moment, and later to Dr. Vasquez via e-mail, how proud they were of them. They were incredulous that these undergraduate students were able not only to maintain their composure, but also to reframe the experience in the current context of the struggles that faced the district: cultural mismatch between teachers and students—leading to academic disengagement and heightened discipline of students of color.

STUDENT FACILITATOR REFLECTIONS

The following are some excerpts from reflections that Dr. Vasquez asked the student facilitators to write after this BaFa BaFa experience:

> *The faculty tried exchanging the ribbons they were given and even simply refused to take the ribbon they were given. I am curious to know how they would respond if their students in their classrooms had behaved similarly.*—Biracial female, junior

> *We then split into our specified cultures and began training. In my group, a few of the teachers tried to see how far they could push us right off the bat. Some trying to manipulate the rules, and some even trying to get out of*

participating. I shut these attitudes down immediately, and made it very clear that I was not someone who could be pushed. My group was largely very attentive during the training, and several teachers approached me afterwards to clarify some of the rules. We went immediately into playing the game.—White LBGTQ+ male, junior

I was furious. Teachers were either on their phones, or they were chatting to their neighbors. I felt as if the teachers were actually the high school students whom they taught. I felt awful for the students who are educated in this district. My cofacilitators were constantly disrespected, and I cannot imagine how these teachers interact with their students. I do not want to think about how many students have left that high school feeling worthless or disrespected because of the environment the teachers create. This experience opened my eyes to the problems in inner-city high schools. It pushed me even harder to someday teach in an inner-city school myself. These students deserve better.—White female, freshman

Teaching is about listening. It is about adjusting your methods to help the kids. It is not about pride. It is not about tradition. Teaching is about innovation and empathy. There is no point in which a teacher can consider him or herself successful and then proceed to stop trying to improve. There is no tangible medal of success to mark the end of improvement. The only point in which a teacher can stop trying to be better is when he or she leaves the classroom for the very last time and retires. Otherwise, there is always room for improvement. A teacher must listen; there is nothing more important than that skill.—African American female, sophomore

TEACHING NOTES

Carol Dweck's research on stereotypes and bias encourages educators to consider how we develop our perceptions of individuals unlike ourselves (2013). An individual with an entity perspective judges others quickly and firmly based on the fixed traits they observe and even acts on those stereotypical theories, whereas individuals with incremental perspectives recognize that any one group comprises a variety of individuals with different traits and behaviors (Dweck, 2013). Incremental mindsets are developed through a wide variety of experiences with individuals who have different backgrounds and beliefs.

The concept of colorblindness nurtures the entity perspective by ignoring historical and current forms of discrimination, dehumanization, and implicit bias, and encourages deficit-minded and stereotyped thinking. As Samuels (2014) indicates, colorblindness, "also known as oppression-blindness . . . or identity-blindness is rampant in U.S. society. . . . Many white Americans believe that if they pretend not to see a person's race, then they cannot be racist" (p. 12).

One strategy to negate the entity mindset, and even nurture individuals to adapt to a more incremental mindset, might be to deemphasize specific stereotypes and focus on multiculturalism with the goal of a more holistic message of equality and tolerance. Schools are typically champions of multicultural experiences, but not of multicultural immersion. Multicultural immersion and anti-racist pedagogy with explicit instruction on implicit bias for both teachers and students must occur in order to achieve true education equity. According to Singleton and Linton (2006), "Anti-racism can be defined as conscious and deliberate efforts to challenge the impact and perpetuation of institutional White racial power, presence, and privilege. . . . To be anti-racist is to be active" (p. 45). Anti-racist schools do not ignore the history of oppressed peoples, as do so many of our schools.

Samuels (2014) provides eight transformative steps to building cultural inclusiveness: (1) discovering our own biases, (2) reflecting on our (systemic) socialization, (3) challenging our assumptions, (4) reflecting on our own identities, (5) contemplating our emotions, (6) reflecting on our own behavior, (7) considering our purpose, and (8) committing to this work.

Nieto (2005) argues that in order to become effective teachers for all students, educators must do the following:

1. Connect learning to students' lives.
2. Have high expectations for all students, even for those whom others may have given up on.
3. Stay committed to students in spite of obstacles that get in the way.
4. Place a high value on students' identities (culture, race, language, gender, and experiences, among others) as a foundation for learning.
5. View parents and other community members as partners in education.
6. Create a safe haven for learning.
7. Dare to challenge the bureaucracy of the school and district.
8. Be resilient in the face of difficult situations.
9. Use active learning strategies.
10. Be willing and eager to experiment and able to "think on their feet."
11. View themselves as lifelong learners.
12. Care about, respect, and love their students.

QUESTIONS FOR DISCUSSION

1. Many of the students who Dr. Vasquez encountered in her undergraduate classroom, plagued with colorblindness, reflected similar sentiments of the teachers in the urban district who experienced the BaFa BaFa simulation. How do Dr. Vasquez's experiences in her undergraduate classroom translate to the BaFa BaFa experi-

ment? Why do you think the teachers were largely so resistant to this experience?
2. Why do you think the white teachers refused to confront Trene about their anger and resistance for being "subjected to" diversity training, yet felt free to lodge these complaints with the white trainers?
3. In this case, students at the university live in a relatively small world. The school functions as a microorganism of the demographics of the surrounding community, again, a small-world perspective. With a homogeneous student body, can a learner more easily develop an entity or an incremental mindset where diversity is concerned? Do the educational experiences we provide hurt or hinder transformation from an entity to an incremental mindset?
4. Would a person with an entity mindset, without sufficient evidence, be more apt to develop stereotypes and identify some groups as superior to others? How do educators in schools that lack diversity offset the strong beliefs of an entity theory and the subsequent bias that occurs?
5. Should we celebrate Black History Month in this compartmentalized manner or should our efforts be directed toward integrating multiculturalism in our formal curriculum? Please explain and defend your answer.

ADDITIONAL ACTIVITIES

1. Read the following article: http://www.tolerance.org/magazine/number-53-summer-2016/feature/why-talk-about-whiteness (Chiariello, 2016). Then discuss how the aspects of whiteness noted in the article play out in this case.
2. Using Samuels's (2014) eight transformative steps to building cultural inclusiveness (discovering our own biases, reflecting on our [systemic] socialization, challenging our assumptions, reflecting on our own identities, contemplating our emotions, reflecting on our own behavior, considering our purpose, and committing to this work), evaluate Dr. Vasquez's teaching methods. Does she attempt to challenge her students to utilize these steps? Next, evaluate your own teaching. Have you thought about Samuels's transformative steps? What do you still need to work on to become more culturally inclusive?
3. Investigate Project Implicit. Take a few of the tests and discuss in small groups: https://implicit.harvard.edu/implicit/takeatest.html
4. Divide the class into two groups: an entity perspective group and an incremental perspective group. Have each group debate whether institutionalizing awareness of marginalized groups with

monthlong observances in areas of Black History, Mental Health, Child Abuse and Neglect, Autism, Birth Defects, Dyslexia, or Childhood Obesity helps to build knowledge and compassion or feeds the entity mentality with oversimplified stereotypes and corresponding traits. By choosing to designate a period of time to recognize a group of individuals who have shared conditions or traits, are we reinforcing a message of strength in numbers rather than appreciating individual differences in everyday life? Do our students become better educated with monthly commemorations or do they become more compartmentalized in their thinking?

REFERENCES

Anderson, M. (2016, February 22). Black history month in schools—retire or reboot? *The Atlantic.* Retrieved from http://www.theatlantic.com/education/archive/2016/02/black-history-monthretire-or-reboot/470124/

Chiariello, E. (2016, summer). Why talk about whiteness? *Teaching Tolerance, 53*. Retrieved from http://www.tolerance.org/magazine/number-53-summer-2016/feature/why-talk-about-whiteness

Dweck, C. (2013). *Self-theories: Their role in motivation, personality, and development* (Essays in Psychology). Hove, UK: Psychology Press.

Goff, P. A., Jackson, M. C., Di Leone, B. A. L., Culotta, C. M., & DiTomasso, N. A. (2014). The essence of innocence: Consequences of dehumanizing black children. *Journal of Personality and Social Psychology, 106*(4), 526–545.

Gorski, P., & Swalwell, K. (2015, March). Equality literacy for all. *Educational Leadership, 72*(6), 34–40.

Lensmire, T. J., & Snaza, N. (2010). What teacher education can learn from blackface minstrelsy. *Educational Researcher, 39*(5), 413–422.

Nieto, S. (Ed.). (2005). *Why we teach.* New York, NY: Teachers College Press.

Penner, A. M., & Saperstein, A. (2013). Engendering racial perceptions: An intersectional analysis of how social status shapes race. *Gender & Society, 27*(3), 319–344.

Project Implicit. (2011). *Implicit association test.* Retrieved from https://implicit.harvard.edu/implicit/takeatest.html

Samuels, D. R. (2014). *The culturally inclusive educator: Preparing for a multicultural world.* New York, NY: Teachers College Press.

Simulation Training Systems. (n.d.). *BaFa' BaFa'–Culture/diversity for schools & charities.* Available from http://www.simulationtrainingsystems.com/schools-and-charities/products/bafa-bafa/

Singleton, G. E., & Linton, C. (2006). *Courageous conversations about race: A field guide for achieving equity in schools.* Thousand Oaks, CA: Corwin Press.

Spencer, J. P. (2012). "Cultural deprivation" to cultural capital: The roots and continued relevance of compensatory education. *Teachers College Record, 114*(6), 1–5.

SEVEN

A Racist Display in the University Library: Action, Reaction, or Inaction?

The library's curriculum resource area (CRA) is a place where education students can check out books, manipulatives, and various other resources in their pursuit of acquiring the skills necessary to become teachers. Within the CRA is an "African American" display, conceivably revealing African American culture, as the display reads, but actually offering Jim Crow-esque caricatures of Aunt Jemima and Uncle Ben in the form of salt and pepper shakers as representations of African American culture. Working at a predominantly white institution (PWI), Dr. Groves understood that the majority of her students would not understand this display as containing symbols of the dehumanization of African Americans. There was no context within this display that revealed that these were historic symbols of racism and Jim Crow. Being fairly new to the institution and not yet tenured, Dr. Groves was troubled by what action she should take.

THE CASE

Dr. Groves, a third-year assistant professor of education at Great Lakes University, was asked to serve as library liaison for the Education Department. Although she was unsure exactly what this entailed, she agreed. She was already embroiled in many controversial issues: she was the chair of the committee in charge of diversity issues at a predominantly white institution (PWI) without tenure. She often found herself fighting battles alone that she could not believe were battles, herself coming from a very diverse university environment, as will be illustrated below.

Dr. Groves's chair, Dr. Vrummer, invited Dr. Groves to visit the library's curriculum resource area (CRA), a site where education students could check out books, manipulatives, and various other resources in their pursuit of acquiring the skills necessary to become teachers. There was also a classroom with an observation window and a whiteboard in the CRA. Dr. Vrummer was anxious to get Dr. Groves acquainted with the CRA because, as a new chair, she saw problems with the site, and although she was not ready to address them, she knew that Dr. Groves would.

At the start of fall semester, Dr. Vrummer invited Dr. Groves to visit the CRA to determine what needs were most urgent. Nothing had been updated in many years. Although the Education Department had a large amount of funds to spend, previous leadership did nothing with these funds, and the librarians were free to spend at will. They did their best to meet the needs of the students; however, they did not always know how to select the best resources for the CRA. Although questions were asked on behalf of the education professors, most were answered without any immediacy.

When Dr. Groves and Dr. Vrummer entered the CRA, they were escorted by the librarian, Ms. Thompson, to a table where they discussed the inner workings of the CRA. Dr. Groves found it hard to focus on the matters at hand, because she was transfixed by the display just above her sight line: a display, purportedly revealing African American culture, as the display read, actually exposed Jim Crow-esque caricatures of Aunt Jemima and Uncle Ben in the form of salt and pepper shakers.

Although Dr. Groves was a white woman, she understood that these figures were representative of Jim Crow, caricatures that served to dehumanize African Americans. She was disturbed. This was not a display portraying the racism of the past; there was no historical context. This "African American" display was nestled in between innocuous displays, one entitled "Germany" and another entitled "Asian American."

The librarian and the department chair talked of inviting the community into this space so that they could utilize the resources. Unbeknownst to anyone, Dr. Groves took a picture of the display on her phone. Upon leaving, she said to her chair, "We cannot have any community members visit this space. Did you see that display?" Dr. Vrummer looked confused. "Look at this." Dr. Groves revealed the photo that she took. "I cannot endorse any community member visiting this space. This display needs to come down. There is no context at all for this representation. This will be confusing to our white students, who already have no context or historical frame of reference to understand this."

That was September. By October, nothing had happened. Dr. Vrummer never mentioned the display to Dr. Groves again. However, Dr. Groves continued to be troubled by the display.

Figure 7.1. Aunt Jemima and Uncle Ben Salt and Pepper Shakers

Dr. Groves, chair for the diversity committee and a person of action, knew she needed to do something. Although she was not acquainted with the librarian who had created this display, she was acquainted with another librarian. Dr. Groves considered the latter librarian, Ms. Sharika, a friend, so she showed Ms. Sharika the display. Ms. Sharika was equally troubled. Ms. Sharika suggested that Dr. Groves broach the issue with the library boss, Mr. Deedis.

Dr. Groves, a fairly new faculty member without tenure, considered this option. She knew it was the right thing to do. But during her process of consideration, Ms. Sharika emailed her to say that she had already informed Mr. Deedis of the situation, that it was handled, and that Dr. Groves would no longer have to worry.

Dr. Groves was elevated. She had already been embroiled in many other racial issues on the campus, and she felt relieved that this matter would be handled without her intervention. However, her relief was premature. Weeks later, she learned that still nothing had been done. The display was still up. She labored over what to do.

After the inaction of her chair and the head of the library, in November Dr. Groves confided in the assistant dean of students, whom she considered a friend. She told Dean Chambers of the situation, showed him the picture on her phone, and asked his advice. "Take it to the students," he suggested. "If the students respond, they will have to take it down."

Dr. Groves called two trusted students to her office; both were African American and education students. As she waited, three other students came to her office for an advising session, all, coincidentally, African American, although only one, Torrence, was an education major. As Torrence sat down, he pulled out his phone and handed it to her. "I have to show you something I saw today. That junk pissed me off, so I Snapchatted it." Dr. Groves looked at the phone and saw a disturbing image of a Black doll holding out her hands to reveal a pile of cotton.

"Where did you see this?" Dr. Groves asked. "In the library. In the CRA," Torrence replied. "This is more than a grand coincidence," Dr. Groves thought. She showed Torrence the photo on her phone. Just then, the two students she had called to her office, John and Charles, arrived. She asked them to enter. She and Torrence proceeded to explain the displays that were housed in the CRA. John, stated, "Yeah, I have seen those. I have a class in there. I do not get it. What is this supposed to mean?"

Kedrick, another student but not an education major, stated, "I can understand how this happens. I know that most of the white students who go here have not had Black History Month in their high schools. So they think we are stereotypes." Dr. Groves looked confused, but after she thought for a moment she realized what Kedrick was saying. "You mean, you thought the display was put up by students?" Kedrick nodded. "Unfortunately, the librarian put together this display," Dr. Groves informed them, thinking to herself that the librarian should have known better.

The students sat in silence for a moment. "I want to go see this for myself," Kedrick replied. "I want to go tell someone off," Torrence muttered. Torrence was visibly upset. Dr. Groves suggested that the students go together to the CRA to observe the displays. She would then speak to them later about what should be done.

It was 4:00 p.m. on a Friday when Dr. Groves suggested the students go visit the CRA. She asked them to text her later with their thoughts, and she left for the day. Approximately thirty minutes later, Kedrick called her and asked her to return to the school, which she did.

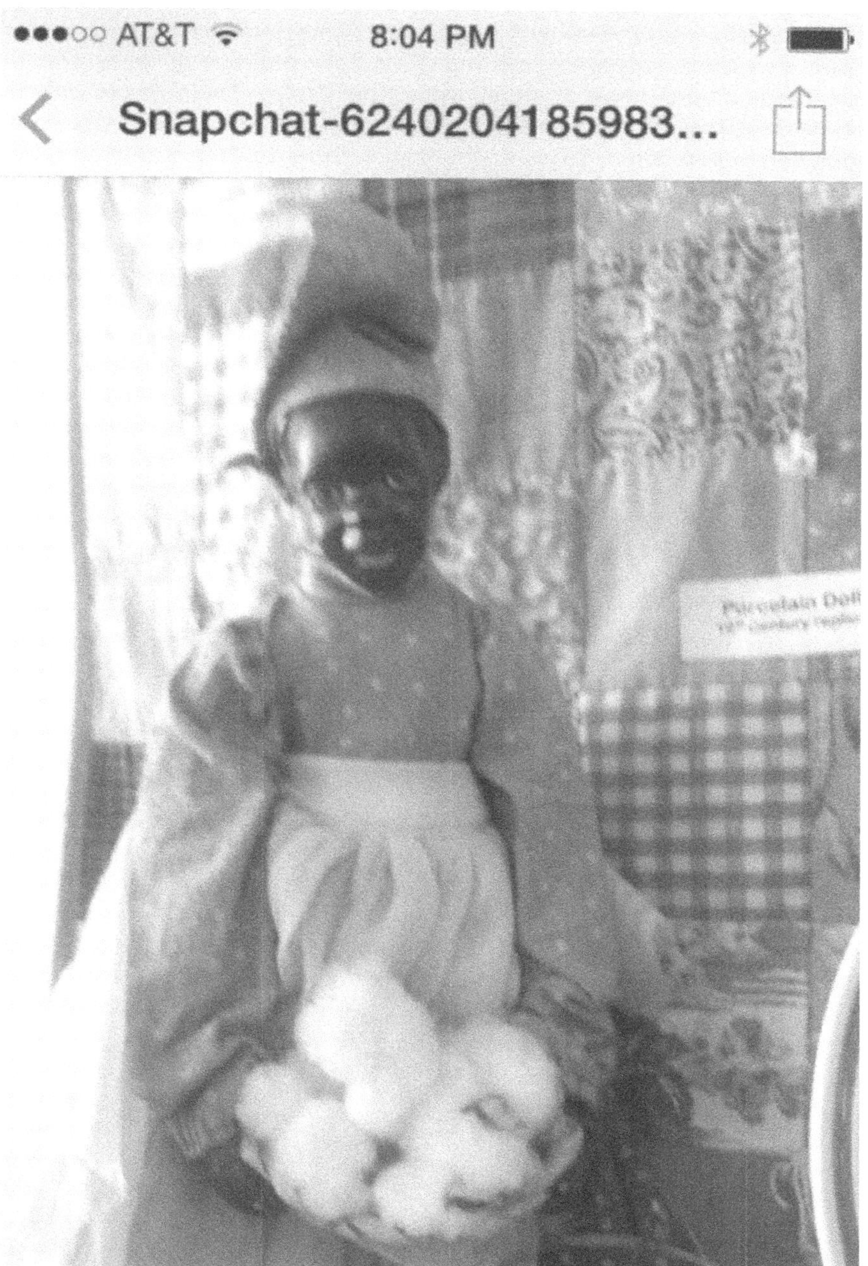

Figure 7.2. Black Doll Holding Bowl of Cotton

Upon much discussion, the students decided that they would use CRA materials to protest the CRA display. They ended up covering the display with brown paper, printing out a "parental advisory" warning, and taping it onto the paper that covered the display. Their plan was then to speak to the librarian and to help to create a new display, one that positively represented African American culture. In the meantime, John created a flyer to take to the Black Student Union to discuss the library situation.

Dr. Groves was not conflicted about what the students were doing. She felt it was their right to protest such a representation that was situated in a public university space. However, she was frightened. She questioned whether she should speak personally to the librarian who had created the display.

Figure 7.3. Flyer Protesting CRA Display

Two considerations prevented her from doing so. First, as the chair of the diversity committee, she had already been associated with controversial issues at her conservative and predominantly white institution, such as updating the language in the faculty handbook to be more inclusive, advocating for gender-neutral bathrooms on campus, and advocating for a harassment-free culture of collegiality on campus. Second, she had been warned by colleagues in her department to avoid extensive contact with this librarian because the librarian was often rude and dismissive.

A few weeks later, Dr. Groves led a diversity committee meeting. Toward the end of the meeting, Dean Chambers, who was required to attend as part of his duties as the Diversity and Inclusion Officer, spoke up about the need for students to do more to solve their own problems.

The committee looked at him for further explanation. Dean Chambers elaborated, "I attend the Black Student Union meetings every week, and students will complain about things on campus, yet they are unwilling to stand up for themselves. For instance, Dr. Groves brought an issue to my attention with the library, and students talked about it, but I do not know what they are willing to do."

Dr. Groves looked at Dean Chambers with a shocked expression. She was not prepared to speak of this issue with the committee, and it was not on the agenda. The committee members, made up of faculty, staff, and students, all looked to her. She already had her computer projected onto a screen in the room. She gave a bit of backstory and showed the picture of the salt and pepper shakers. She then explained that the students had created a protest of the display using CRA materials. She added that she was in the process of helping students determine how they would respond to the display in addition to their "paper protest."

The committee expressed their collective horror at the display and offered their assistance if any of the students needed them for support. Dr. Groves left the meeting feeling a bit "thrown under the bus" by Dean Chambers. She wished he would have consulted with her first about bringing this issue up at the meeting.

The next morning, Dr. Chambers awoke to an e-mail from a staff member who had attended the committee meeting the day before. She read the following:

> I am struggling with what you discussed at the meeting. I understand why students question how to respond to concerns like a display of stereotypic representations of African Americans, but why would you show us those pictures? Why did you take pictures in the first place? Why not go directly to the source? Why would you not take the opportunity to approach the librarian directly to share your concerns? We are all part of the same community, and all of us need to grow and change. It feels awkward to me to know that this mistake is hanging out there without Ms. Thompson's knowledge. I want her to hear your concerns directly. I want her to have the opportunity to remove the offensive

display or if it has relevance to display it accompanied by the proper explanation.

In one of my women's groups a few years ago we celebrated the 50th year of our pancake breakfast. To promote this within the club, one of our members included a copy of the original ticket from the first year of the breakfast on our newsletter. It contained a classic Aunt Jemima photo. There was nothing to indicate that we had come to understand the inappropriateness of such a graphic. I was horrified. I went right to the person who put together the newsletter. Initially, she did not understand, thinking it was simply an artifact. It took her a while to discern that something that is historically accurate may be offensive to modern sensibilities.

Perhaps you are approaching the current situation from the "teachable moment" perspective with your students. I also think it is such a moment for our community member. I encourage you to speak to Ms. Thompson about your concerns. Taking a direct, assertive approach to such situations may set a good example for students.

Respectfully,
Lark

Dr. Groves was livid when she read this e-mail. She thought to herself, "This is not a pancake breakfast. This is a university." Dr. Groves desired to rifle off an angry e-mail back, but she refrained. Instead, she set up a meeting to speak with Lark in person. Dr. Groves informed Dean Chambers via e-mail that Lark was upset with her because of the issue he had broached at the diversity team meeting. He never responded to her e-mail.

When she met with Lark, Dr. Groves was very angry. She was outraged by the display and by the inaction, but, most of all, she was impacted by her students' feelings of being unwelcome at the institution as represented by the display. Dr. Groves attempted to pinch her own leg to stave off tears during the conversation, but her tried-and-true technique no longer worked. Tears flowed as she defended her position.

The meeting ended with Lark agreeing to view the CRA display on her own. Dr. Groves followed up via e-mail to inquire what Lark thought, but she received no response. Lark had also offered to speak to Ms. Thompson about the display. When Dr. Groves inquired about this, she again received no reply.

In late November, Ms. Thompson inquired of Dr. Groves when the protest display might come down, as students had informed her that the brown paper covering the display was a project for Dr. Groves's Multicultural Education course. Unsure what to say, Dr. Groves stated, "I am not sure, but I will find out." Other students began asking Dr. Groves what the display meant.

Later, Dean Chambers suggested to Dr. Groves that she have the students come and meet with him, because this situation was not over. Although the paper hung in front of the display into the month of December, the students still had not been able to meet with Dean Chambers. Dr. Groves met again with her students, and Charles ultimately decided he would be the spokesperson for the group.

In late December, Charles set up a meeting with Ms. Thompson to discuss the original display. Charles met with Ms. Thompson and wrote an e-mail to Dr. Groves immediately following his conversation with Ms. Thompson to explain what had transpired:

> I talked to the librarian in the CRA today and tried to explain to her our purpose of covering it up. She told me that she would just take it all down and put books up. I tried to tell her that's not what we want, that all we wanted was to put some positive things up. She did not understand what was negative about her display. I attempted to tell her that the salt shakers were created to dehumanize African Americans and she proceeded to tell me that they were "Americana like *Huckleberry Finn*." I told her that we would work with her to put up some positive things, but she said she would just take it all down and put up books that she does not currently have room for on the shelves. I was respectful and professional in my approach, but I sensed anger and sarcasm from her. I will have an update for the other students tomorrow.

By late December all of the displays were removed from the CRA and replaced with books. Except for the five students involved in the paper protest, no one ever spoke to Dr. Groves of this incident again.

TEACHING NOTES

A framework of social justice should guide a leader's behaviors and actions. This framework includes principles of equity and diversity, safeguarding democratic values (Chouhoud & Zirkel, 2008; Gavin & Zirkel, 2008; Holler & Zirkel, 2008); and understanding the interplay between school culture and climate, social justice, and student success (Bustamante, Nelson, & Onwuegbuzie, 2009; Flanagan, Cumsille, Gill, & Gallay, 2007; Leithwood, Patten, & Jantzi, 2010; Marks & Printy, 2003). Leaders must use self-awareness, reflective practice, transparency, and ethical behavior as related to their roles within the school in order to develop and model cultural competency.

Best practice as it relates to inclusive leadership (Leithwood & Mascall, 2008; Ryan, 2006) and leadership diversity (Tillman, 2004) affirms the central role that reflective practice has for educational leaders if they are to model principles of self-awareness and ethical behavior (Sparks, 2005). A leader who embodies the values of social justice is one who reflects on their own personal beliefs and through that process gains a sense of self awareness and perception about their own beliefs, assumptions, behaviors, and motivations.

While cultural, ethnic, and racial difference are often recognized in schools, the concepts of diversity and cultural competency are more complex. They involve confronting the privileges some children have compared to others who are different, and working to confront these inequities (Lopez, 2006). Leaders can promote the values of democracy, equity, and diversity in their schools through communication, symbols, and structures (Cooper, 1996) and through the development and implementation of a professional development plan that addresses democratic values, equity, and diversity (Burch, Theoharis, & Rauscher, 2010; Theoharis, 2007).

Beyond the typical professional development, professional learning communities support teacher growth (Talbert, 1996). Leaders who model equitable practices and democratic values better serve the needs of diverse students (Rusch, 1998). Reciprocity and collaboration are fostered through professional learning communities that facilitate an increased awareness and appreciation of cultural differences (Bustamante et al., 2009; Leithwood & Mascall, 2008; Nazinga-Johnson, Baker, & Aupperlee, 2009). The goal is to equip faculty with the skills necessary to make sure that school curriculum, programs, and policies ensure social fairness and justice, acceptance, and respect between teachers and students and the community (Burch et al., 2010; Goddard, Goddard, & Tschannen-Moran, 2007).

QUESTIONS FOR DISCUSSION

1. What would you do if you were Dr. Groves? Did Dr. Groves overstep her bounds by taking the issue to the students? Explain your answer.
2. What do you make of the culture of silence around issues of race at this university? Why did Lark make promises that she did not keep? Why did Dean Chambers bring up the issue of the racist display at the meeting without first consulting Dr. Groves? Why did he ignore e-mails from Dr. Groves about the subsequent fallout?
3. What actions were not taken or should have been taken by the department chair and the head of the library?
4. What policies and procedures could be developed to support democratic values, equity, and diversity issues?
5. Discuss the relationship between social justice, school culture, and student achievement. What evidence is there in the research literature to support your conclusions?
6. Critique school policies and practices in this case that did not support issues of social justice, equity, confidentiality, acceptance, and respect between and among students and faculty.

7. How would you personally develop the resiliency to uphold core values and persist in the face of adversity?
8. In your estimation, was this situation resolved in a satisfactory manner? Please explain your answer.

ADDITIONAL ACTIVITIES

1. Explore the Jim Crow Museum of Racist Memorabilia website and discuss your thoughts on a university library showcasing racist artifacts without context: http://www.ferris.edu/jimcrow/
2. On the same website, explore the "Caricatures" option in the "The Museum" dropdown menu and discuss how these images have created and still reinforce stereotypes of the African American community. Discuss what you learned from this examination. How do these images persist in our culture today?

REFERENCES

Burch, P., Theoharis, G., & Rauscher, E. (2010). Class size reduction in practice: Investigating the influence of the elementary school principal. *Educational Policy, 24*(2), 330–358.

Bustamante, R. M., Nelson, J. A., & Onwuegbuzie, A. J. (2009). Assessing schoolwide cultural competence: Implications for school leadership preparation. *Educational Administration Quarterly, 45*(5), 793–827.

Chouhoud, Y., & Zirkel, P. (2008). The Goss progeny: An empirical analysis. *San Diego Law Review, 45*(2), 353–82.

Cooper, R. (1996). Detracking reform in an urban California high school: Improving the schooling experiences. *Education, 65*(2), 190–208.

Flanagan, C. A., Cumsille, P., Gill, S., & Gallay, L. S. (2007). School and community climates and civic commitments: Patterns for ethnic minority and majority students. *Journal of Educational Psychology, 99*(2), 421–431.

Gavin, I., & Zirkel, P. (2008). An outcome analysis of school employee-initiated litigation: A comparison of 1977–81 and 1997–2001 decisions. *West's Education Law Reporter, 232*(1), 19–36.

Goddard, Y. L., Goddard, R. D., & Tschannen-Moran, M. (2007). A theoretical and empirical investigation of teacher collaboration for school improvement and student achievement in public elementary schools. *Teachers College Record, 109*(4), 877–896. Retrieved from http://www.tcrecord.org/

Holler, R., & Zirkel, P. (2008). Section 504 and public schools: A national survey concerning "Section 504-only" students. *NASSP Bulletin, 92*(1), 19–43.

Leithwood, K., & Mascall, B. (2008). Collective leadership effects on student achievement. *Educational Administration Quarterly, 44*(4), 529–561. doi:10.1177/0013161X08321221

Leithwood, K., Patten, S., & Jantzi, D. (2010). Testing a conception of how school leadership influences student learning. *Educational Administration Quarterly, 46*(5), 671–706. doi:10.1177/0013161X10377347

Lopez, G. (2006). Diversity. In F. English (Ed.), *Encyclopedia of Educational Leadership and Administration* (pp. 297–300). Thousand Oaks, CA: Sage.

Marks, H. M., & Printy, S. M. (2003). Principal leadership and school performance: An integration of transformational and instructional leadership. *Educational Administration Quarterly, 39*(3), 370–397. doi:10.1177/0013161X03253412

Nazinga-Johnson, S., Baker, J. A., & Aupperlee, J. (2009). Teacher–parent relationships and school involvement among racially and educationally diverse parents of kindergartners. *The Elementary School Journal, 110*(1), 81–91.

Rusch, E. A. (1998). Leadership in evolving democratic school communities. *Journal of School Leadership, 5*(3), 214–250.

Ryan, J. (2006). *Inclusive leadership*. San Francisco, CA: Jossey-Bass.

Sparks, D. (2005). *Leading for results: Transforming teaching, learning and relationships in schools*. Alexandria, VA: Association for Supervision and Curriculum Development.

Talbert, J. E. (1996). Primacy and promise of professional development in the nation's education reform agenda: Sociological views. In K. Borman, P. Cookson, A. Sadovnik, & J. Spade (Eds.), *Implementing educational reform: Sociological perspectives on educational policy* (pp. 283–311). Norwood, NJ: Ablex Publishing Corporation.

Theoharis, G. (2007). Social justice educational leaders and resistance: Toward a theory of social justice leadership. *Educational Administration Quarterly, 43*(2), 221–251.

Tillman, L. C. (2004). African American principals and the legacy of Brown. *Review of Research in Education, 28*, 101–146.

EIGHT

"He Looks Like a Terrorist!": Special Education and Stereotype Threat

The key here is not the kind of instruction but the attitude underlying it. When teachers do not understand the potential of the students they teach, they will underteach them no matter what the methodology—Lisa Delpit (1995, p. 175).

In 1975, the Education for All Handicapped Children Act (EAHCA) established the terms *disability* and *high risk* and new requirements were established for educators. EAHCA was considered landmark federal legislation that secured and protected access to general and individualized education services for K–12 students identified with cognitive and/or physical disabilities (Ballard & Zettel, 1978; EAHCA, 1975; Keogh, 2007). Consequently, schools were required to administer diagnostic assessments to identify and to create individualized educational service plans for students with disabilities (Ballard & Zettel, 1978).

In 1990, the United States Congress reauthorized EACHA and changed the title to the Individuals with Disabilities Act (IDEA) (Pub. L. No. 94-142). IDEA is composed of six main elements: the Individualized Education Program (IEP), Free and Appropriate Public Education (FAPE), Least Restrictive Environment (LRE), appropriate evaluation, parent and teacher participation, and procedural safeguards with additional consideration given to confidentiality of information, transition services, and discipline (Hulett, 2009). IDEA expanded operational definitions, including additional disability identifications authorizing research to continue to define disabilities and propose recommendations to Congress (Aleman, 1991; Alexander & Alexander, 2008; Alexander, 2012).

Nine years after EAHCA was implemented there was a 16% increase in students identified with handicaps, and a 119% increase in students identified with learning disabilities (Wang, Reynolds, & Walberg, 1986).

These data suggest that specific groups of students who may demonstrate gaps in learning or learning challenges, as opposed to learning disabilities, were being misidentified as learning disabled and inappropriately receiving special education services (Keogh, 2007).

The No Child Left Behind Act of 2001 (NCLB) raised the issue of accurate identification of students who do, and do not, possess a learning disability. However, discerning students with disabilities as opposed to students with learning deficiencies was not operationally defined until the passage of the Every Student Succeeds Act (ESSA, 2015). ESSA defined the achievement gap as the discrepancy between students who do, and do not, meet state academic standards and students who are identified as at risk for failure (2015, p. 52); this new guidance will hopefully alleviate some of the mischaracterizations of students with learning needs being referred for special education services.

We hope that new interventions will be created for students who are caught in this achievement gap and fall behind academically, but not necessarily because of identified learning disabilities. Rather, the students impacted by the achievement gap may be attending failing schools with underprepared teachers, may have missed instructional time because of family transience or illness, or may be impacted by a variety of other reasons. In the continuum of student performance, there are at-risk students who face gaps in learning or learning challenges alongside students who have been appropriately identified as possessing learning disabilities.

THE CASE

Mr. Vincent Robbins was hired at a middle school in a large urban school district in the South to teach special education. Mr. Robbins is a Muslim man of Pakistani descent. He has lived in the United States his entire life. After receiving his teaching degree, he worked as a middle school English teacher for six years and recently finished his master's in special education. In his new position, he was hired to assist students with IEPs in traditional academic courses, as full inclusion was the law in the state.

Upon his hire at Lincoln Middle School, Mr. Robbins was given one week to observe other special education teachers as they made their rounds to their various classes. His first observation was that team teaching was not the norm.

Team teaching is an instructional strategy where two teachers collaborate to teach a group of students or a specific class. There are a number of different types of team teaching that can be used in both special education and general classroom settings. A few examples are the tag-team format, whereby two teachers deliver instruction together; the "one teach, one assist method," whereby one teacher provides instruction while the other teacher walks around the room and assists students; and a method of grouping whereby one teacher works with a small group based upon their learning needs, and the other with the larger group (Vanderbilt, 2016). Some of the benefits of team teaching are that low-performing students receive individualized attention and small-group time, students experience different teaching styles that may better match their learning styles (Coffey, 2008), and the co-planning process produces stronger and more creative lessons (Kaplan, 2012). Team teaching requires teachers to coordinate their schedules to make time to engage in collaborative, interdisciplinary planning.

As Mr. Robbins noted during his observations, the special education teachers typically sat at the back of the classroom and waited for students to come to them if they needed assistance, which was rare. He did not notice any effective methods of team teaching. In fact, he was concerned that for students to approach the special education teacher, they would be singling themselves out as deficient or "less than" their noncertified peers. Mr. Robbins never witnessed the general education teacher consulting with or bringing in the special education teacher on any lesson in any classroom—and he observed many classes: math, science, language arts, and social studies.

Mr. Robbins also was allowed to observe the "discipline room": the room in which students who were disruptive in class were sent for a "time-out," prior to interventions from the administration. Mr. Robbins noticed that the vast majority of the students sent to the discipline room were minority students; however, minority students made up only half of the overall student population. Likewise, most of the minority students were also certified for special education services. Mr. Robbins wondered if the implicitly held biases of the teachers were contributing to this disparity.

According to the US Department of Education Office for Civil Rights (2014), African American students are three and a half times more likely to be suspended or expelled. Although they make up only 18% of the overall student population, African American students make up 46% of those students suspended more than one time. One in four African American students is suspended at least once, compared to one in eleven white students (US Department of Education Office for Civil Rights, 2014). New data show inequitable discipline practices enacted upon minority children in general beginning in preschool (US Department of Education Office for Civil Rights, 2014).

Mr. Robbins's observations led him to ask the administration for discipline records and special education referrals for the last five years. He did so on the presumption that this would better allow him to do his job. The administration freely divulged the records. Upon examination, Mr. Robbins learned not only that minority students were disproportionately being referred for special education services, but also that they were disproportionately disciplined, and at greater risk for retention, suspension, and expulsion.

Mr. Robbins was aware of the research on the overrepresentation of students in special education who are not learning disabled, as many special education determinations are simply learning deficits that are misdiagnosed as learning disabilities, or *false positives* (Kavale, Kauffman, Bachmeier, & LeFever, 2008, p. 139). He personally wanted to successfully navigate any learning challenges or gaps in learning that students possessed through instructional interventions.

During this time, the district and the school were in jeopardy of being taken over by the state for underperformance. Thus, they were in need of making institutional changes that would lead to student success.

Upon his first day of teaching, Mr. Robbins was given a strict schedule: he was to "team teach" in two language arts classes with Ms. Porter, two social studies classes with Mr. Bishop; he would manage the resource room for one hour; and the final hour of the day would be his planning hour. The resource room was a space where special education students were sent, whether by individual or teacher request in order to receive special academic or social attention and support. Mr. Robbins's planning hour was the same as the two teachers with whom he was to collaborate, and the presumption was that this common planning time would be used to create team-based lessons.

Mr. Robbins attempted to communicate with veteran teachers Ms. Porter and Mr. Bishop, who had taught at the school for five and seven years, respectively, several times in person and via e-mail to ask that they meet as a team. Ms. Porter, a thirty-three-year-old white woman, and Mr. Bishop, a forty-two-year-old white male, both indicated to Mr. Robbins in person that they were too busy grading papers to meet with him, and that things would be just fine as they were—with him assisting when needed and as requested by students.

Immediately following this conversation, Mr. Robbins sought out the principal, Mr. Horgan, to communicate his situation. Mr. Horgan, a white male with forty-two years of experience in education, began his career as a math teacher in a suburban district where he taught for eight years; during the last three of those years he earned his master's degree in educational administration and principal licensure. It had been almost thirty-four years since he decided to move to an urban setting so that he could make a difference in the lives of inner-city children. However, Mr. Horgan felt increasing disillusioned by the high turnover rate of his teachers, a common occurrence in urban schools. He knew that he probably should have retired years ago, lacking the energy it takes to lead a staff, particularly one that requires so much training and professional development on how best to serve the current student population, which was rapidly becoming more diverse.

Mr. Robbins indicated to Mr. Horgan that he desired to be an integral part of the team, and asked for his advice on how to do so. Mr. Horgan, although too exhausted to fight with teachers, sympathized with Mr. Robbins; on the spot, he devised a plan.

"I mean no disrespect, Mr. Robbins, but I am going to assume that you are of the Muslim faith." Mr. Robbins wondered why Mr. Horgan would assume this, for he had neither made proclamations of his faith nor worn any religious symbols. He also wondered why, if Mr. Horgan were so concerned and assured of his faith, he did not provide a location for Mr. Robbins to adhere to the Muslim call to prayer, but he readily dismissed these negative thoughts and listened to what Mr. Horgan had to say.

Mr. Horgan continued, "We have a student, Adeeb, who wears a religious headdress. He has been teased by other students, and some faculty feel that since he is now in America that he should not be allowed to wear this to school—citing the dress code policy of 'no hats' in school. I am wondering if your open planning time may be a blessing in disguise. How about you spend this time with Adeeb?" Mr. Horgan still faced ill will from staff members who had lost the dress code battle over Adeeb's turban during the previous school year. Word traveled fast, and Mr. Horgan navigated many angry meetings with concerned staff members and phone calls from parents.

Mr. Robbins, a bit surprised, replied, "Well, I am happy to help, but what about this student's academics? Won't he be missing a class if he is with me during last period?"

"Well, yes," Mr. Horgan replied, "but we attempt to educate the whole child here, and I think Adeeb would benefit from some one-on-one time with another male to whom he can relate during the school day."

Mr. Robbins quickly agreed, not wanting to alienate himself from the administration in his brand-new job. He asked to review the file on Adeeb, and Mr. Horgan enthusiastically provided it.

From his file, Mr. Robbins quickly learned that Adeeb Singh was a recent immigrant from India who spoke both English and Punjabi. Mr. Robbins determined to seek him out the next day prior to the start of classes.

Upon first glance, Mr. Robbins recognized that Adeeb was a Sikh. Per his religious tradition, Adeeb was permitted to wear his turban to school, despite many previous protestations from parents and staff. Turbans are worn by males of the Sikh religion because it is seen as their commitment to their own higher consciousness, and is a symbol of spirituality and holiness.

Many staff members, students, and parents confused Adeeb with being Muslim and feared that he might be a terrorist. Mr. Robbins was not only concerned that his colleagues and his community would automatically assume that any Muslim would be a terrorist, but also that they could not differentiate a Sikh from a Muslim, and did not seem to care about the obvious religious differences.

Mr. Horgan was worried that Adeeb would be subject to bullying by other students and differential treatment by his teachers. Mr. Horgan felt that special attention from Mr. Robbins might be an additional source of support for a vulnerable student. After meeting Adeeb, Mr. Robbins asked Mr. Horgan if he could become more involved with Adeeb's case by checking in with his teachers and overseeing his grades and overall academic progress. Mr. Horgan readily accepted Mr. Robbins's offer. However, Mr. Robbins was troubled by the fact that there was no training for staff or even the slightest recognition of Adeeb's faith, and the unique challenges he might face within the school because of it.

When Mr. Robbins met with Adeeb again at the end of the day, he was confused about why Adeeb was a special education student, which he had learned from reading his file. "This student is fluent in two languages, and likely proficient in more. Why is he in special education?" he wondered to himself after speaking with Adeeb for five minutes.

Mr. Robbins was aware of the disproportionate number of English language learners (ELLs) classified in special education, a national trend (Sullivan, 2011). Their learning needs, and rudimentary exposure to or proficiency in the English language, were often perceived to be a language learning disability. However, this did not pertain to Adeeb, for he was proficient in English.

Mr. Robbins spent his first planning hour engaging in conversation with Adeeb and simply getting to know him. He learned that Adeeb and his family had been in the United States for about six months, and that this was his first experience with schooling in America. His family had moved here because his father was a biochemist, and his company had transferred him to their home office in the United States.

Mr. Robbins asked what subjects Adeeb struggled with. Adeeb stated that he did not have many struggles with the academics, but rather with the customs in the United States. On his first day, when called upon by one of his teachers to answer a question, he stood—as is the custom in India. When he did so, the teacher looked confused and commanded Adeeb to keep his seat. Adeeb did so, and subsequently put his head down on the desk in deference. The teacher took this to be an additional act of disrespect and sent Adeeb down to the principal's office, as opposed to the discipline room—bypassing a step in the required discipline policies and procedures. She also requested that Adeeb be tested for special education services, and requested that he be removed from her class.

For years, Mr. Horgan had been unsettled by the number of negative comments he heard from his staff about immigrant children from Eastern and Middle Eastern countries. His teachers had made negative assumptions regarding the overall intelligence of these students, and presumed that these students were not as invested in their academics as their white counterparts. After years of trying to combat these stereotypes and their corresponding mindsets, Mr. Horgan gave up and stayed quiet. The battle over the dress code took quite a toll on him.

Mr. Horgan was deeply troubled when Mr. Robbins came into his office with his concerns. Mr. Robbins wanted answers about and validation for his feelings when he heard a stereotypical comment made by one of Adeeb's teachers: "Arab-American students are underachievers, and receiving special needs services will be a support to Adeeb and others like him."

Mr. Robbins attempted to indicate to this teacher that Adeeb was not, in fact, Arab American, but his protestations fell on deaf ears. It was as if this teacher did not want to become educated about Adeeb, or any other student that was not white, Christian, and native born. Mr. Robbins wondered why this teacher went into the education profession in the first place, if he was unwilling to become educated himself.

For Mr. Robbins, this statement, and others like it, was highly offensive. Mr. Robbins engaged Mr. Horgan in a discussion of the school's over-identification (for special education) of some subgroups within the student population. Mr. Robbins asked, "Why are so many minority students identified as having disabilities? If you look at the data, it is not an anomaly; as a district it appears that either our minority kids are identified as special needs more frequently than their white counterparts, or there is a societal or evaluative bias at work in the identification process. The observable behaviors, which may very well be linked to cultural differences or a lack of dialogue, are used to attribute disability."

Mr. Robbins continued, "Why? Why are minority students over-represented in our special education population? Why are they appearing at a more frequent rate in our test data when we look at the scores of our failing students?"

Mr. Horgan questioned the results of the process that resulted in Adeeb, and others, being referred for special education services, but he felt compelled to adhere to the results because of pressure from his staff. Most of the staff seemed afraid to deal with Adeeb.

TEACHING NOTES

According to Steele and Aronson (1995), stereotype threat is the fear of being judged by negative stereotype from others not possessing the same identities that are often subject to stereotypes in society, and/or the fear of acting in such a way to confirm the preexisting stereotypes that exist for one's particular identity or group. This heightened fear to "represent" for one's racial/ethnic/gender (or other) group may result in higher stress and lower performance.

For example, if a math teacher holds the stereotype that girls are not as good at math as their male counterparts, the females in the class may feel additional pressure to perform well in order to disconfirm the stereotype that the teacher holds. This added pressure and stress may cause the stereotyped individuals to perform poorly, thus perpetuating said stereotypes. It becomes a vicious circle, and one that serves to reinforce stereotypes. According to Hill, Corbett, and St. Rose (2010), "Stereotype threat arises in situations when a negative stereotype is relevant to evaluating performance" (p. 39). Stereotype threat can impact individuals both psychologically and physiologically. Fortunately, stereotype threat can be counteracted by teaching students about it (Hill et al., 2010). Unfortunately, this is not often the case.

Steele (2010) pinpoints the identity categories that are often rife for stereotype threat: age, sexual orientation, race, gender, ethnicity, political affiliation, mental illness, disability, etc. Steele (2010) further illuminates the danger of stereotype threat: "We know what 'people think.' We know that anything we do that fits the stereotype could be taken as confirming it" (p. 5). Thus, the vicious circle is perpetuated. If teachers are unaware of their implicit biases and of the phenomenon of stereotype threat, they are likely to perpetuate it. According to Benjamin Bloom, "After forty years of intensive research on school learning in the United States as well as abroad, my major conclusion is: What any person in the world can learn, *almost* all persons can learn *if* provided with the appropriate prior and current conditions of learning" (Bloom, as cited in Dweck, 2006, pp. 65–66). However, Bloom's sentiment as well as knowledge and understanding of implicit bias and stereotype threat are not explicitly taught in many teacher education programs, and thus do not trickle down to classrooms and schools.

According to Dweck (2006), some teachers have "fixed mindsets," believing that the students who enter their classrooms with lower academic achievement levels are somehow different from their other students, and that this fact is unchangeable. On the other hand, other teachers possess "growth mindsets," and believe that all students can learn and develop their skills. As Dweck states, "The group differences had simply disappeared under the guidance of teachers who taught for improvement, for these teachers had found a way to reach their 'low-ability' students" (p. 66). Furthermore, according to Dweck:

> The fixed mindset limits achievement. It fills people's minds with interfering thoughts, it makes effort disagreeable, and it leads to inferior learning strategies. What's more, it makes other people into judges instead of allies. Whether we're talking about Darwin or college students, important achievements require a clear focus, all-out effort, and a bottomless trunk full of strategies. Plus allies in learning. This is what the growth mindset gives people, and what's why it helps their abilities grow and bear fruit. (p. 67)

It is important for all teachers to possess growth mindsets in order to cultivate the abilities of all of their students.

Finally, the phenomenon of stereotype threat can affect the strongest and most capable students, indicating that the pressure from without (or "situational pressure") can impact student performance (Steele, 2010). According to Steele (2010), stereotype threat "causes rumination, which takes up mental capacity, distracting us from the task at hand—from the questions on the standardized test we're taking or from the conversation we're having with persons of a different race. So beyond the physiological reactions that identity threat causes, it also impairs performance and other actions by interfering with our thinking" (p. 121).

QUESTIONS FOR DISCUSSION

1. What role do implicit bias and stereotype threat play in this case?
2. How do you think minority students at Lincoln Middle School are impacted by stereotype threat?
3. What types of training should be required of the staff at Lincoln Middle School?
4. What should the school do for Adeeb, and for students like him?
5. Discuss the leadership style of Mr. Horgan. Is it adequate for this school?
6. What should Mr. Robbins do about his concerns?
7. Students and educators with an entity perspective judge others quickly and firmly on fixed traits they observe, and even act on those stereotypical theories. Incremental mindsets recognize that any one group comprises a variety of individuals with different traits and behaviors. An entity mindset, without sufficient evidence, would be more apt to develop stereotypes and identify some groups as superior to others. How do school officials in districts that lack diversity offset the strong beliefs of an entity mindset and the subsequent bias that occurs?

ADDITIONAL ACTIVITIES

1. Read the following article:

Murphy Paul, A. (2012, October 6). It's not me, it's you. *The New York Times*. Retrieved from http://www.nytimes.com/2012/10/07/opinion/sunday/intelligence-and-the-stereotype-threat.html

Demonstrate your understanding of stereotype threat, and indicate how this phenomenon is relevant to this case.

2. Think first about the concept of judging the personality and character of an individual from observable behavior. Then consider the saying by Charles Horton Cooley: "I am not who you think I am; I am not who I

think I am; I am who I think you think I am" (Landvatter, 2013, p. 1). Begin with a dissection of the quotation. In a reflective sense, individuals draw identity, and subsequently engage in a pattern of behavior, that reinforces an image that they believe others have of them. In a small group, discuss this quotation, specifically addressing how each one of us is aware of the ways in which we think others see us and make judgments of us based upon our behavior. Then relate these ideas to the facts of this case.

REFERENCES

Aleman, S. R. (1991). Education of the Handicapped Act Amendments of 1990, PL 101-476: A summary. CRS Report for Congress.

Alexander, K., & Alexander, M. D. (2008). *American public school law* (8th ed.). Boston, MA: Cengage Learning.

Alexander, M. (2012). *The new Jim Crow: Mass incarceration in the age of colorblindness*. New York, NY: The New Press.

Ball, A. F., & Tyson, C. A. (Eds.). (2011). *Studying diversity in teacher education*. Lanham, MD: Rowman & Littlefield.

Ballard, J., & Zettel, J. J. (1978). The managerial aspects of Public Law 94-142. *Exceptional Children, 44*(6), 457–462.

Banaji, M. R., & Greenwald, A. G. (2013). *Blindspot: Hidden biases of good people*. New York, NY: Delacorte Press.

Chandler, P. T. (Ed.). (2015). *Doing race in social studies: Critical perspectives*. Charlotte, NC: Information Age Publishing.

Coffey, H. (2008). Team teaching. *University of North Carolina School of Education*. Retrieved from http://www.learnnc.org/lp/pages/4754

Delpit, L. (1995). *Other people's children*. New York: New Press.

Dweck, C. S. (2006). *Mindset: The new psychology of success*. New York, NY: Ballantine Books.

Education for All Handicapped Children Act, Public Law No. 94-142 § 6. (1975).

Elias, M. (2012, spring). The school-to-prison pipeline: Policies and practices that favor incarceration over education do us all a grave injustice. *Teaching Tolerance, 43*, 39–40.

Every Student Succeeds Act of 2015, Public Law No. 114-95 § 114 Stat. 1177. (2015–2016).

Feistritzer, C. E. (2011, July). *Profiles of teachers in the U.S. 2011*. National Center for Education Information. Retrieved from http://www.edweek.org/media/pot2011final-blog.pdf

Giroux, H. A. (2012). *Education and the crisis of public values: Challenging the assault on teachers, students, and public education*. New York, NY: Peter Lang.

Hill, C., Corbett, C., & St. Rose, A. (2010). *Why so few? Women in science, technology, engineering, and mathematics*. Washington, DC: AAUW.

Hulett, K. E. (2009). *Legal aspects of special education*. Upper Saddle River, NJ: Pearson Education.

Individuals with Disabilities Education Act of 1990, Public Law No. 94-142, U.S.C. 20 § 1400 *et seq.*

Kaplan, M. (2012, May 10). Collaborative team teaching: Challenges and rewards. *Edutopia*. Retrieved from http://www.edutopia.org/blog/collaborative-team-teaching-challenges-rewards-marisa-kaplan

Kavale, K. A., Kauffman, J. M., Bachmeier, R. J., & LeFever, G. B. (2008). Response-to-intervention: Separating the rhetoric of self-congratulation from the reality of specific learning disability identification. *Learning Disability Quarterly, 31*(3), 135–150. doi:10.2307/25474644

Keogh, B. K. (2007). Celebrating PL 94-142: The Education of All Handicapped Children Act of 1975. *Issues in Teacher Education, 16*(2), 65–69.

Landvatter, R. (2013). *I am what you think I am* (Master's thesis) Retrieved from http://digitalcommons.usu.edu/gradreports/328/

Michie, G. (1999). *Holler if you hear me: The education of a teacher and his students.* New York, NY: Teachers College Press.

Milner, H. R. (2013). *Start where you are, but don't stay there: Understanding diversity, opportunity gaps, and teaching in today's classrooms.* Cambridge, MA: Harvard Education Press.

Murphy Paul, A. (2012, October 6). It's not me, it's you. *The New York Times.* Retrieved from http://www.nytimes.com/2012/10/07/opinion/sunday/intelligence-and-the-stereotype-threat.html

National Education Policy Center. (2016, June 21). How effective is class size reduction? Retrieved from http://nepc.colorado.edu/newsletter/2016/06/class-size

Niedenfuer, J. D. (2015). The overrepresentation of African American students in special education: A review of the literature (Master's thesis). *Culminating Projects in Special Education,* Paper 3, St. Cloud State University.

Nieto, S. (Ed.). (2005). *Why we teach.* New York, NY: Teachers College Press.

No Child Left Behind Act of 2001, Public Law No. 107-110, § 115, Stat. 1425. (2002).

Samuels, D. R. (2014). *The culturally inclusive educator: Preparing for a multicultural world.* New York, NY: Teachers College Press.

Singleton, G. E. (2013). *More courageous conversations about race.* Thousand Oaks, CA: Corwin Press.

Singleton, G. E., & Linton, C. (2006). *Courageous conversations about race: A field guide for achieving equity in schools.* Thousand Oaks, CA: Corwin Press.

Steele, C. M. (2010). *Whistling Vivaldi and other clues to how stereotypes affect us.* New York, NY: W. W. Norton & Company.

Steele, C. M., & Aronson, J. (1995). Stereotype threat as the intellectual test-performance of African-Americans. *Journal of Personality and Social Psychology,* 69(5), 797–811.

Sullivan, A. (2011). Disproportionality in special education identification and placement of English language learners. *Exceptional Children,* 77(3), 317–334.

US Department of Education Office for Civil Rights. (2014, March). *Civil rights data collection data snapshot: School discipline.* Retrieved from http://www2.ed.gov/about/offices/list/ocr/docs/crdc-discipline-snapshot.pdf

Vanderbilt University. (2016). Team/collaborative teaching. *Vanderbilt University Center for Teaching.* Retrieved from https://cft.vanderbilt.edu/guides-sub-pages/teamcollaborative-teaching/

Wang, M. C., Reynolds, M. C., & Walberg, H. J. (1986). Rethinking special education. *Educational Leadership,* 44(1), 26–31.

Williamson, P., Mercurio, M., & Walker, C. (2013). Songs of the caged birds: Literacy and learning with incarcerated youth. *English Journal, 102*(4), 31–37.

Young, S. (2007). *Micromessaging: Why great leadership is beyond words.* New York, NY: McGraw-Hill.

NINE

Hostile Environment, Sexual Harassment, and a BB Gun

This case is inspired by the Catherine Ferguson Academy in Detroit, Michigan. Catherine Ferguson is a public school for pregnant teens and young mothers created to support these young women with real coursework and day care so the students can bring their children to school with them.

For generations young women had a place to go that held them to high standards with the expectation that they would attend college after graduation. The school's vision is "Success by choice, not by chance."

In 2011, a state-appointed emergency manager for Detroit schools ordered Catherine Ferguson Academy to close. It was that year that girls and alumni took it upon themselves to save their school. They staged a very public sit-in. They chanted over police sirens as they were escorted out of the building in handcuffs. Catherine Ferguson Academy was spared that year and remained open. But several years later, Catherine Ferguson closed its doors because of inadequate funding (Maddow, 2014).

Of the 70% of all students who drop out of school early, teen pregnancy is the number one reason. Among pregnant teens, 90% leave school because young mothers encounter financial struggles and economic insecurity as they try to raise their children; Hispanic and African American students with low socioeconomic status leave in even higher numbers (Teen Pregnancy Statistics, 2009).

Although the location, type of school, and student protest of the school's closing in this case are based on the Catherine Ferguson Academy, the facts of this case are entirely fictionalized. However, both the real story of the Catherine Ferguson Academy and the fictionalized account presented in this chapter highlight the real need for services for students who are pregnant and/or raising children. The Catherine Ferguson Academy was an anomaly in advocating for the education of pregnant students and young female parents.

THE CASE

Ms. Olivia Sidhwa teaches at a small urban school for pregnant teens and young mothers, a unique teaching situation. Seen as a beacon for at-risk girls, the Madame C. J. Walker School made national news a few years prior when the district, a large and struggling urban district, threatened to close it; a state-appointed emergency manager for Detroit schools ordered the school to close in order to cut costs. It was that year that girls and alumni took it upon themselves to save their school. Girls protested and refused to leave the premises, police were called, and reporters from across the country were there to record the protest, along with support from the National Organization for Women (NOW) and the United Auto Workers (UAW). National news outlets showed police forcing protesting young women from their school and into police cars, often restrained in handcuffs.

Alumni and current students desperately fought for the school to stay open because they knew the support they had been given by the school and its faculty and staff: prenatal care; parenting classes; childcare resources, such as diapers, furniture, clothing, and food; and childcare, before, during, and after school hours. The C. J. Walker School provided free childcare one hour before school started so that students could have some social time with friends before class, and two hours after school so that students could study, read, and complete their homework. Students past and present indicated that the school made a huge difference in the outcome of their lives.

The school managed to stay open via local support and was eventually taken over by a charter company. The local school district, which could no longer feasibly fund the school, granted the school charter. Charter schools, which are state subsidized, are often seen as alternative education, and this certainly fit the mission of C. J. Walker.

Although Ms. Sidhwa did not support charters, she decided to stay on for a few years to ensure that her girls were in good hands—despite a significant pay cut. Ms. Sidhwa bonded with untold students during her ten-year tenure at C. J. Walker. She created a course in intersectional feminism, which taught students the history of women's accomplishments throughout history, stories often hidden within traditional curricula; she also taught students their rights not only within the school, but also within their workplaces and their communities. Many of Ms. Sidhwa's students lived in rental homes or apartments in the city and were subjected to substandard living conditions; Ms. Sidhwa taught herself about tenants' rights, and passed on what she learned so that students and their families could advocate for better living conditions.

Ms. Sidhwa taught primarily science and health at C. J. Walker for ten years prior to the charter takeover. She had seen teachers and administrators come and go, but this did not trouble her too much. Although she desired longevity in her colleagues, she was relieved when principals and teachers left who were not a good "fit": those who did not believe in the program or the students, or those who were simply biding their time until a "better" opportunity came along.

Ms. Sidhwa was an effective teacher, and had managed to create a sustainable science and health program at the school largely due to her own tenacity and help from state grants and local businesses. On the school's vast grounds, she created an urban farming plot and taught her students to grow and cultivate food. The school's farm was also a useful resource for her science courses. Both made lab work practical for her students, and ideal for meeting her learning targets.

Student discipline was never a problem for Ms. Sidhwa, but other teachers and administrators struggled with the girls' transience, conduct, and seeming lack of commitment to their studies. Ms. Sidhwa, a self-proclaimed feminist, was committed to ensuring her girls received a stellar education, and often advocated for higher expectations among the other teachers, who she felt expected too little of girls who came from poverty and were or would soon become teen mothers.

Ms. Sidhwa was pleased when Dr. Orhan became principal of the school five years earlier. Dr. Orhan also had high expectations for the students, and did not abide the tradition of low expectations for the students who attended the school. Dr. Orhan had been an urban teacher for twenty years before completing her PhD and becoming an administrator. She was an administrator for five years in the district before transferring to C. J. Walker when the opportunity presented itself. She believed in the program, as she knew that many teen mothers struggled to stay in school while caring for their children, and felt grateful to be a part of the school and its innovative offerings, such as on-site childcare.

Dr. Orhan worked hard to bring the needs of her girls to the community to garner their support. She had developed partnerships with several area churches and local organizations. These partnerships provided needed resources such as afterschool parenting classes and a clothing closet containing maternity and infant clothing.

In Ms. Sidhwa's estimation, this idyllic atmosphere changed when the charter company hired a security officer for the school, after the CEO of the company visited the school once and deemed the students "unruly." Mr. John Sullivan, a very large white male in his fifties, was hired as the security officer the following week. He had no education past high school except for his security officer training, which he had completed six years earlier.

Ms. Sidhwa was troubled by the fact that many classroom sites are not places of intellectual struggle, particularly in low-income and urban areas; instead, they are places of behavioral struggle, where students are perceived as entities worthy only of control, discipline, and punishment (Milner, 2015; Morris, 2016). The addition of the security officer only made her beliefs in the systematic control of urban students more pronounced, and she was not happy.

Ms. Sidhwa feared the unwarranted presence of security on campus. She understood that her girls were already primed for the school-to-prison pipeline, and she feared that the addition of a security officer, with self-proclaimed experience in policing, might have a direct line to bring police into the school for small infractions that could escalate to arrests.

The school-to-prison pipeline contributes to the atmosphere of increased surveillance of schools, including police presence in schools, zero-tolerance policies, physical restraint tactics, and automatic consequence policies, resulting in suspensions from school (Alexander, 2012). The phenomenon of the school-to-prison pipeline leads to more students being introduced to the criminal justice system, and, ultimately, to more juveniles being incarcerated (Heitzeg, 2009).

Subject to disproportionate numbers of behavior referrals, students of color are more negatively impacted by these policies than their white counterparts (Alexander, 2012; Hilberth & Slate, 2014). Juveniles of color are perceived differently by the justice system than their white counterparts; prosecutors tend to attribute white criminal behavior to external factors, such as family problems, whereas criminal behavior exhibited by youth of color is often attributed to internal factors, such as personality flaws and disrespect (Alexander, 2012; Goff, Jackson, Di Leone, Culotta, & DiTomasso, 2014). Overuse of suspension and expulsion impacts student success and leads to increased arrests and imprisonment, higher drop-out rates, placement in alternative schools, and greater chance of continued aggressive behavior (Freeman, 2007). These detrimental effects are often the result of zero-tolerance policies and harsh punishments by school authorities.

Despite Ms. Sidhwa's knowledge of the research on the school-to-prison pipeline, she attempted to keep her politics to herself and be professional when she came into contact with Officer Sullivan. She greeted him upon his introduction to the school, and attempted to engage him in pleasant conversation. All was well for a few weeks, but things soon became uncomfortable when Officer Sullivan began complimenting Ms. Sidhwa in strange and inappropriate ways. "Smile for me, *Ms. Sidhwa,*" was a refrain she heard all too often from Officer Sullivan and in front of her students—he placed the stress on her title, as he was commonly referred to as John by students and staff. Ms. Sidhwa wondered if Officer Sullivan was threatened in some way by her title; otherwise, she thought, "Why would he stress it sarcastically?" Although Officer Sullivan "rang her bells," so to speak, meaning that her intuition informed her that something was amiss, she choose to let it be. Yet she was on guard.

In the following months, Officer Sullivan's comments to Ms. Sidhwa escalated to more provocative comments about her walk, her clothing, and her appearance in general. Comments such as, "Aren't you looking fine today?" "Walk that walk," and "Um, um, um, aren't you something today?" began to occur more frequently, and often in front of the students.

The last straw for Ms. Sidhwa was when she and a colleague were leaving the building for a long holiday weekend. As the two women walked past Officer Sullivan, they said good-bye and wished him well for a restful weekend. Officer Sullivan replied only to Ms. Sidhwa, stating, "That pretty smile . . . I'll be thinking about that pretty smile while I'm alone in my deer blind this weekend."

Shocked, Ms. Sidhwa did not say a word. She simply hurried to her car, her colleague in tow. When the two were safely in the parking lot, Ms. Sidhwa inquired to her colleague, Ms. Rose, "Can you believe he just said that to me?" "What?" Ms. Rose responded. Ms. Sidhwa quickly tried to communicate to Ms. Rose how uncomfortable she felt, for she could feel that her tears would betray her, and she did not want Officer Sullivan to see her crying. But Ms. Rose laughed and dismissed the comment as "no big deal." Ms. Sidhwa quickly cut the conversation short, and got into her car to drive home. On the drive she wondered about Ms. Rose's minimization of Officer Sullivan's comment: did she truly believe it was "no big deal," or did she simply not want to get involved? All weekend, Ms. Sidhwa could do nothing but think about that comment, and its sexualized implications.

Upon her return to school, Ms. Sidhwa called a meeting with the principal, Dr. Orhan. Ms. Sidhwa explained all that she had experienced in the last few months. She stated, "I do not want you to do anything. I just wanted to make you aware."

Dr. Orhan looked sideways at Ms. Sidhwa and stated, "Olivia, are you serious? Do you *hear* yourself? You teach your students about this very stuff, yet you do not want to *do* anything? I think you should file a formal complaint against him. We need to have this behavior on the record."

Ms. Sidhwa took a pause and remembered herself. She thought for a moment. Confiding in her principal, with whom she had a great amount of trust and respect, she stated, "I truly cannot believe this is happening. I am experiencing classic victim characteristics right now. I think I must be in self-protection mode. Give me a day to think about this. I am really confused."

Dr. Orhan complied with the request, and Ms. Sidhwa took some time to critically reflect, but she knew that Dr. Orhan was correct. She was the feminist teacher. She taught her students about sexual harassment, about how to advocate for themselves, about what they should do when they experience discrimination, yet she, knowing all that she knew, effectively shut down when facing harassing treatment herself. So, she thought of a plan.

Ms. Sidhwa did not feel that simply reporting Officer Sullivan's behavior to Human Resources would be an effective strategy. She surmised that Officer Sullivan would simply deny his behaviors, and they would be back to square one, with Ms. Sidhwa potentially having to also deal with retaliation, for Officer Sullivan would undoubtedly be angry if Ms. Sidhwa filed a report with Human Resources. So, with the endorsement of Dr. Orhan, Ms. Sidhwa devised a plan where she would confront Officer's Sullivan's behavior from a position of power; she would meet with Officer Sullivan, along with the school counselor/Title IX coordinator, Ms. Hamrick, in the principal's office to talk with him about his inappropriate behavior. Ms. Sidhwa felt this was the correct course of action before filing a formal complaint with Human Resources.

On the day of the meeting, Ms. Sidhwa was prepared with information on the district's sexual harassment policy, along with Title IX information. Although she could feel her heart pulsing through her body, she knew she had to project confidence. She sat in the principal's chair at the request of the principal, as Dr. Orhan was needed in the hallways (with much of the staff in attendance at this meeting).

Ms. Hamrick, having full knowledge of the aforementioned incidents, was in full support of the plan. Ms. Hamrick began by noting the reason for the meeting: that Officer Sullivan had made Ms. Sidhwa feel uncomfortable on several occasions with his inappropriate and sexually charged comments. She then indicated that she would be mediating as a neutral party, and would end the meeting if "things got heated," or if further actions were necessary that she could not undertake.

Officer Sullivan looked confused. Ms. Sidhwa then cited several examples of the comments that Officer Sullivan had made to her, particularly the one about the deer blind, and reiterated that these comments made her uncomfortable. Officer Sullivan indicated that he had no recollection of making this comment or any other inappropriate or sexualized comments. Officer Sullivan did indicate that he had innocently complimented Ms. Sidhwa, and that he would refrain from doing so in the future.

Ms. Sidhwa was quite sure that Officer Sullivan was minimizing his comments now that he was sitting in front of a third party. However, she was pleased that Ms. Hamrick asked that he read the literature Ms. Sidhwa provided. Officer Sullivan indicated that he would complete the reading prior to arriving at work the next day. Ms. Sidhwa left the meeting thinking this was a small win.

When Dr. Orhan debriefed the meeting with Ms. Sidhwa at the end of the day, Ms. Sidhwa communicated that she felt the situation would get better. Dr. Orhan hoped that this would be the case, but she also thought that Ms. Sidhwa was being overly optimistic. Dr. Orhan thought it interesting that Ms. Sidhwa, who was very knowledgeable on issues such as sexual harassment, would be so naïve, but she also hoped for the best. She wondered if Ms. Sidhwa's optimism had something to do with what victims of harassment commonly experience.

Despite Ms. Sidhwa's optimism, things did not get better; they just got different. In the weeks following the meeting, Officer Sullivan began a campaign of microaggressive behavior against Ms. Sidhwa. For example, each morning Officer Sullivan would stand at the one unlocked entrance door to the school building. Students would be gathered around this entrance, chatting with their peers prior to entering the building. Students were witness to Officer Sullivan greeting every staff member by name, and holding the door for them.

When Ms. Sidhwa would approach the door, literally seconds after the previous faculty member had entered, Officer Sullivan would stand silent, saying nothing and standing in front of the door—barring her entrance. Ms. Sidhwa would either have to walk around him or ask him to move. He neither greeted her nor opened the door for her. Students not only noticed Officer Sullivan's strange behavior toward Ms. Sidhwa, but also brought it to her attention, asking why Officer Sullivan was disrespecting her. Ms. Sidhwa attempted to dismiss the behavior and maintain professionalism, but she could not mask Officer Sullivan's passive-aggressive behavior, which always took place in front of students.

Unbeknownst to her at the time, Ms. Sidhwa began to stare at her shoes instead of holding her head up as she walked into the building from her car or through the hallways, attempting to avoid the aggressive glare of Officer Sullivan. This attempt at self-protection became a routine in her walk. She did not even realize she was doing this; her students pointed it out to her. It was years before she would break herself of this habit of looking down at her shoes while walking. Ms. Sidhwa felt a pit in her stomach while driving to work, while walking into the building each morning, and while walking through the hallways; any time she might encounter Officer Sullivan she felt sick, and he would, verbally or physically, make his presence known to her. Ms. Sidhwa was uncomfortable and troubled, but she was also worried for her students. This was not a professional situation for them to be witnessing. She also did not want them to implicitly learn that women in the workplace should expect to face gendered microaggressions. She knew that she was working in a very hostile environment, yet she could not say anything to her students about what she was facing daily.

Although Ms. Sidhwa kept a record of these microaggressive incidents and continued to rely on Dr. Orhan for support, she did not feel she had enough evidence of harassment and retaliation to report to Human Resources. But from all of her research on sexual harassment, she knew there would be a "final straw."

The "final straw" incident occurred during lunch a few weeks later. Ms. Sidhwa was walking down the hallway toward her classroom, well past Officer Sullivan, and she just managed to overhear a student being noncompliant with a directive issued by him. She kept walking. Much to her dismay, Officer Sullivan then yelled down the hallway at the top of his lungs, "That was very disrespectful, *Ms. Sidhwa*. Aren't you going to say anything? That is not very professional of you!" Ms. Sidhwa continued to walk to her classroom.

As Officer Sullivan was the security officer, Ms. Sidhwa did not believe it her place to step in, neither did she want any further interactions with him. So, she kept walking. She was shocked when she heard Officer Sullivan's footsteps behind her. Officer Sullivan had jogged down the hallway to catch up to Ms. Sidhwa in order to confront her.

As soon as she felt his presence behind her, Ms. Sidhwa turned around to face Officer Sullivan. She raised her eyebrows. "How dare you disrespect me in front of the students," he bellowed. Ms. Sidhwa stood silent, waiting for more accusations. "You think you have something on me? You have nothing! These students, who you believe love you, talk nothing but trash about you. They think you are too harsh and stuck up, and you are! You think they only disrespect me, which you saw, and did nothing, but they disrespect you too. They just do it behind your back!"

Ms. Sidhwa, saying nothing, continued to walk to her classroom, with Officer Sullivan following. Not wanting to turn her back on him, Ms. Sidhwa backed into her classroom, just as Officer Sullivan slammed the door in her face. Taylor, a student who had overheard this exchange, was running to catch up with Ms. Sidhwa and then stopped when she saw Officer Sullivan slam the classroom door.

As Officer Sullivan walked back down the hallway, Taylor knocked on the door. Ms. Sidhwa first asked who it was, and when hearing Taylor acknowledge herself, opened the door a crack. "Ms. Sidhwa, are you okay? That was crazy! He just went 'gansta' on your ass! What the hell is wrong with him?"

Ms. Sidhwa did not know what to say in response to Taylor. She was embarrassed. Knowing not what to do, she assured Taylor that she was okay, shut the door, and spent her lunch break alone.

Ms. Sidhwa later realized that Officer Sullivan felt that she implicitly accused him of unprofessionalism, and, although unwarranted, he was trying to do the same to her. She reported this incident to Dr. Orhan and reiterated Officer Sullivan's previous microaggressive comments and behaviors. Dr. Orhan, in turn, encouraged Ms. Sidhwa to file an incident report with Human Resources.

Ms. Sidhwa knew that she needed to do something. Although individually they were seemingly small incidents, taken together they constituted a repeated pattern of microaggressive comments and behaviors that were retaliatory. She thus wrote an incident report and filed it with Human Resources.

Mr. Van Allen, director of Human Resources, was a veteran of the district, having been both a teacher and an administrator for over twenty-five years. He was currently in his first year as director of HR, coming directly from another central office administrative position. Ms. Sidhwa wondered whether he had any knowledge of or experience in dealing with sexual harassment.

When she was called to meet with Mr. Van Allen, she learned that Human Resources representatives had already met with Officer Sullivan. Officer Sullivan had assured the Human Resources representatives that he would indeed now hold the door for Ms. Sidhwa. Ms. Sidhwa could barely contain her outrage that Human Resources was making this a case of a woman being upset about a door not being held for her. Mr. Van Allen then indicated to Ms. Sidhwa that no sexual harassment had occurred because Officer Sullivan had not actually propositioned Ms. Sidhwa for sex.

Ms. Sidhwa, aware of her rights, responded that what she had experienced was indeed hostile environment sexual harassment, and that this was more than about holding a door; she then provided Mr. Van Allen with a chronology of events, including times, dates, and specific comments (many of which were made in front of students), along with an account of how these incidents made her feel, and a definition of hostile environment sexual harassment.

Although she had done her due diligence, Ms. Sidhwa left Human Resources feeling unsatisfied. She believed that Mr. Van Allen neither had the required knowledge of sexual harassment befitting a director of Human Resources, nor the experience to adequately contextualize this case and follow through with a proper investigation.

Ms. Sidhwa walked into the building the next day, eyes trained upon her shoes. Officer Sullivan opened the door widely and loudly proclaimed, "Good morning *Ms. Sidhwa,*" sarcasm palpable. Ms. Sidhwa replied "Good morning" because there were students around, although she desired not to respond at all. For weeks, this sarcastic greeting continued each morning, but Ms. Sidhwa experienced no additional incidents.

Approximately one month later, two students, Eve (a young mother) and Asia (a pregnant teen) came to Ms. Sidhwa and informed her that Officer Sullivan had been making strange comments to them—statements that confused them and made them feel "uncomfortable." When Ms. Sidhwa probed further, Eve, replied, "He told Asia that he could see the color of her underwear through her pants." Ms. Sidhwa sighed. "What else?" she inquired. Asia and Eve both paused. "He looks at us, kind of up and down, and like he wants us to see what he is doing, and to know. He has said stuff to other girls too, and we don't like it. He says stuff to us about you, Ms. Sidhwa—making up stuff about why you're not married and don't have kids of your own, and how the school should not give handouts to us pregnant girls. We don't like him. What should we do?"

Ms. Sidhwa asked the girls to write up what had happened. Then she immediately went to Dr. Orhan's office, angry. She stood with her hands on her hips, the allegations of her students spilling from her mouth along with her outrage: "These are just two students. What else is he saying and doing that we do not know about?" Ms. Sidhwa then demanded, "Are we going to do anything now?"

Dr. Orhan sighed, but before she could respond, both women heard yelling from the hall just outside the office. Eve's social worker was there to take her back to a juvenile lock-up facility. A resident of a group home for young mothers, Eve was subject to random drug screens. Just after Eve's meeting with Ms. Sidhwa, her worker had come to do a screening, and she had "dropped dirty" for marijuana.

When Ms. Sidhwa ran from the office into the hallway to investigate the screams, she saw Eve on the floor and Officer Sullivan and Eve's worker attempting to restrain her. Ms. Sidhwa was angered by Officer Sullivan's tactics: he had Eve's legs spread open and was placing pressure, his full body weight, upon her inner thighs. Eve began screaming for Ms. Sidhwa. Ms. Sidhwa was aware that Eve was a victim of prior sexual abuse, and was horrified at these aggressive tactics. Ms. Sidhwa began screaming, "Let her go. Let her up. Stop touching her like that!"

Dr. Orhan and Ms. Sidhwa were able to calm Eve down, and Officer Sullivan and the worker allowed her to sit up. The worker escorted Eve, tears streaming down her face, from the premises to a juvenile lock-up facility. This was on Friday.

Ms. Hamrick had been called in over the weekend to make phone calls to students about the incidents reported by Eve and Asia. Following her initial phone investigation, Ms. Hamrick was determined to find out if Officer Sullivan had sexually harassed any of the girls. She had a good relationship with a few of the girls, and invited them to come in and talk to her. She had uncovered ongoing questionable conduct and comments made by Officer Sullivan toward many students.

By the following Monday, prompted by Ms. Hamrick and the initial student reporters, many additional students came forward with written statements about Officer Sullivan's comments and behaviors. Dr. Orhan, in consultation with the superintendent and the director of Human Resources, relieved Officer Sullivan of his duties, with pay, pending further investigation.

The investigation of Officer Sullivan's comments resulted in his termination from the Madame C. J. Walker School by Friday of the same week. Ms. Sidhwa was more than relieved. She slept soundly that Friday evening, but the next morning she found the driver's window of her car, parked in front of her house, shot out by a BB gun. She called the police and filed a report informing them of possible retaliation by a former coworker, but nothing ever came of it.

It was many years before Ms. Sidhwa could teach herself to walk again with her head held high, without looking at her shoes.

TEACHING NOTES

Sexual Harassment

Sexual harassment is a complex phenomenon involving various interrelated factors such as gender, patriarchal norms (most specifically, hegemonic or hostile masculinity), and issues of power. Brandenburg (1997) defines sexual harassment as "unwanted sexual attention that would be offensive to a reasonable person and that negatively affects the work or school environment" (p. 1).

Sexual harassment is defined by the American Association of University Women Educational Foundation (2001/1993) as "*unwanted* and *unwelcome* sexual behavior that interferes with your life. Sexual harassment is *not* behaviors that you *like* or *want* (for example wanted kissing, touching, or flirting)" (p. 2). Research indicates that over 40% of women and 32% of men have experienced sexual harassment at some point during their work lives (Das, 2009). The literature on sexual harassment suggests that over 90% of the time, males are the perpetrators of sexual harassment against females (Fineran & Bennett, 1999).

According to a 2011 report published by the American Association of University Women (Hill & Kearl, 2011), based on a nationally representative survey of 1,965 students in grades 7–12, sexual harassment continues to negatively impact the climate of US middle and high schools. Approximately half of the students surveyed experienced some form of sexual harassment; 87% indicated that sexual harassment had a negative effect on them. Girls were the most likely victims of sexual harassment.

Gender is a key factor in enabling a culture of harassment according to Rospenda, Richman, and Nawyn (1998). Coined by Katherine Benson (1984), *contrapower sexual harassment* occurs when the victim has formal power over the abuser. Benson argues that the power relation essential to sexual harassment is not formal, organizational power, but the differential relation that exists between men and women in society. Countrapower sexual harassment "serves to reinforce gender status by negating organizational status for women targets" (Rospenda et al., 1998, p. 56). Contrapower sexual harassment is common when women are in positions of authority, particularly in nontraditional situations (Rospenda et al., 1998).

Countrapower sexual harassment has much to do with informal power based on privilege that enables perpetrator behaviors, "influencing the ability of lower-status perpetrators to harass those at higher levels in organizational hierarchies" (Rospenda et al., 1998, p. 56). These sources of informal power can include dominant statuses such as race, class, and gender; contrapower sexual harassment is used to reestablish the subordinate position of the target. Contrapower sexual harassment may be used when the target of harassment is acting in ways that somehow disrupt traditional roles.

Title IX Defined

Passed in 1972, Title IX of the Educational Amendments prohibits sex discrimination in schools. Title IX also protects all students of all genders and sexual orientations from sexual harassment. Students in federally funded institutions, public and private schools, colleges and universities, have a right to an education free from discrimination on the basis of sex, including equitable access to all academic programs, activities, athletics, course offerings, admissions, recruitment, scholarships, and free from harassment (including assault) based upon sex, gender, gender identity and expression, and sexual orientation. Title IX also protects students from discrimination in academic and nonacademic activities because of pregnancy, birth, miscarriage, and abortion and protects faculty, staff, and whistleblowers from sexual harassment, sex discrimination, and retaliation (Martin, Kearl, & Murphy, 2013).

Microaggressions

Microaggressions are "verbal, behavioral, or environmental indignities . . . intentional or unintentional, that communicate hostile, derogatory, or negative slights and insults" toward people possessing minority status (Sue et al., 2007, p. 271). Microaggressive comments can be racial, sexualized, or gendered in nature.

Microaggressions are oftentimes the byproduct of implicit bias. According to Young (2007), "Micromessages reveal what is behind our masks, including hidden assumptions that connect underachievement in the workplace with race, gender, nationality, religious preference, class, and appearance" (p. 26). People who hold internalized ideologies about women and/or minorities may sometimes engage in microaggressive behavior without realizing it.

There are three different types of microaggressive behaviors: (1) Micro-insults are racially, sexually, or gender-charged statements that speak to the biases commonly held for that group, e.g., "You are really good at math, for a girl." (2) Micro-invalidations involve invalidating the lived reality of others, e.g., "You're too sensitive—it was just a joke." Micro-invalidations are common when a member of the dominant culture minimizes the experiences of someone in the minority, because they have never experienced indignities based upon minority status themselves. (3) Micro-inequities involve differential treatment of racial, gender, and/or sexual minorities, e.g., not calling on black students or other minorities (Sue et al., 2007). According to Young (2007), "The negative impact of micromessages builds up over time, hampering performance, and even causing emotional maladjustment" (p. 27).

Dealing with Sexual Harassment

Strategies and tools for reducing sexual harassment in schools include the following: a designated person that victims can confide in; online resources for victims of harassment, including information on their legal rights and appropriate reporting procedures; support groups for those who have experienced or witnessed harassment; proper protocols for the anonymous reporting of harassment; enforcing sexual harassment policies; and holding harassers accountable for their behavior.

School districts are required to appoint, train, and make available to the public a Title IX coordinator to oversee compliance and to deal with complaints and oversee reporting procedures of sexual harassment in its many forms. Although this is a federal mandate, many school districts are not in compliance with this Title IX requirement; thus victims of harassment often have no recourse in dealing with their harassers within the school.

School districts can apply restorative justice models, which involve the idea that perpetrators of crimes (in this case, sexual harassment) can be rehabilitated through reconciliation with victims and the school community at large.

The implementation of restorative justice models for dealing with sexual harassment will, in the short term, minimize the impact of sexual harassment, and in the long term, reduce its occurrence. The first step in this process is to include antiharassment statements in school handbooks, accompanied by detailed instructions on how to report incidents of harassment, including antiretaliation statements. Institutions should publicize these initiatives, so all are aware of them. Support systems and mentoring programs are crucial for victims of harassment, but particularly for those possessing marginalized identities; institutions should create, monitor, and support such systems. Restorative justice models should be created as an option for victims, but utilized only if they desire to address their perpetrators in such a manner.

Policy Prescriptions

School districts are advised to:

- Conduct a Title IX compliance review to determine if they are in compliance with the law by examining school policies and procedures, course advising, sports scheduling, and facilities to ensure gender equity.
- Create an antiharassment policy that provides details for reporting, investigation and resolution, and policies enumerating categories to include sexual minorities. Include an antiretaliation statement and provide for prompt and equitable investigation and resolution of complaints.
- Make contact information for the Title IX coordinator easily accessible. It be posted publicly and made available to students, parents, and employees. Posting this information on the district's website is ideal.
- Provide resources and materials on Title IX to parents and students. Create and disseminate a handbook for students and parents defining harassment and providing examples of behaviors that are prohibited (Martin et al. 2013).
- Train all faculty, staff, and students in sexual harassment prevention, including information on microaggressions.

QUESTIONS FOR DISCUSSION

1. What recourse was available to Ms. Sidhwa in this case? What support systems should be in place in a school? Discuss alternative measures Ms. Sidhwa could have taken to address the situation with Officer Sullivan.
2. As an administrator, what would you do if Ms. Sidhwa came to you with her concerns? How should these types of concerns be handled by an administrator?
3. Ms. Sidhwa's initial meeting with Officer Sullivan and Ms. Hamrick was an attempt on her part for restorative justice. What is required for a successful restorative justice mediation? Why do you think Ms. Sidhwa's attempt was unsuccessful?
4. What role should Ms. Hamrick, the Title IX coordinator, have played in this case? Should she have done more? What steps might she have taken to resolve the issues?
5. Is there a difference between the allegations raised by Ms. Sidhwa versus the students in this case? How should each be handled? Who is responsible for carrying out the investigation?
6. What is your position on hiring nondegreed individuals to work in schools in a security capacity? Do you see similar issues in both urban and suburban schools? Please defend your position.

7. How should security officers working in schools be trained? What were the various issues caused by the employment of Officer Sullivan?
8. After reviewing information on Title IX, determine if Title IX was violated in this case. If so, in what ways?
9. How were the students in this case impacted by the employment of Officer Sullivan? Did the employment of a security officer in this school reflect the larger problem of the school-to-prison pipeline? If so, how?
10. How did the inexperience of the Human Resources director, Mr. Van Allen, play into the outcome in this case? What actions should Human Resources have taken when Ms. Sidhwa initially filed her incident report?

ADDITIONAL ACTIVITIES

1. Investigate restorative justice models by reading the following two articles:http://www.edutopia.org/blog/restorative-justice-resources-matt-davis (Davis, 2013) and https://www.skidmore.edu/campusrj/documents/Kosspublication.pdf (Koss, Wilgus, & Williamsen, 2014). When, if ever, would these models be appropriate to use in cases of sexual harassment?
2. Wink (2005) states that hegemony continues when students are "quiet because (a) it is the polite, appropriate way to behave; (b) they have been schooled to behave that way; and/or (c) it is safe" (p. 94); these expectations are similar to what we see in most urban schools today, where the emphasis is on strict discipline, punitive policies, and "pushout," particularly for Black girls (Morris, 2016). As Guillard (2012) states, "To practice counter-hegemony is to be honest, authentic, and, most likely, to painfully or uncomfortably process and put into words how we position, and are positioned by, others in society" (p. 59). Read the following two articles on the criminalization of Black girls: http://www.theatlantic.com/education/archive/2016/03/the-criminalization-of-black-girls-in-schools/473718/ (Anderson, 2016) and http://www.npr.org/sections/ed/2016/03/23/471267584/the-untold-stories-of-black-girls (Kamenetz, 2016). Then work in groups to determine how to create acceptance of counterhegemonic beliefs and practices at Madame C. J. Walker School that will support students. What programs might you develop? What types of professional development would you provide to faculty and staff?
3. Investigate the Microaggression Project by utilizing the following website: http://www.microaggressions.com/. Work in groups not only to paraphrase the definition of microaggression, but to exam-

ine the site for common patterns/themes in the lived experiences of nondominant populations. Discuss how microaggressions can impact students, and develop a plan to raise awareness of this issue and to reduce incidents of microaggressive behavior in your school.

4. Optional activity: Encourage participants to share their stories about experiencing or witnessing sexual harassment and/or microaggressions if they feel comfortable.

REFERENCES

Alexander, M. (2012). *The new Jim Crow: Mass incarceration in the age of colorblindness.* New York, NY: The New Press.

American Association of University Women. (2004). *Harassment-free hallways: How to stop sexual harassment in schools, a guide for students, parents, and schools.* Washington, DC: American Association of University Women. Retrieved from http://history.aauw.org/files/2013/01/harassment_free.pdf

American Association of University Women Educational Foundation. (2001/1993). *Hostile hallways: Bullying, teasing, and sexual harassment in school.* Washington, DC: The American Association of University Women Educational Foundation. Retrieved from http://www.aauw.org/files/2013/02/hostile-hallways-bullying-teasing-and-sexual-harassment-in-school.pdf

Anderson, M. D. (2016, March 15). The black girl pushout. *The Atlantic.* Retrieved from https://www.theatlantic.com/education/archive/2016/03/the-criminalization-of-black-girls-in-schools/473718/

Benson, K. A. (1984). Comment on Crocker's "An analysis of university definitions of sexual harassment." *Signs: Women, Culture, & Society, 9*(3), 516–519.

Brandenburg, J. B. (1997). *Confronting sexual harassment: What schools and colleges can do.* New York, NY: Teachers College Press.

Conrad, S., Dortch, G. N., & DeNoon, B. (2011). Feminist pedagogy: Theory to practice. *National Forum of Multicultural Issues Journal, 8*(1), 99–105.

Das, A. (2009). Sexual harassment at work in the United States. *Archives of Sexual Behavior, 38*(6), 909–921. doi:10.1007/s10508-008-9354-9

Davis, M. (2013, October 4). Restorative justice: Resources for schools. *Edutopia.* Retrieved from https://www.edutopia.org/blog/restorative-justice-resources-matt-davis

DeSouza, E. R., & Solberg, J. (2003). Incidence and dimensions of sexual harassment across cultures. In M. Paludi & C. A. Paludi Jr. (Eds.), *Academic and workplace sexual harassment: A handbook of cultural, social science, management, and legal perspectives* (pp. 3–30). Wesport, CT: Praeger Publishers/Greenwood Publishing Group.

Fineran, S., & Bennett, L. (1999). Gender and power issues of peer sexual harassment among teenagers. *Journal of Interpersonal Violence, 14*(6), 626–641.

Freeman, S. M. (2007). Upholding students due process rights: Why students are in need of better representation at, and alternatives to, school suspension hearings. *Family Court Review,* 45(4), 638–656.

Goff, P. A., Jackson, M. C., Di Leone, B. A. L., Culotta, C. M., & DiTomasso, N. A. (2014, February). The essence of innocence: Consequences of dehumanizing black children. *Journal of Personality and Social Psychology.* Retrieved from http://www.apa.org/pubs/journals/releases/psp-a0035663.pdf

Guillard, J. (2012). Potentialities of participatory pedagogy in the women's studies classroom. *Feminist Teacher, 23*(1), 50–62.

Heitzeg, N. (2009). Education or incarceration: Zero tolerance policies and the school to prison pipeline. *Forum on Public Policy, 2,* 1–21.

Hilberth, M., & Slate, J. R. (2014). Middle school black and white student assignment to disciplinary consequences: A clear lack of equity. *Urban Education, 46*(3), 312–328.

Hill, C., & Kearl, H. (2011). *Crossing the line: Sexual harassment at school.* Washington, DC: American Association of University Women. Retrieved from http://www.aauw.org/files/2013/02/Crossing-the-Line-Sexual-Harassment-at-School.pdf

Kamenetz, A. (2016, March 23). The untold stories of black girls. *NPR.* Retrieved from http://www.npr.org/sections/ed/2016/03/23/471267584/the-untold-stories-of-black-girls

Koss, M. P., Wilgus, J. K., & Williamsen, K. M. (2014). Campus sexual misconduct: Restorative justice approaches to enhance compliance with Title IX guidance. *Trauma, Violence, and Abuse, 15*(3), 242-257. Retrieved from https://www.skidmore.edu/campusrj/documents/Kosspublication.pdf

Maddow, R. (2014, June 4). School for young mothers in Detroit to close. *The Rachel Maddow Show.* MSNBC. Retrieved from http://www.msnbc.com/rachel-maddow-show/watch/school-for-young-mothers-in-detroit-to-close-273886787725

Martin, J. L. (In press). Bullying, gender-based. In K. Nadal (Ed.), *The SAGE encyclopedia of psychology and gender.*

Martin, J. L., Kearl, H., & Murphy, W. J. (2013). Bullying and harassment in schools: Analysis of legislation and policy. In M. A. Paludi (Ed.), *Women and management: Global issues and promising solutions. Volume 2: Signs of solutions* (pp. 29–51). Santa Barbara, CA: Praeger.

Milner, H. R. (2015). *Rac(e)ing to class: Confronting poverty and race in schools and classrooms.* Cambridge, MA: Harvard Educational Press.

Morris, M. W. (2016). *Pushout: The criminalization of black girls in schools.* New York, NY: The New Press.

Paludi, M., Nydegger, R., DeSouza, E., Nydegger, L., & Dicker, K. A. (2006). International perspectives on sexual harassment of college students: The sounds of silence. *Annals of the New York Academy of Sciences, 1087*, 103–120.

Rospenda, K. M., Richman, J. A., & Nawyn, S. J. (1998). Doing power: The confluence of gender, race, and class in contrapower sexual harassment. *Gender & Society, 12*(1), 40–60.

Sheffield, C. J. (1989). Sexual terrorism. In J. Freeman (Ed.), *Women: A feminist perspective* (4th ed.) (pp. 3–19). Mountain View, CA: Mayfield Publishing Company.

Sue, D. W., Capodilupo, C. M., Torino, G. C., Bucceri, J. M., Holder, A. M. B., Nadal, K. L., & Esquilin, M. (2007). Racial microaggressions in everyday life: Implications for clinical practice. *American Psychologist, 62*(4), 271–286. Retrieved from http://www.cpedv.org/sites/main/files/file-attachments/how_to_be_an_effective_ally-lessons_learned_microaggressions.pdf

Teen Pregnancy Statistics. (2009). Drop out rates among pregnant teens. *Teen Pregnancy, Help, Treatment, and Counseling.* Retrieved from http://www.teenpregnancystatistics.org/content/drop-out-rates-among-pregnant-teens.html

Wink, J. (2005). *Critical pedagogy: Notes from the real world* (3rd ed.). Boston, MA: Pearson Education.

Young, S. (2007). *Micromessaging: Why great leadership is beyond words.* New York, NY: McGraw-Hill.

TEN

Violence Erupts at Oakhill High School

The issue of school safety has become of paramount importance to legislators, administrators, teachers, and parents. Incidents of violence in schools such as those at Columbine, Sandy Hook, and Red Lake Senior High have graphically illustrated the cause for alarm and action in order to provide secure educational environments. The causes of school violence are complicated and deeply rooted. According to Dogutas (2013), there is a strong association between physical abuse and aggression in children, and the factors that increase children's risk for violence, which include gender (males are at higher risk), poverty, having been a victim of violence, or witnessing violent acts in early childhood (Hofman, 1996).

Violent acts like hitting or pushing can cause physical harm, but bullying can result in great emotional harm. In 2012, there were 749,200 non-fatal victimizations in schools affecting students 12 to 18 years old; zero percent of teachers reported having been threatened, with 5% reporting being attacked by a student (School Violence, 2015). In a 2013 study, a nationally representative sample of students in high school determined that 8% of students reported fighting on school property, 19.6% of students reported being bullied on school property, 14.8% of students were bullied electronically, and 5.2% of students reported carrying a weapon onto school property within the past academic year (Dogutas, 2013).

The impact of violence on student behavior and performance is significant. Research shows that there is a direct relationship between victims of violence and a victim who displays violent behavior. Victimized students can experience extreme feelings of loneliness, low self-esteem, and depression (Luk, Wang, & Simmons-Morton, 2010). Further, researchers have found an indirect relationship between victimization and overt violent behavior (Povendano, Jesus-Cava, Carmen-Monreal, Varela, & Musitu, 2015). According to Carrell and Hoekstra (2008), "Children from troubled families or those having reported domestic violence decrease their peers reading and math test scores significantly and increase misbehavior by others in the classroom" (p. 17). Being bullied or victimized in some manner is also positively associated with substance use (Luk, Wang, & Simmons-Morton, 2010).

Based upon these startling findings, effective interventions relating to violent behavior must be created based on the specific issues that have manifested, and tailored to the needs of the school and community. Schools must consider the specific context of their community in order to design a process that will address issues of safety and violence (Chadwick, 2004). Such plans should be based on assessment and include plans for the facility, comprehensive staff training, a process for eliminating bullying, and an emphasis on responsive security within the school (Furlong, Felix, Sharkey, & Larson, 2015).

Another approach is to prevent school violence by recognizing early warning signs. Schools that encourage and empower students, faculty, and parents/caregivers to speak up and raise concerns about what they observe, and to assist others when they need help are likely to have school climates with less bullying, aggressive behaviors, and violence (Early Warning, 2015). Early interventions are vital to the successful curtailment of violence; providing educators with the necessary training and resources to identify such issues is paramount.

Conversely, there are serious negative impacts of zero tolerance policies and increased school security. There is an atmosphere of increased surveillance of schools, including: police presence in schools, physical restraint tactics, and automatic consequence policies, resulting in suspensions from school (Alexander, 2012). Such policies have contributed to the school to prison pipeline (Heitzeg, 2016). Constant surveillance of students within the school functions as an oppressive educational practice by reinforcing the prison of the mind, that of low expectations and negative self-fulfilling prophesies (Kozol, 2005; Pane, Rocco, Miller, & Salmon, 2014; Weis & Fine, 2005). It is a daunting task to successfully secure an educational environment, while at the same time promote freedom of expression and critical thinking in accordance with diverse perspectives.

BACKGROUND TO THE CASE

Oakhill High School within the Rockwood School District serves approximately 1,500 students in grades 9 through 12, with the student population consisting of 72% African American, 15% Hispanic, 3% Multiracial, and 9% white, non-Hispanic in a large urban city in Northeastern United States. Thirty-five percent of students at Oakhill High School are diagnosed with disabilities. This community is not immune to poverty, with 99% of students receiving free and reduced lunch. Students from the school live in poverty for different environmental reasons. A depressed local economy makes finding and attaining employment difficult, and generational poverty exists as an environmental factor in the community. As research indicates, children living in poverty in the U.S. are less likely to be able to rise out of poverty than in any other developed nation (Wagmiller & Adelman, 2009).

The latest state report card indicates that the Rockwood School District is ranked as one of the worst in the state, with the high school receiving the grade of "F." Oakhill High School received "Fs" in every measurement on the state report card with no indicators met for achievement, progress, gains in the closing of the achievement gap, or graduation rate. The graduation rate is 67%, with chronic absenteeism at 56%.

A review of the professional staff presents some insight into possible areas requiring attention. Ninety-six percent of the teaching staff possess a bachelor's degree, while 4% of the teaching staff do not. This means that not all teachers who are providing instruction to students have a degree, and are therefore not certified or licensed to teach. Only 75% of the district's building administrators have a master's degree. With a master's degree being a prerequisite for principal licensure, it is significant that 25% of the building administrators in the district are not licensed principals with leadership training. The use of non-certified teachers in the classroom, and unlicensed building administrators, not only presents a credibility issue in terms of educational accountability, but also raises important questions related to the legality of such actions on the part of the board of education and central office administration.

Henrietta Johnson: Citizen Politician

The Rockwood School District is perceived by many as being "in chaos," having received failing grades under the State Report Card System for years. There has been a historical divide between the school and the community for quite a few years. Henrietta Johnson, an African American woman in her 70s, was born and raised in the community, attending Rockwood District schools, and graduating from Oakhill. She remembers being one of the few African American students in the school before white flight. She remembers the area being prosperous, with manufacturing jobs in abundance, and hope in the air. In the mid-'80s, all of that began to change. Johnson watched as people and factories moved out. She witnessed the schools' decline.

"My kids were taught in Rockwood schools. Back in the '70s and '80s, my husband and I were active parents. The schools wanted us around; we volunteered and were at every school event. Now I'm a grandparent and it's different. We don't receive any communication from the school. They don't invite us in. I am retired now, and I have all the time in the world to help."

In the summer of 2015, Johnson began a community group to bridge the divide between the school and community. At the first meeting, attendees encouraged her to run for the open position on the board of education. Never thinking of herself as a leader, she did. She ran and she won. "Sometimes you need to see yourself through the eyes of others to believe you can do something. That was the case for me."

Johnson's main focus was on school discipline. During her first year, another seat opened on the board. Johnson suggested that Winnie Dodson, another member of the community group, run for the open seat. Dodson accepted the challenge, and eventually won. Both became crusaders for increased academic standards, and a full revision of the discipline policies and practices. Johnson used his personal influence and relationships to commission a study within the district on discipline, conducted by two researchers from the nearest university. The researchers interviewed teachers over the summer, and determined that many held perceptions such as:

Students at Oakhill do not value education or have respect for themselves or their school.
These students have very little self-worth.
They [students] are followers not leaders.
The students at Oakhill High School are poor and the families they come from are poor.
The community is poor.
The students do not feel education can significantly change their lives.

As Johnson stated at the September board meeting, "There are so many reasons for the poor school performance of students in the district." Winnie Dodson, followed with, "Our kids are getting cheated of a good education. They are getting cheated, we are getting cheated, and we have to do something to change this." Veteran school board member William Blithe recently joined Henrietta's community group, which inspired him to become more of an activist for the students and the community. In this new role, he encouraged community members to attend school board meetings, and to speak up about their concerns during the time given for public participation. This way, he surmised, issues important to the community would be voiced by the community, forcing the school board to address these issues; the meeting minutes would serve as a record.

The overriding concern expressed by Johnson, Dodson, and Blithe at the first board meeting of the new academic year was how discipline issues were being handled, and the frequency in which students were removed from their classes for what they perceived to be "subjective" discipline infractions such as "disrespect." As Blithe stated at the September board meeting, "The number of students who are given in-school suspensions and spend their day in rooms where they are not doing school work is astounding! These students are not receiving an education—they are being pushed out of the system."

According to the U.S. Department of Education Office for Civil Rights (2014), African American students are 3.5 times more likely to be suspended or expelled. Although they make up only 18% of the overall student population, African American students make up 46% of those students suspended more than one time. One in four African American students are suspended at least once compared to one in 11 white students (U.S. Department of Education Office for Civil Rights, 2012). New data show inequitable discipline practices enacted upon minority children beginning in preschool (U.S. Department of Education Office for Civil Rights, 2014). Additionally, African American girls are four times more likely to be suspended as white girls; African American girls with disabilities are five times more likely to be suspended as white girls, and experienced more instances of informal removal from schools, such as being asked to go home early (National Women's Law Center, 2016).

After learning about the board meeting from the local paper, a civil rights organization, along with other community leaders in the Rockwood area, called a Community Civil Rights Education Summit to discuss issues in the district, leading to a call for more equity in academics. Soon after, a national civil rights organization held a public forum on the issue. Parents, students, and community members indicated that their individual concerns with the problems in the district were never addressed. Some of the concerns included textbook and teacher shortages, poor attendance rates from students and teachers, and high rates of in and out of school suspensions.

Mary Reading, a representative from this national civil rights organization, listened to the concerns of community members who were outspoken—blaming the school board for not providing the necessary faculty and resources students needed to be successful. Another parent whose child attended Oakhill was upset that students went part of the year without a math teacher. She stated, "The per pupil allocation this year is more than $16,000. There's no reason for them to be lacking anything." Reading, replied, "Our organization views the problems at Oakhill as a civil-rights issue." Reading, on behalf of her organization, and the citizens of the Rockwood School District, filed a civil rights claim with the Department of Education's Office for Civil Rights. Ignoring requests to meet with state leaders, the State Department of Education made plans to bring in a CEO to reform the district.

The Appointment of the CEO in Rockwood School District

Hundreds of community members descended on the October school board meeting to voice their concerns about the appointment of a CEO by the state. Parents and teachers felt they were under attack by the state, and they did not feel the CEO would do anything to address the punitive discipline policies and practices occurring within the district. For the past three years, the state oversight commission had been present in the district and active in an advisement capacity to both the superintendent and the board of education with little accomplished to ameliorate the differences between the parties; additionally, under the state's control, the school board became powerless and could not affect change. New legislation was introduced to place the district under CEO direction.

The community was also concerned about the lack of teachers and administrators of color working at the schools within the Rockwood School District. They indicated that the appointment of a white CEO would only exacerbate the alienation and disconnection that students, parents, and community members experienced. The national civil rights organization agreed. Reading argued that it was important for the district to recruit more teachers and administrators that reflected the overall student demographics of the district.

The sentiment, here and reflected in many schools throughout the country, was that local leaders were more informed and better qualified to run the schools (Demske, 2016). As one parent was quoted in the press, "We want to run our own schools—its our kids and our right! We will do everything we can to keep the CEO out of the district!" The district filed a lawsuit in the Court of Claims against the School Reform Office, its office, and the CEO. This lawsuit is still pending.

A recent problem facing schools in this country, especially in large urban areas, is the shortage of school superintendents for lack of qualified candidates (Danitz, 2000). Candidate pools for superintendent jobs are limited, and, to exacerbate this issue, the average tenure for a school superintendent is seven to ten years, with turnover in urban areas every 2.5 years (Wheeler, 2014). More districts are looking to businesspeople and former military officers as potential superintendents to widen the candidate pool (Danitz, 2000).

The issue of noneducators being appointed as superintendents has found its way into legislation and schools throughout the country. In Detroit, a temporary restraining order was issued that prevented the state from appointing a chief executive to run the district's schools (Mitchell, 2016). Others examples are the Chicago School System and the Cleveland

Municipal School District, which are under the mayoral leadership—both are noneducators. This trend of appointing noneducators in administrative roles has taken hold in many of the larger urban districts in the country.

The move to noneducators being appointed as superintendents is a contentious issue. In a report for the Center for American Progress, Wong and Shen (2013) analyzed the impact of mayoral control in 11 different school districts across the U.S. They found while they can be effective in some schools, it does not work everywhere. Where some improvement in student achievement was evidenced in some districts, mayoral control was less effective in large urban cities like Cleveland, Ohio, and Yonkers, New York. Turning around a low-performing district is a challenge and it requires strong leadership skills. Some of the urban districts are equivalent to large corporations in the U.S. (Quinn, 2007).

Additionally, educational reformers, researchers, and experts in urban education remain concerned that noneducators will not have a complex understanding of the systemic factors within the community that impact children being educated in urban schools, such as: poverty, underemployment of parents, historical discrimination, housing instability, as well as factors impacting children urban school children within the school: underprepared and inexperienced teachers, lack of resources, cultural mismatch, and low expectations for students (Dyrli, 2013). While noneducators might be well versed in contract negotiation, resource allocation, and budgeting, possessing expertise in pedagogy and teaching practices is a necessity for school administrators.

Public school administration today requires a working knowledge of school finance, school law and policy, and experience in interpersonal relationships with staff, community, and caregivers. Increased involvement with special education programming and issues dealing with the myriad of student-related functional impairments necessitates a specialized knowledge of special education law and its financial and curricular implications for any school district. Understanding student assessment practices, teacher-directed and state mandated, requires a knowledge of curriculum and instruction. Such knowledge is also necessary for understanding teacher accountability and best practices for evaluation of performance. Noneducators from the private sector neither have such preparation nor the insights from experience to administer such programs.

Dr. Fred Myers was eventually appointed to run the Rockwood School District. Despite Myers's seemingly limitless power, he had neither a degree in education, nor any previous background in the field of education. The district had searched for a superintendent for two years prior to Myer's appointment and found many applicants were certified, but most lacked the experience and criteria they desired in their leader.

Myers had a military and business background, and saw as his main goal to increase school performance by developing a sound fiscal plan that would entice the best teachers they could hire, negotiate contracts for staff and faculty, and develop policies that would provide a smooth running organization. Oakhill High School was the only high school in the district, but because of its poor performance, many parents had chosen to enroll their children in local charter schools.

The district was top heavy with 56 administrative positions, and the promise of adding more middle management to the district. Most of these positions had experienced considerable turnover with all of the administrative positions at the board office being replaced except for one within the last three years.

Mirroring the district, Oakhill High School had seen considerable turnover in principals in the past five years. Oakhill seemed to be a revolving door for ineffective leaders who did not gain staff buy in or the respect of the students.

The current African American administrator, Donna Dardon, had only been on the job a month when the fight occurred. Although Dardon had been in the district for more than twenty years, this was her first administrative position and she felt overwhelmed. With the state appointment of Fred Myers as superintendent, the power of principals to suspend students was removed. More concerning to Dardon was the fact that all major administrative decisions needed to be approved by the superintendent. Dardon knew that this was a dangerous decision. She knew that teachers and administrators often needed to act fast in order to prevent conflicts within schools. She was fearful of the implications of this short-sighted decision.

THE FIGHT

Kendrick was a lonely introverted junior. He was studious, and often teased for being a "poindexter." He hurried to his classes to avoid seeing James in the hallway. James, a senior, was often his tormenter. Previous friends in elementary school, James, now a popular athlete, was embarrassed that he was once friends with Kendrick who he perceived now to be awkward and strange.

One fateful day, Kendrick did not make it to class early. Because he needed to use the restroom, which was only open at certain times during the school day, he got caught in a particularly congested hallway. He was trapped in the crowd when he came face-to-face with James who had crossed from the other side of the hallway, headed in the opposite direction.

Kendrick closed his eyes and sighed. He knew this would not end well. Just as he finished this thought, he felt his body being slammed into the lockers. As he struggled to pick up his belongings from the floor, James began to yell that Kendrick had scuffed his shoe. James threated that he was going to make him pay.

By the end of the day, Kendrick learned that there was a video of him being pushed into the lockers on several social media sights. In the comments section, students were starting to repeat a rumor that Kendrick was going to "Columbine" the school.

The next day, just before lunch, the senior class was holding a meeting about prom in the commons near the front of the building. Principal Dardon had heard there was going to be retaliation for the video posting. Although she desired to bring in both students and speak to them separately, her directive from the superintendent was to report all major incidents to central office. In so doing, Superintendent Myers positioned police officers in the office and around the building in preparation for the worst case scenario. As the seniors were exiting their meeting, Kendrick found himself surrounded by a group of students, James included. Principal Dardon was ready, and called them into the office immediately. In so doing, she felt that she could shield them from possible arrest.

At the same time, the hallways were filled with students as they were leaving their classes for lunch. Tricia Mullhollen was a first-year African American math teacher, and a member of the 2010 graduating class. She had lived in the area her whole life. She was proud to live and work in the community where she was raised. She was standing at her classroom door greeting her students when she heard fighting.

Ms. Mullhollen followed procedure, told her students to press the panic button, and locked her door before going out into the hall to determine what was happening. Ms. Mullhollen could not see the source of the commotion, but she saw dozens of students looking at their phones. She asked a nearby student what was happening. The student replied, "Students are posting on social media that SWAT teams are here. Everyone is saying there are bombs about to go off, and that a shooter is on the loose. We gotta get out of here!" Students in the hallway began to run in every direction. Ms. Mullhollen unlocked her classroom and ran to the phone. Her students were looking out the window. Some were crying. She called the main office, and reported what the students had told her.

Very shortly after Kendrick and James were pulled into the office, the police began to fight their way through the crowd. The school went into lockdown, as police, teachers, and the administration tried to move students out of the way and into classrooms. Officers wearing gas masks warned students many times to move or pepper spray would be used. As the crowd expanded and the noise escalated, officers began to pepper spray the air. Students hit with the spray began screaming.

The office began to fill up with students who had been pepper sprayed. Students continued to capture everything on their cell phones, sent pictures and videos to their families, and posted them on social media. A large crowd of parents and concerned citizens gathered outside the building, as well as several press trucks, and members of the board of education.

Some students were being escorted out of the building by police. There was no nurse employed by the school, so the secretaries attempted to treat the students who had been pepper sprayed. The phones were ringing off the hook. Faculty and staff needed direction, but Donna Dardon had limited administrative power. She had called the superintendent, and was waiting for him to arrive to help with the situation.

Outside, the local news station was reporting the incident. Reporter Josh Walsh asked a few of the students who managed to exit the school what was happening inside.

A student stated, "They called the SWAT team to the school. The police blocked all of doors so that no one could get in or out of the building."

Christine Brown, a sophomore, was visibly upset. She stated, "I couldn't see where I was walking and I was trying to get up the stairs and out of the hallway. My eyes were burning from the pepper spray and tears were streaming down my face. I couldn't see through the tears."

Josh Walsh recognized Rockwood City School Superintendent Fred Myers talking on his cell phone near the parking lot. He walked over, and waited for Myers to end his call, then he asked, "What is happening inside the school now? Are the students safe?" Myers said, "The situation is chaotic." He stated, "The Rockwood Police Department has advised up to close school for a few days until the situation has calmed down."

TEACHING NOTES

Though concerns about crisis are not exclusive to any segment of society, the development of practical guidelines for educational leaders related to effective communication have served as the specific initiative behind the 2001, National School Public Relations Association's *The Complete Crisis Communication Management Manual.* Educational leaders must have knowledge of how to communicate information about what is happening in the school to the community (Kowalski, 2004). School administrators understand that family, community, and school partnerships take sustained effort to build relationships and trust, mechanisms that support effective communication.

In order to put forth a strategic plan for communication, leaders must possess strategies for effective communication with stakeholders and ways to promote open communication within their school community (Epstein, 2005; Sanders, 2008). Crisis situations will test the communication management of even the best school administrator.

During a crisis, everyone wants to be and stay informed on what is happening in the school (Schneider & Hollenczer, 2006). People inside and outside the school are looking for information from as many sources as possible: the principal, of course, but also the media, the neighbors, their children, classroom teachers, and the internet (Schneider & Hollenczer, 2006).

During a crisis, it is crucial for the administration to communicate frequently and truthfully with key stakeholders about events as they are unfolding because in today's breaking news environment and with cell phones, if they do not, stakeholders will get their information elsewhere and that information may be flawed. Students and teachers inside the school may send inaccurate information out through their cell phones. Parents and members of the community will settle for whatever information they can find even if that information comes from second-hand sources and may be inaccurate. The problem is that once inaccurate information is released, the truth will not be received as readily as it would have been had the misinformation not been received.

Although crises are frequently shocking when reported on the news, a typical thought is, "That would never happen at our school or in our community." Principals, district offices, and communities must now prepare for crises that were once unthinkable. Crisis prevention is all about preparing for the unimaginable. Crisis management plans typically consist of a written document in a three-ring binder that includes checklists, contact information, step-by-step guidelines, and fact sheets that are coordinated with local police and fire departments and social service agencies.

The development of a crisis management plan takes place at the district level, but principals are expected to play a particular role in the safety of the people in their building. What generally happens in a crisis is that the concern for safety blocks out the concern for communication, which, in turn, can create serious problems for the principal. Those who look to the principal for leadership expect safety to be the highest priority, of course, but they also expect to be kept informed about what is happening.

In times of crisis, the building principal must communicate clearly and make crucial decisions in the name of safety for their staff and students. In this case, Donna Dardon is a high school principal facing violence in her building. The principal faced many decisions about communication and crisis management. According to Stuart (2013), "When disasters occur, principals often find themselves in unfamiliar territory, making decisions in an environment of uncertainty" (pp. 25–31). The pressure for Principal Dardon to handle this critical situation was paramount from a leadership standpoint. In this case, the building principal has to identify the resources that can be used to assist them with decision-making and implement communication strategies.

During a crisis, the first three questions that parents will ask will be basic: Is my child safe? What is being done at the school? And, how do I get to my child? A principal must communicate with parents as soon as possible, even if all the answers are not yet available. The first message may convey that there has been an incident at the school; the children have been secured, and the school has gone into lockdown. The school communicates that the situation remains under investigation, and parents will be informed of the status within the next hour. At that time, they will learn some basic steps for the remainder of the day. The key for principals is to keep a steady stream of information coming from the school to alleviate worries and keep parents, partners, and the district office up-to-date.

School administrators should be equipped to deal with the media in the time of a crisis. The media is an essential communication medium in which news can be delivered, and developing a plan to deal with reporters is a good idea. Educators should be responsive to reporters with news. The statement, no comment, should be avoided. Instead, leaders should find out accurate information, and provide reporters with honest answers (Schneider & Hollenczer, 2006).

QUESTIONS FOR DISCUSSION

1. What are the major issues in this case?
2. What contextual circumstances contributed to the crisis?
3. Who do you think is most responsible for the crisis and why? Who is responsible for communicating about the crisis to parents and the community?
4. Consider the highly specialized process of preparing someone for school administration, especially at the highest level. Does it stand to reason that an individual from the private sector with no such preparation could competently assume the responsibilities of running a complex school system in today's educational culture? Should noneducators assume leadership roles in public administration?
5. Discuss your reaction to CEO Myers decision to install police in the school building as a precaution. Was this the correct course of action? Please explain your answer.

6. What were the consequences of involving police in this situation, and how were the students impacted?
7. What steps should Principal Dardon have taken during this crisis?
8. What mistakes were made in response to the dissemination of information and how can this be improved?
9. In what ways can students feel connected and have a voice at Oakhill High School? How might the situation described in this case have exacerbated student alienation from the school?
10. What should Superintendent Fred Myers to repair the damage caused in this case?

ADDITIONAL ACTIVITIES

1. Review the National School Public Relations Association's The Complete Crisis Communication Management Manual (2001) and the National School Safety and Security Web site at www.schoolsecurity.org
2. Determine what a noneducator need to become familiar with the intricacies associated with school finance and the important issues associated with the day to day operations of running a school district.

REFERENCES

Alexander, M. (2012). *The new Jim Crow: Mass incarceration in the age of colorblindness.* New York, NY: The New Press.

Batsche, G. M., & Knoff, H. M. (1994). Bullies and their victims: Understanding a pervasive problem in the schools. *School Psychology Review, 23*(2), 165–174.

Carrell, S. E., & Hoekstra, M. L. (2008). *Externalities in the classroom: How children exposed to domestic violence affect everyone's kids* (Working paper). Cambridge, MA: National Bureau of Economic Research.

Center for Disease Control. (2016). *Understanding School Violence.* Retrieved from https://www.cdc.gov/violenceprevention/pdf/school_violence_fact_sheet-a.pdf

Chadwick, K. G. (2004). *Improving schools through community engagement: A practical guide for educators.* Thousand Oaks, CA: Corwin Press.

Danitz, T. (2000, February 24). States confronting school superintendent shortage. *The Pew Charitable Trusts.* Retrieved from http://www.pewtrusts.org/en/research-and-analysis/blogs/stateline/2000/02/24/states-confronting-school-superintendent-shortage

Demske, K. E. (2016, June 30). Community protests appointment of CEO for schools. *C & G Newspapers.* Retrieved from http://www.candgnews.com/news/community-protests-appointment-ceo-schools-94082#.V4fHvULJbVg.email

Dogutas, A. (2013). School violence in American schools: Teachers perceptions. *International Journal of Academic Research, 5*(3), 87–92.

Dyrli, K. E. (2013, September 15). Administrators move from private sectors to public schools: Outsiders bring expertise to K12 administration, but must learn the mission of education. *District Administration.* Retrieved from https://www.districtadministration.com/article/administrators-move-private-sector-public-schools

Early warning timely response. (2015). Retrieved from http://cecp.air.org/guide/files/4.asp

Epstein, J. L. (2005). A case study of the Partnership Schools Comprehensive School Reform (CSR) model. *The Elementary School Journal, 106*(2), 151–170.

Foucault, M. (1979). *Discipline and punish: The birth of the prison.* New York, NY: Vintage.

Furlong, M. J., Felix, E. D., Sharkey, J. D., & Larson, J. (2015). A plan for safe and engaging schools. *National Association of School Psychologists.* Retrieved from http://www.nasponline.org/resources/principals/Student%20Counseling%20Violence%20Prevention.pdf

Heitzeg, Nancy A. (2016). *The school-to-prison pipeline: Education, discipline, and racialized double standards.* Santa Barbara, CA: Praeger.

Hofman, A. M. (1996). *Schools, violence and society.* Westport, CT: Praeger Publishing.

Howard, D. S. (2016, October 28). Suspended and removed: How to enforce a student's right to school (Webinar). *National Women's Law Center.* Retrieved from https://nwlc.org/resources/webinar-suspended-and-removed-how-to-enforce-a-students-right-to-school/

Kaufman, R. (2016). *The Complete Crisis Communication Management Manual for Schools* (4th ed.). Rockville, MD: National School Public Relations Association.

Kowalski, T. J. (2004). School public relations: A new agenda. In T. J. Kowalski (Ed.), *Public relations in schools* (3rd ed., pp. 3–29). Upper Saddle River, NJ: Merrill, Prentice Hall.

Kozol, J. (2005). *The shame of the nation: The restoration of apartheid schooling in America.* New York, NY: Crown.

Luk, J. W., Wang, J., & Simmons-Morton, B. G. (2010, April 27). Bullying victimization and substance use among U.S. adolescents: Mediation by depression. *Prevention Science, 11*(4), 355–359.

Mitchell, C. (2016, July 8). Judge's order temporarily halts CEO oversight of schools. *Education Week.*

Pane, D. M., Rocco, T. S., Miller, L. D., & Salmon, A. K. (2014). How teachers use power in the classroom to avoid or support exclusionary school discipline practices. *Urban Education, 49*(3), 297–328.

Povendano, A., Jesus-Cava, M., Carmen-Monreal, M., Varela, R., & Musitu, G. (2015). Victimization, loneliness, overt and relational violence at school from a gender perspective. *International Journal of Clinical and Health Psychology, 15*(1), 44–51.

Quinn, T. (2007). Preparing non-educators for the superintendency. *School Administrator, 64*(7), 22–29.

Sanders, M. G. (2008). How parent liaisons can help bridge the home-school gap. *The Journal of Educational Research, 101*(5), 287–298.

Schneider, E. J., & Hollenczer, L. L. (2006). *The principal's guide to managing communication.* Thousand Oaks, CA: Corwin Press.

Smith Howard, D. (2016, October 28). Webinar. Suspended and removed: How to enforce a student's right to school. National Women's Law Center. Retrieved from https://nwlc.org/resources/webinar-suspended-and-removed-how-to-enforce-a-students-right-to-school/

Stuart, K. L., Patterson, L. G., Johnston, D. M., & Peace, R. (2013). Managing temporary school closure due to environmental hazard: Lessons from New Zealand. *Management in Education, 27*(1), 25–31.

Understanding school violence fact sheet [Fact Sheet]. (2015). Retrieved from http://www.cdc.gov/violenceprevention/pdf/school_violence_fact_sheet-a.pdf

U.S. Department of Education Office for Civil Rights. (2014, March). *Civil rights data collection data snapshot: School discipline.* Retrieved from http://www2.ed.gov/about/offices/list/ocr/docs/crdc-discipline-snapshot.pdf

U.S. Department of Education. (2015). *Early warning timely response: A guide to safe schools.* Retreived from https://www.tes.com/us/teacher-lessons/early-warning-timely-response-safe-schools-7162061

Wagmiller, R. L., & Adelman, R. M. (2009). Childhood and intergenerational poverty: The long-term consequences of growing up poor. *National Center for Children in Poverty.* Retrieved from http://www.nccp.org/publications/pub_909.html

Weis, L., & Fine, M. (Eds.). (2005). *Beyond silenced voices: Class, race, and gender in United States schools.* Albany, NY: State University of New York Press.

Wheeler, Jo. (2014). North Carolina superintendent turnover. Proquest.

Wong, K. K., & Shen, F. S. (2013, March 22). Mayoral governance and student achievement: How mayor-led districts are improving school and student performance. *Center for American Progress.* Retrieved from https://www.americanprogress.org/issues/education/reports/2013/03/22/56934/mayoral-governance-and-student-achievement/

Appendix A
Multicultural Resources for Teachers and Administrators

TERMS AND NOTIONS IN THE PROGRESSION OF OUR THINKING ABOUT RACE AND CULTURE

For most of the history of American education, students of color and students in poverty were viewed as culturally deprived, and thus not capable of achieving on par with their white, middle-class counterparts. Instead, they were provided with tracked classes and watered-down curriculums, less qualified or capable teachers, and fewer academic resources. According to Paris (2012), "Deficit approaches to teaching and learning, firmly in place prior to and during the 1960s and 1970s, viewed the languages, literacies, and cultural ways of being of many students and communities of color as deficiencies to be overcome in learning the demanded and legitimized dominant language, literacy, and cultural ways of schooling" (p. 93). One of the goals of these approaches was to eradicate the home cultures and literacy practices that many students brought to school from their homes and communities in order to replace them with what were considered to be correct, proper, and superior practices (Morris & Monroe, 2009; Paris, 2012).

Lee (2003) argues that although we have progressed beyond the pejorative terms of "culturally deprived" and "culturally disadvantaged," we still have terms such as "inner-city," "at-risk" (p. 3), and "urban," which are codes for those not classified as white.

According to Lee (2003), "the European-American middle class is consistently used as the point of reference from which to compare cultural practices with other national and international ethnic groups" (p. 3). Although the terms "culturally deprived" and "culturally disadvantaged" are used with less frequency within the current educational milieu, the implications are still with us.

Various scholars have outlined the progression of how educators (most of whom historically have been white) think about and talk about race and culture within education. To summarize:

- *Culturally deprived* (Lee, 2003) is the notion that people of color do not have a meaningful culture, or that nonwhite culture is somehow "less than."
- *Deficit approaches* (Paris, 2012), which dominated the twentieth century, view children and the cultures of which they are a part through negative comparisons with white, middle-class culture, instead of viewing cultures on their own terms, e.g., Indian boarding schools.
- *Difference approaches* (Paris, 2012) began to develop in the 1970s as a progression to viewing language/culture/community as "equal to, but different from" in-school knowledges.
- *Resource pedagogies* (Moll & Gonzalez, 1994) involve viewing communities of color as resources to explore, e.g., Moll and Gonzalez's (1994) conception of "funds of knowledge," which refers to "historically accumulated and culturally developed bodies of knowledge and skills essential for household or individual functioning and well being" (p. 133).
- *Third space* (Gutierrez, 2008) addresses an imagined future, where "curriculum and its pedagogy. . . grounded in the historical and current particulars of students' everyday lives, while at the same time oriented toward an imagined possible future" is key (Gutierrez, 2008, p. 154). According to Paris (2012), this third space requires that "teaching and learning is not simply about building bridges for students between the often disparate knowledges of home, community, and school spaces but that teachers and students must bring together and extend the various activities and practices of these domains in a forward-looking third space" (p. 94).
- *Critical Race Theory* (Bell, 1992), according to Ladson-Billings (2012), argues that racism is a normative aspect of US society. In their analysis of CRT, DeCuir and Dixson (2004) argue that counternarratives are crucial in dismantling myths and stereotypes of students of color: ". . . by telling their stories in their own words, their counter-narratives allow them to contradict the Othering process, and, thus, challenge the privileged discourses that are often found at elite, predominantly White, independent schools" (p. 27). CRT also necessitates a critique of Whiteness, which is made virtually impossible by the liberal ideology of colorblindness.
- *Culturally relevant pedagogy,* according to Ladson-Billings (1995), should do three things: "produce students who can achieve academically, produce students who demonstrate cultural competence, and develop students who can both understand and critique

the existing social order" (p. 474). According to Paris (2012), Ladson-Billings's conception of CRP involves "supporting students in maintaining their community and heritage ways with language and other cultural practices in the process of gaining access to dominant ones. In her third tenet, Ladson-Billings also called for the development of an explicitly critical and praxis-oriented stance in students" (p. 94).

- *Critical multiculturalism* (Castro, 2010) "strives to bring about the transformation of society to accomplish the goals of social justice by confronting and disrupting institutions and the structures of power that maintain disparities across race, class, and gender" (p. 199).
- *Culturally sustaining pedagogy* (Paris, 2012) is an alternative to Ladson-Billings's use of the term *relevance,* which Paris sees as being inadequate. Culturally sustaining pedagogy "requires that our pedagogies be more than responsive of or relevant to the cultural experiences and practices of young people—it requires that they support young people in sustaining the cultural and linguistic competence of their communities while simultaneously offering access to dominant cultural competence" (Paris, 2012, p. 95).

REFERENCES

Bell, D. (1992). Racial realism. *Connecticut Law Review, 24*(2), 363–379.

Castro, A. J. (2010). Themes in the research on preservice teachers' views of cultural diversity: Implications for researching millennial preservice teachers. *Educational Researcher, 39*(3), 198–210.

DeCuir, J. T., & Dixson, A. D. (2004). "So when it comes out, they aren't that surprised that it is there": Using critical race theory as a tool of analysis of race and racism in education. *Educational Researcher, 33*(5), 26–31.

Gutierrez, K. (2008). Developing a sociocritical literacy in the third space. *Reading Research Quarterly, 43*(2), 148–164.

Ladson-Billings, G. (2012). Through a glass darkly: The persistence of race in education research and scholarship. *Educational Researcher, 41*(4), 115–120.

Ladson-Billings, G., & Tate, E. (1995). Toward a critical race theory of education. *Teachers College Record, 97*(1), 47–67.

Lee, C. D. (2003). Why we need to re-think race and ethnicity in educational research. *Educational Researcher, 32*(5), 3–5.

Lutterloh, C., Cornier, J., & Hassel, B. C. (2016). Measuring school turnaround success. *Public Impact.* Retrieved from www.schoolturnaroundsupport.org/sites/default/files/resources/Measuring_School_Turnaround_Success.pdf

Mathis, W. J., & Trujillo, T. (2016, July 20). School turnaround report fails to meet standard of evidence. *National Education Policy Center.* Retrieved from http://nepc.colorado.edu/newsletter/2016/07/turnaround

Mathis, W. J., & White, T. (2016, July 26). Report oversteps in attempt to portray Denver as reform exemplar. *National Education Policy Center.* Retrieved from http://nepc.colorado.edu/newsletter/2016/07/report-oversteps

Moll, L., & Gonzalez, N. (1994). Lessons from research with language minority children. *Journal of Reading Behavior, 26*(4), 23–41.

Morris, J. E., & Monroe, C. R. (2009). Why study the U.S. South? The nexus of race and place in investigating black student achievement. *Educational Researcher, 38*(1), 21–36.

Paris, D. (2012). Culturally sustaining pedagogy: A needed change in stance, terminology, and practice. *Educational Researcher, 41*(3), 93–97.

Trujillo, T., & Rivera, M. (2016, July 20). Review of *Measuring School Turnaround Success. National Education Policy Center.* Retrieved from http://nepc.colorado.edu/thinktank/review-turnaround

ACTIVITIES/INFORMATION (TOPICAL)

Curriculum

Colorin Colorado. (n.d.). Multicultural resources for the classroom. Retrieved from http://www.colorincolorado.org/web_resources/by_topic/multicultural_resources_for_classroom/

Deshmukh Towery, I., Oliveri, R., & Gidney, C. L. (2007). Peer-led professional development for equity and diversity: A report for teachers and administrators based on findings from the SEED Project (Seeking Educational Equity and Diversity). *Schott Foundation for Public Education.* Retrieved from http://www.racialequitytools.org/resourcefiles/deshmukh.pdf

Kea, C., Campbell-Whatley, G. D., & Richards, H. V. (2006). Becoming culturally responsive educators: Rethinking teacher education pedagogy. *National Center for Culturally Responsive Educational Systems: Education for All.* Retrieved from http://glec.education.iupui.edu/equity/Becoming_Culturally_Responsive_Educators.pdf

Loyola University. (n.d.). Curriculum resources on the Internet: Multicultural resources. *Loyola University.* Retrieved from http://libguides.luc.edu/c.php?g=49783&p=320646

Talking about Race

Hannah-Jones, N. (2015, June 29). What Abigail Fisher's affirmative action case is really about. *ProPublica.* Retrieved from http://www.rawstory.com/2015/07/what-abigail-fishers-affirmative-action-case-is-really-about/

Johnson, C. (2015, June 24). Bryan Stevenson on Charleston and our real problem with race. *The Marshall Project.* Retrieved from https://www.themarshallproject.org/2015/06/24/bryan-stevenson-on-charleston-and-our-real-problem-with-race

Lurie, J. (2015, April 17). Just how racist are schoolteachers? *Mother Jones.* Retrieved from http://www.motherjones.com/kevin-drum/2015/04/teachers-racism-bias-stanford

Milner, H. R. (2015, July 1). Educators shouldn't avoid the tough conversations. *Education Week.* Retrieved from http://blogs.edweek.org/edweek/op_education/2015/07/educators_shouldnt_avoid_the_tough_conversations.html

Milner, H. R. (2015, July 1). Getting race and poverty right in education. *Diverse Issues in Higher Education.* Retrieved from http://diverseeducation.com/article/76058/

ARTICLES

Bemak, F., & Chi-Ying Chung, R. (2008, summer). New professional roles and advocacy strategies for school counselors: A multicultural/social justice perspective to move beyond the nice counselor syndrome. *Journal of Counseling & Development, 86,* 372–382. Retrieved from http://edresearch.yolasite.com/resources/BemakChung.pdf

Chesler, M. (2003, January). Teaching well in the diverse/multicultural classroom. *American Association for Higher Education and Accreditation Bulletin.* Retrieved from http://www.aahea.org/articles/sociology.htm

Chou, H. (2007, summer). Multicultural teacher education: Toward a culturally responsive pedagogy. *Essays in Education, 21,* 139–162. Retrieved from https://gsueds2007.pbworks.com/f/multiculturalism%20teacher%20education.pdf

Gorski, P. (n.d.). Stages of multicultural school transformation. *EdChange.* Retrieved from http://www.edchange.org/multicultural/resources/school_transformation.html

ORGANIZATIONS

EdChange: Bringing equitable and just schools, communities, and organizations through transformative action: http://www.edchange.org/

National Alliance for Partnerships in Equity (NAPE): http://www.napequity.org/

The National Association for Multicultural Education (NAME): http://www.nameorg.org/

Southern Poverty Law Center: https://www.splcenter.org/

Teaching Tolerance: http://www.tolerance.org/

Urban Research-Based Action Network (URBAN): http://urbanresearchnetwork.org/

RESOURCES

AAUW. (n.d.). Find your Title IX coordinators. Retrieved from http://www.aauw.org/resource/find-your-title-ix-coordinator/

Center for Research on Learning and Teaching. (n.d.). Diversity and inclusion. *The University of Michigan.* Retrieved from http://www.crlt.umich.edu/multicultural-teaching

John Jay College of Criminal Justice. (2016). Teaching resources for difficult times. Retrieved from http://www.jjay.cuny.edu/teaching-resources-difficult-times

National Education Association. (2015). Resources for addressing multicultural and diversity issues in your classroom: Books, websites and other resources help you learn about multicultural and diversity issues. Retrieved from http://www.nea.org/tools/resources-addressing-multicultural-diversity-issues-in-your-classroom.htm

National MultiCultural Institute: http://www.nmci.org/

Southern Poverty Law Center. (2016, August 9). SPLC complaint: Schools in Alabama town discriminating against black children. Retrieved from https://www.splcenter.org/news/2016/08/09/splc-complaint-schools-alabama-town-discriminating-against-black-children

Scholastic. (n.d.). Lesson plan: Multiculturalism and diversity. Retrieved from http://www.scholastic.com/teachers/lesson-plan/multiculturalism-and-diversity

Teaching Tolerance. (n.d.). Family and community engagement. Retrieved from http://www.tolerance.org/publication/family-and-community-engagement

Teaching Tolerance. (n.d.). The Southern Poverty Law Center. Retrieved from http://www.tolerance.org/

SIMULATIONS

BaFa BaFa. Can be found at http://www.simulationtrainingsystems.com/corporate/products/bafa-bafa/

Crossing the Line. Facilitation guidelines can be found at http://freechild.org/Firestarter/CrossingTheLine.htm

The Dance of Structural Inequality. Can be found at https://www.yumpu.com/en/document/view/49609798/dance-of-structural-inequality-in-pdf-format (see Buzzfeed video example below)
Harvard Implicit Bias Tests: https://implicit.harvard.edu/implicit/takeatest.html

VIDEOS

Buzzfeed. (2015). What is privilege? *YouTube.* Retrieved from https://www.youtube.com/watch?v=hD5f8GuNuGQ
Jane Elliott: Blue eyes/brown eyes. *YouTube.* Retrieved from https://www.youtube.com/watch?v=Nqv9k3jbtYU
Jane Elliot: How racist are you? *YouTube.* Retrieved from https://www.youtube.com/watch?v=XAv8JA_9uKI
Jane Elliot: *Oprah* racism experiment. *Huffington Post.* Retrieved from http://www.huffingtonpost.com/2015/01/02/jane-elliott-race-experiment-oprah-show_n_6396980.html

WEBSITES

Brown, S. (2002, fall). In it together: Teacher networks support multicultural education. *The Notebook.* Retrieved from http://thenotebook.org/fall-2002/021465/it-together-teacher-networks-support-multicultural-education
Walsh, B. (2015, January 26). Getting to excellence with equity: Ron Ferguson talks about opportunity, achievement, and raising the bar for all students. *Usable Knowledge: Connecting Research to Practice.* Retrieved from http://www.gse.harvard.edu/news/uk/15/01/getting-excellence-equity

FOR FURTHER READING

Adams, M., Blumenfeld, W. J., Castaneda, R., Hackman, H. W., Peters, M. L., & Zuniga, X. (Eds.). (2013). *Readings for diversity and social justice* (3rd ed.). New York, NY: Routledge.
Adams, M., Bell, L. E., & Griffin, P. (Eds.). (1997). *Teaching for diversity and social justice.* New York, NY: Routledge.
Adams, V. (2013). *Markets of sorrow, labors of faith: New Orleans in the wake of Katrina.* Durham, NC: Duke University Press.
Akiba, M. (2011). Identifying program characteristics for preparing pre-service teachers for diversity. *Teachers College Record, 113*(3), 658–697.
Allport, G. W. (1954). *The nature of prejudice.* Reading, MA: Addison-Wesley.
Artiles, A. J. (2011). Toward an interdisciplinary understanding of educational equity and difference: The case of the racialization of ability. *Educational Researcher, 40*(9), 431–445.
Asanti, M. (1988). *Afrocentricity: The theory of social change.* Trenton, NJ: African World Press.
Asher, N. (2007). Made in the (multicultural) U.S.A.: Unpacking tensions of race, culture, gender, and sexuality in education. *Educational Researcher, 36*(2), 65–73.
Baker, G. C. (1988). Recognition of our culturally pluralistic society and multicultural education in our schools. *Education and Society, 1*(1), 23–28.
Banks, J. A. (2009). *Teaching strategies for ethnic studies* (8th ed.). Boston, MA: Pearson Allyn and Bacon.
Banks, J. A. (2007). *Educating citizens in a multicultural society* (2nd ed.). New York, NY: Teachers College Press.

Banks, J. A. (2006). *Cultural diversity and education: Foundations, curriculum, and teaching* (4th ed.). Boston, MA: Allyn and Bacon.

Banks, J. A. (2006). *Race, culture, and education: The selected works of James A. Banks*. New York, NY: Routledge.

Banks, J. A. (2001). Citizenship education and diversity: Implications for teacher education. *Journal of Teacher Education, 52*(1), 5–16.

Banks, J. A., & McGee Banks, C. A. (1998). *Teaching strategies for the social studies: Decision-making and citizen action* (5th ed.). New York, NY: Longman.

Banks, J. A. (1988). *Multicultural education: Theory and practice*. Boston, MA: Allyn and Bacon.

Bartolome, L. I. (1994). Beyond the methods fetish: Towards a humanizing pedagogy. *Harvard Educational Review, 64*(2), 172–194.

Bell, D. (1992). Racial realism. *Connecticut Law Review, 24*(2), 363–379.

Biklen, R. (1985). *The complete school: Integrating special and regular education*. New York, NY: Columbia University Press.

Blanchett, W. J. (2006). Disproportionate representation of African American students in special education: Acknowledging the role of white privilege and racism. *Educational Researcher, 35*(6), 24–28.

Bogdan, R. (1986). The sociology of special education. In R. J. Morris & B. Blatt (Eds.), *Special education: Research and trends*. Elmsford, NY: Pergamon.

Bolotin Joseph, P., Luster Bravmann, S., Windschitl, M. A., Mikel, E. R., & Stewart Green, N. (2000). *Cultures of curriculum*. Mahwah, NJ: Lawrence Erlbaum Associates.

Brown, P., Reay, D., & Vincent, C. (2013). Education and social mobility. *British Journal of Sociology of Education, 34*(5–6), 637–643.

Bullivant, B. (1989). *Multicultural education: Issues and perspectives*. Boston: Allyn and Bacon.

Cantu, N. V., & Heumann, J. E. (2000, July 25). Prohibited disability harassment: Reminder of responsibilities under section 504 of the Rehabilitation Act of 1973 and Title II of the Americans with Disabilities Act. US Department of Education, Office for Civil Rights. Retrieved from http://www2.ed.gov/about/offices/list/ocr/docs/disabharassltr.html

Carter Andrews, D. J. (2012). Black achievers' experiences with racial spotlighting and ignoring in a predominantly white high school. *Teachers College Record, 114*(10), 1–46.

Casella, R. (2003, November). Punishing dangerousness through preventive detention: Illustrating the institutional link between school and prison. *New Directions for Youth Development. Special Issue: Deconstructing the School-to-Prison Pipeline, 99*, 55–70.

Castro, A. J. (2010). Themes in the research on preservice teachers' views of cultural diversity: Implications for researching millennial preservice teachers. *Educational Researcher, 39*(3), 198–210.

Center for Evidence-Based Crime Policy. (2014). *Broken windows policing*. George Mason University. Retrieved from http://cebcp.org/evidence-based-policing/what-works-in-policing/research-evidence-review/broken-windows-policing/

Chapman, T. K. (2007). Interrogating classroom relationships and events: Using portraiture and critical race theory in education research. *Educational Researcher, 36*(3), 156–162.

Chappell, M. (2010). *The war on welfare: Family, poverty, and politics in modern America*. Philadelphia, PA: The University of Pennsylvania Press.

Charity Hudley, A. H., & Mallinson, C. (2012). *Understanding English language variation in U.S. schools*. New York, NY: Teachers College Press.

Clinchy, E., & Kolb, F. (1989). *Planning for schools of choice: Achieving equity and excellence*. Andover, MA: Network, Inc.

Cortes, C. (2000). *The children are watching: How the media teach about diversity*. New York, NY: Teachers College Press.

Costa, M. D., & James, S. (1975). *The power of women and the subversion of the community*. London, UK: Falling Wall Press.

Counts, G. (1932). *Dare the school build a new social order*? Carbondale, IL: Southern Illinois University Press.

Daniels, H. A. (1990). *Not only English: Affirming America's multilingual heritage*. Urbana, IL: National Council of Teachers of English.

DeCuir, J. T., & Dixson, A. D. (2004). "So when it comes out, they aren't that surprised that it is there": Using critical race theory as a tool of analysis of race and racism in education. *Educational Researcher, 33*(5), 26–31.

Delpit, L. (2003). Educators as "seed people": Growing a new future. *Educational Leadership, 7*(32), 14–21.

Delpit, L. (1995). *Other people's children: Cultural conflict in the classroom*. New York, NY: The New Press.

Dewey, J. (1916). *Democracy and education*. New York, NY: Macmillan.

DiAngelo, R. (2012). Nothing to add: The role of white silence in racial discussions. *Journal of Understanding and Dismantling Privilege, 2*(2), 1–17.

Dover, A. G. (2013). Getting "up to code": Preparing for and confronting challenges when teaching for social justice in standards-based classrooms. *Action in Teacher Education, 35*(2), 89–102.

Fagan, J., & Davies, G. (2000). Street stops and broken windows: Terry, race, and disorder in New York City. *Fordham Urban Law Journal, 28*(3), 457–504.

Farrington, C. A. (2014). *Failing at school: Lessons for redesigning urban high schools*. New York, NY: Teachers College Press.

Feistritzer, C. E. (2011, July). *Profiles of teachers in the U.S. 2011*. National Center for Education Information. Retrieved from http://www.edweek.org/media/pot2011final-blog.pdf

Fine, M. (1991). *Framing dropouts: Notes on the politics of an urban high school*. Albany, NY: State University of New York Press.

Fraschl, M., & Sprung, B. (1986). *Building community: A manual exploring issues of women and disabilities*. Women and Disabilities Awareness Project. New York, NY: Equity Concepts, Inc.

Fraser, N., & Linda G. (1994). A genealogy of dependency: Tracing a keyword of the U.S. welfare state. *Signs, 19*(2), 309–336.

Freire, P. (1974). *Pedagogy of the oppressed*. New York: Seabury Press.

Furnin, T. L. (2009). *Combating hatred: Educators leading the* way. Lanham, MD: Rowman & Littlefield.

Gaines, L. K., & Miller, L. E. (2014). *Criminal justice in action: The core* (7th ed.). Belmont, CA: Wadsworth.

Gay, G. (2000). *Culturally responsive teaching: Theory, research and practice*. New York, NY: Teachers College Press.

Gay, G., & Howard, T. (2000). Multicultural teacher education for the 21st century. *The Teacher Educator, 36*(1), 1–16.

Ginsberg, A. E. (2012). *Embracing risk in urban education: Curiosity, creativity, and courage in the era of "no excuses" and relay race reform*. Lanham, MD: Rowman & Littlefield.

Giroux, H. A., & McLaren, P. (Eds.). (1989). *Critical pedagogy, the state, and cultural struggles*. Albany, NY: The State University of New York.

Goff, P. A., Jackson, M. C., Di Leone, B. A. L., Culotta, C. M., & DiTomasso, N. A. (2014). The essence of innocence: Consequences of dehumanizing black children. *Journal of Personality and Social Psychology, 106*(4), 526–545. Retrieved from https://www.apa.org/pubs/journals/releases/psp-a0035663.pdf

Goldberg, G. S., & Collins, S. D. (2001). *Washington's new poor law: Welfare reform and the roads not taken—1935 to the present*. New York, NY: Apex Press.

Good, T. L., & Brophy, J. E. (1987). *Looking in classrooms* (4th ed.). New York, NY: Harper and Row.

Gordon, A. (1979). *The nature of prejudice*. Cambridge, MA: Addison-Wesley.

Gordon, L. (1994). *Pitied but not entitled: Single mothers and the history of welfare, 1890–1935*. New York, NY: Free Press.

Grady, S. (2000). *Drama and diversity: A pluralistic perspective for educational drama*. Westport, CT: Heinemann.

Grayson, D. (1986). *The equity principal: An inclusive approach to excellence*. Los Angeles, CA: County Office of Education.

Grayson, D. A. (1985). *Infusing an equity agenda into schools districts*. Downey, CA: Los Angeles County Office of Education.

Gregory, A., Skiba, R. J., & Noguera, P. A. (2010). The achievement gap and the discipline gap: Two sides of the same coin? *Educational Researcher, 39*(1), 59–68.

Grossman, H. (1984). *Educating Hispanic children: Cultural implications for classroom instruction, classroom management, counseling, and assessment*. Springfield, IL: C.C. Thomas.

Guimond, S. (2000). Group socialization and prejudice: The social transmission of intergroup attitudes and beliefs. *European Journal of Social Psychology, 30*(3), 335–354.

Gutierrez, K. (2008). Developing a sociocritical literacy in the third space. *Reading Research Quarterly, 43*(2), 148–164.

Hancock, A. M. (2004). *The politics of disgust: The public identity of the welfare queen*. New York, NY: New York University Press.

Hatzenbuehler, M. L., McLaughlin, K. A., Keyes, K. M., & Hasin, D. S. (2010). The impact of institutional discrimination on psychiatric disorders in lesbian, gay, and bisexual populations: A prospective study. *American Journal of Public Health, 100*(3), 452–459.

Henkel, K. E., Dovidio, J. F., & Gaertner, S. L. (2006). Institutional discrimination, individual racism, and Hurricane Katrina. *Analyses of Social Issues and Public Policy, 6*(1), 99–124.

Hill, J. D., & Flynn, K. M. (2006). *Classroom instruction that works with English language learners*. Alexandria, VA: Association for Supervision and Curriculum Development.

Iwamoto, D. (2003). Tupac Shakur: Understanding the identity formation of hypermasculinity of a popular hip-hop artist. *The Black Scholar, 33*(2), 44–49.

Jenlink, P. M. (Ed.). (2009). *Equity issues for today's educational leaders: Meeting the challenge of creating equitable schools for all*. Lanham, MD: Rowman & Littlefield.

Kessler-Harris, A. (2003). *Pursuit of equity: Women, men, and the quest for economic citizenship in twentieth-century America*. Oxford, UK: Oxford University Press.

Ladson-Billings, G. (2012). Through a glass darkly: The persistence of race in education research and scholarship. *Educational Researcher, 41*(4), 115–120.

Ladson-Billings, G. (2004). Landing on the wrong note: The price we paid for *Brown*. *Educational Researcher, 33*(7), 3–13.

Ladson-Billings, G. (1995). Toward a theory of culturally relevant pedagogy. *American Educational Research Journal, 32*, 465–491.

Ladson-Billings, G., & Tate, E. (1995). Toward a critical race theory of education. *Teachers College Record, 97*(1), 47–67.

Lan Rong, X. (1996). Effects of race and gender on teachers' perceptions of the social behavior of elementary students. *Urban Education, 31*(3), 261–290.

Landsman, J. (2009). *A white teacher talks about race*. Lanham, MD: Rowman & Littlefield.

Laycock, D., & Picarello Jr., A. (2008). *Same-sex marriage and religious liberty: Emerging conflicts*. Lanham, MD: Rowman & Littlefield.

Lee, C. D. (2003). Why we need to re-think race and ethnicity in educational research. *Educational Researcher, 32*(5), 3–5.

Lemert, C., & Bhan, E. (1998). *The voice of Anna Julia Copper: Including a voice from the South and other important essays, papers, and letters* (Legacies of Social Thought series). Lanham, MD: Rowman & Littlefield.

Lensmire, T. J., & Snaza, N. (2010). What teacher education can learn from blackface minstrelsy. *Educational Researcher, 39*(5), 413–422.

Lewis, C. W., Butler, B. R., Bonner, I. I., Fred, A., & Joubert, M. (2010). African American male discipline patterns and school district responses resulting impact on academic achievement: Implications for urban educators and policy makers. *Journal of African American Males in Education, 1*(1), 7–25.
Lickel, B., Schmader, T., & Hamilton, D. L. (2003). A case of collective responsibility: Who else was to blame for the Columbine High School shootings? *Personality and Social Psychology Bulletin, 29*(2), 194–204.
Lightfoot, S. L., & Carew, J. (1979). *Beyond bias: Perspectives on classrooms*. Cambridge, MA: Harvard University Press.
Livingston, J. N., & Nahimana, C. (2006). Problem child or problem context: An ecological approach to young black males. *Reclaiming Children and Youth, 14*(4), 209.
Martin, J. L. (Ed.). (2015). *Racial battle fatigue: Insights from the front lines of social justice advocacy*. Santa Barbara, CA: Praeger.
Martin, J. L. (Ed.). (2011). *Women as leaders in education: Succeeding despite inequity, discrimination, and other challenges. Volume 1: Women as leaders in higher education*. Santa Barbara, CA: Praeger.
Martin, J. L. (Ed.). (2011). *Women as leaders in education: Succeeding despite inequity, discrimination, and other challenges. Volume 2: Women as leaders in classrooms and schools*. Santa Barbara, CA: Praeger.
Massaro, T. (2011). *Living justice: Catholic social teaching in action* (2nd ed.). Lanham, MD: Rowman & Littlefield.
McCarthy, J. D., & Hoge, D. R. (1987). The social construction of school punishment: Racial disadvantage out of universalistic process. *Social Forces, 65*(4), 1101–1120.
McCrudden, C. (1982). Institutional discrimination. *Oxford Journal of Legal Studies, 2*(3), 303–367.
Milner, H. R. (2015). *Racing to class: What schools should know and do to end poverty*. Cambridge, MA: Harvard Education Press.
Milner, H. R., & Lomotey, K. (Eds.). (2014). *Handbook of urban education*. New York, NY: Routledge Press.
Milner, H. R. (2012). Losing the color-blind mind in the urban classroom. *Urban Education, 47*(5), 868–875.
Milner, H. R. (2010). *Start where you are but don't stay there: Understanding diversity, opportunity gaps, and teaching in today's classrooms*. Cambridge, MA: Harvard Education Press.
Milner, H. R. (Ed.). (2010). *Culture, curriculum, and identity in education*. New York, NY: Palgrave Macmillan.
Milner, H. R. (Ed.). (2009). *Diversity and education: Teachers, teaching, and teacher education*. Springfield, IL: Charles C. Thomas.
Milner, H. R. (2008). Disrupting deficit notions of difference: Counter-narratives of teachers and community in urban education. *Teaching and Teacher Education, 24*, 1573–1598.
Milner, H. R., Tenore, F. B., & Laughter, J. (2008). What can teacher education programs do to prepare teachers to teach high-achieving culturally diverse males? *Gifted Child Today, 31*(1), 18–23.
Milner, H. R. (2006). Preservice teachers' learning about cultural and racial diversity: Implications for urban education. *Urban Education, 41*(4), 343–375.
Milner, H. R., & Ross, E. W. (Eds.). (2006). *Race, ethnicity, and education: The influences of racial and ethnic identity in education*. Westport, CT: Greenwood/Praeger.
Milner, H. R., & Woolfolk Hoy, A. (2003). A case study of an African American teacher's self-efficacy, stereotype threat, and persistence. *Teaching and Teacher Education, 19*, 263–276.
Moghadam, V. M. (2012). *Globalization and social movements: Islamism, feminism, and the global justice movement* (2nd ed.). Lanham, MD: Rowman & Littlefield.
Moll, L., & Gonzalez, N. (1994). Lessons from research with language minority children. *Journal of Reading Behavior, 26*(4), 23–41.

Monroe, C. R. (2005). Why are "bad boys" always black? Causes of disproportionality in school discipline and recommendations for change. *The Clearing House: A Journal of Educational Strategies, Issues and Ideas, 79*(1), 45–50.

Morris, J. E., & Monroe, C. R. (2009). Why study the U.S. South? The nexus of race and place in investigating black student achievement. *Educational Researcher, 38*(1), 21–36.

Morrison, A. M. (1993). *The new leaders: Guidelines on leadership diversity in America*. San Francisco, CA: Jossey-Bass.

Nadasen, P. (2005). *Welfare warriors: The welfare rights movement in the United States*. New York, NY: Routledge.

National Council of LaRaza. (1986). *The education of Hispanics: Status and implications*. Washington, DC.

Neelsen, J. P. (1975). Education and social mobility. *Comparative Education Review, 19*(1), 129–143.

Nieto, S., & Bode, P. (2011). *Affirming diversity: The sociopolitical context of multicultural education* (6th ed.). Boston, MA: Pearson.

Oaks, J. (1985). *Keeping track: How schools structure inequality*. New Haven, CT: Yale University Press.

Obiakor, F. E., & Algorzine, B. (2001). *It even happens in 'good' schools: Responding to cultural diversity in today's classrooms*. Thousand Oaks, CA: Corwin Press.

O'Connor, A. (2001). *Poverty knowledge: Social science, social policy, and the poor in twentieth-century U.S. history*. Princeton, NJ: Princeton University Press.

O'Connor, C., & Fernandez, S. D. (2006). Race, class, and disproportionality: Reevaluating the relationship between poverty and special education placement. *Educational Researcher, 35*(6), 6–11.

Okoye-Johnson, O. (2011). Does multicultural education improve students' racial attitudes? Implications for closing the achievement gap. *Journal of Black Studies, 42*(8), 1252–1274.

Paris, D. (2012). Culturally sustaining pedagogy: A needed change in stance, terminology, and practice. *Educational Researcher, 41*(3), 93–97.

Penner, A. M., & Saperstein, A. (2013). Engendering racial perceptions: An intersectional analysis of how social status shapes race. *Gender & Society, 27*(3), 319–344.

Perry, B. L., & Morris, E. W. (2014). Suspending progress: Collateral consequences of exclusionary punishment in public schools. *American Sociological Review, 79*(6), 1067–1087.

Pignatelli, F., & Pflaum, S. (1993). *Celebrating diverse voices: Progressive education and equity*. Newbury, CA: Corwin.

Pitre, A., Allen, T. G., & Pitre, E. (2015). *Multicultural education for educational leaders: Critical race theory and antiracist perspectives*. Lanham, MD: Rowman & Littlefield.

Purcell-Gates, V. (1995). *Other people's words: The cycle of low literacy*. Cambridge, MA: Harvard University Press.

Quadagno, J. (1994). *The color of welfare: How racism undermined the war on poverty*. New York, NY: Oxford University Press.

Reyhner, J. (1986). *Teaching the Indian child: A bilingual/multicultural approach*. Billings, MT: Eastern Montana College.

Rhoads, R. A. (1998). *Freedom's web: Student activism in an age of cultural diversity*. Baltimore, MD: Johns Hopkins.

Rios, F., & Rogers, C. A. (2011). *Understanding multicultural education: Equity for all students*. Lanham, MD: Rowman & Littlefield.

Ryan, J. (2006). *Inclusive leadership*. San Francisco, CA: Jossey-Bass.

Sadker, M., & Sadker, D. (1990). *Sex equity handbook for schools*. New York, NY: Longman.

Sampson, R. J., & Raudenbush, S. W. (2004). Seeing disorder: Neighborhood stigma and the social construction of "broken windows." *Social Psychology Quarterly, 67*(4), 319–342.

Scherff, L., & Spector, K. (Eds.). (2011). *Culturally relevant pedagogy: Clashes and confrontations*. Lanham, MD: Rowman & Littlefield.

Seller, M. S. (1988). *To seek America: A history of ethnic life in the United States*. Englewood, NJ: Jerome S. Ozer.

Servais, K. (2012). *The courage to grow: Leading with intentionality*. Lanham, MD: Rowman & Littlefield.

Sharma, A., Joyner, A. M., & Osment, A. (2014). Adverse impact of racial isolation on student performance: A study in North Carolina. *Education Policy Analysis Archives, 22*(14).

Sharp-Grier, Martina. (2015). "She was more intelligent than I thought she'd be!": Status, stigma, and microaggressions in the academy. In J. L. Martin (Ed.), *Racial battle fatigue: Insights from the front lines of social justice advocacy* (pp. 29–44). Westport, CT: Prager.

Sleeter, C. E. (2013). Becoming white: Reinterpreting a family story by putting race back into the picture. *Race Ethnicity and Education, 14*(4), 421–433.

Schlesinger, M., Dorwart, R., Hoover, C., & Epstein, S. (1997). The determinants of dumping: A national study of economically motivated transfers involving mental health care. *Health Services Research, 32*(5), 561–590.

Shipler, D. (2005). *The working poor: Invisible in America*. New York: Vintage Books.

Skiba, R. J., Michael, R. S., Nardo, A. C., & Peterson, R. L. (2002). The color of discipline: Sources of racial and gender disproportionality in school punishment. *The Urban Review, 34*(4), 317–342.

Skiba, R., & Peterson, R. (1999). The dark side of zero tolerance: Can punishment lead to safe schools? *Phi Delta Kappan, 80*(5), 372–382.

Smith, W. A., Altbach, P. G., & Lomotey, K. (2002). *The racial crisis in American higher education: Continuing challenges for the twenty-first century* (Frontiers in Education). New York, NY: SUNY Press.

Smitherman, G. (2006). *Word from the mother: Language and African Americans*. New York, NY: Routledge.

Spencer, J. P. (2012). "Cultural deprivation" to cultural capital: The roots and continued relevance of compensatory education. *Teachers College Record, 114*(6), 1–5.

Spencer, M. B. (2008). Lessons learned and opportunities ignored since *Brown v. Board of Education*: Youth development and the myth of a colorblind society. *Educational Researcher, 37*(5), 253–266.

Spencer-Rodgers, J., & McGovern, T. (2002). Attitudes toward the culturally different: The role of intercultural communication barriers, affective responses, consensual stereotypes, and perceived threat. *International Journal of Intercultural Relations, 26*(6), 609–631.

Spring, J. (2012). *Deculturalization and the struggle for equality: A brief history of the education of dominated cultures in the United States*. New York, NY: McGraw-Hill.

Spring, J. (2004). *Deculturalization and the struggle for equality*. Boston, MA: McGraw-Hill.

Spring, J. (1989). *The sorting machine*. White Plains, NY: Longman.

Spring, J. (1985). *American education*. White Plains, NY: Longman.

Steele, C. M., & Aronson, J. (1995). Stereotype threat and the intellectual test performance of African Americans. *Journal of Personality and Social Psychology, 69*(5), 797–811.

Stephan, W. G., & Stephan, C. W. (2000). An integrated threat theory of prejudice. In S. Oskamp (Ed.), *Reducing prejudice and discrimination* (pp. 23–45). Mahwah, NJ: Lawrence Erlbaum and Associates.

Stevenson, B. (2014). *A just mercy: A story of justice and redemption*. New York, NY: Random House.

Straubhaar, R. (2015). The stark reality of the "White saviour" complex and the need for critical consciousness: A document analysis of the early journals of a Freirean educator. *Compare: A Journal of Comparative and International Education, 45*(3), 381–400.

Suad Nasir, N., & Saxe, G. B. (2003). Ethnic and academic identities: A cultural practice perspective on emerging tensions and their management in the lives of minority students. *Educational Researcher, 32*(5), 14–18.

Tatum, B. D. (1997). *"Why are all the black kids sitting together in the cafeteria?" And other conversations about race*. New York, NY: Basic Books.

Teidt, P. L., & Teidt, I. M. (2009). *Multicultural teaching: A handbook of activities, information, and resources*. New York, NY: Pearson.

Tocluk, S. (2010). *Witnessing whiteness: The need to talk about race and how to do it*. Lanham, MD: Rowman & Littlefield.

Thompson, C. (1985). *As boys become men: Learning new male roles*. Cambridge, MA: Resources for Change.

US Department of Justice, Civil Rights Division, & US Department of Education, Office for Civil Rights. (2014, January 8). Dear colleague letter on the nondiscriminatory administration of school discipline. Retrieved from http://www2.ed.gov/about/offices/list/ocr/letters/colleague-201401-title-vi.html

Wallace, T. L., & Chhuon, V. (2014). Proximal processes in urban classrooms: Engagement and disaffection in urban youth of color. *American Educational Research Journal, 51*(5), 937–973.

Ward, J., & Anthony, P. (1992). *Who pays for student diversity? Population changes and educational policy*. Newbury Park, CA: Corwin.

Weinberg, M. (1986). *Because they were Jews: A history of anti-Semitism*. Westport, CT: Greenwood Press.

Wells, A. S. (1989). Hispanic education in America: Separate and unequal. *ERIC Clearinghouse on Urban Education Digest No. 59*, Teachers College, Columbia University.

Wiggins, G. (1991). Standards not standardization: Evoking quality student work. *Educational Leadership, 48*(5), 18–20.

Wildhagen, T. (2012). How teachers and schools contribute to racial differences in the realization of academic potential. *Teachers College Record, 114*(7), 1–27.

Zion, S. D., & Blanchett, W. (2011). (Re)conceptualizing inclusion: Can critical race theory and interest convergence be utilized to achieve inclusion and equity for African American students? *Teachers College Record, 113*(10), 2186–2205.

Appendix B

Social Justice Guidance and Resources for Teachers and Administrators

ACTIVITIES/INFORMATION (TOPICAL)

Differential Discipline Based on Race

Chiles, N. (2015, April 16). Stanford researchers unveil racial stereotypes that lead teachers to discipline black students more severely. *Atlanta Black Star*. Retrieved from http://atlantablackstar.com/2015/04/16/stanford-researchers-unveil-racial-stereotypes-that-lead-teachers-to-discipline-black-students-more-severely/

Dobuzinskis, A. (2015, April 15). U.S. study finds teacher bias in discipline toward black students. *Reuters*. Retrieved from http://www.reuters.com/article/2015/04/16/us-usa-race-schooldiscipline-idUSKBN0N701C20150416

Rowe, C. (2015, June 23). Race dramatically skews discipline, even in elementary school. *The Seattle Times*. Retrieved from http://www.seattletimes.com/education-lab/race-dramatically-skews-discipline-even-in-elementary-school/

U.S. Department of Education. (2015, July). Educators gather at the White House to rethink school discipline. Retrieved from http://www.ed.gov/news/press-releases/educators-gather-white-house-rethink-school-discipline

U.S. Department of Education, Office for Civil Rights. (2014, March). *Civil rights data collection, data snapshot: School discipline*. Retrieved from http://ocrdata.ed.gov/Downloads/CRDC-School-Discipline-Snapshot.pdf

Microaggressions

Examples of racial microaggressions. (n.d.). Retrieved from http://www.uwsp.edu/acadaff/NewFacultyResources/NFSRacialMicroaggressions_Table.pdf

Kaskan, E. R., & Ho, I. K. (2016, April). Microaggressions and female athletes. *Sex Roles, 74*(7), 275–287. Retrieved from http://link.springer.com/article/10.1007%2Fs11199-014-0425-1#page-1

The Microaggression Project. (n.d.). Microaggressions: Power, privilege, and everyday life. Retrieved from http://www.microaggressions.com/

Morris, M. W. (2016). *Pushout: The criminalization of black girls in schools*. New York, NY: The New Press.

Pérez Huber, L., & Solorzano, D. G. (2015). Racial microaggressions as a tool for critical race research. *Race Ethnicity and Education, 18*(3), 297–320. Retrieved from http://dx.doi.org/10.1080/13613324.2014.994173

Sue, D. W. (2010). *Microaggressions in everyday life: Race, gender, and sexual orientation.* Hoboken, NJ: John Wiley & Sons.

Sue, D. W. (2010, October 5). Racial microaggressions in everyday life: Is subtle bias harmless? *Psychology Today.* Retrieved from https://www.psychologytoday.com/blog/microaggressions-in-everyday-life/201010/racial-microaggressions-in-everyday-life

Sue, D. W., Capodilupo, C. M., Torino, G. C., Bucceri, J. M., Holder, A. M. D., Nadal, K. L., & Esquilin, M. (2007). Racial microaggressions in everyday life: Implications for clinical practice. *American Psychologist, 62*(4), 271-286. Retrieved from http://www.cpedv.org/sites/main/files/file-attachments/how_to_be_an_effective_ally-lessons_learned_microaggressions.pdf

Vega, T. (2014, March 21). Students see many slights as racial "microaggressions." *The New York Times.* Retrieved from http://www.nytimes.com/2014/03/22/us/as-diversity-increases-slights-get-subtler-but-still-sting.html?_r=0

[See *I too am Harvard* in Video section.]

Sexual Harassment

Ali, R. (2010, October 26). Dear colleague letter: Harassment and bullying. US Department of Education, Office for Civil Rights. Retrieved from http://www2.ed.gov/about/offices/list/ocr/letters/colleague-201010.html

AAUW. (2016, fall). The simple truth about the gender pay gap. Retrieved from http://www.aauw.org/research/the-simple-truth-about-the-gender-pay-gap/

AAUW. (2016, July 12). Two-thirds of public schools reported zero incidents of sexual harassment in 2013-14. Retrieved from http://www.aauw.org/article/schools-report-zero-sexual-harassment/

Transgender

Manfredo, R. F. (2016, June 3). Office of Civil Rights releases "dear colleague" letter on transgender students. *Higher Education Law Report.* Retrieved from http://www.higheredlawreport.com/2016/06/office-of-civil-rights-releases-dear-colleague-letter-on-transgender-students/

National Center for Transgender Equality & Gay, Lesbian and Straight Education Network. (2016). Model school district policy on transgender and gender nonconforming students. Retrieved from https://www.glsen.org/sites/default/files/Trans%20Model%20Policy.pdf

Orr, A., Baum, J., Brown, J., Gill, E., Kahn, E., & Salem, A. (2015). *Schools in transition: A guide to supporting transgender students in K-12 schools.* Retrieved from https://www.genderspectrum.org/staging/wp-content/uploads/2015/08/Schools-in-Transition-2015.pdf

U.S. Department of Justice, Civil Rights Division, & US Department of Education, Office for Civil Rights. (2016, May 13). Dear colleague letter on transgender students. Retrieved from https://www2.ed.gov/about/offices/list/ocr/letters/colleague-201605-title-ix-transgender.pdf

Whalen, A., & Esquith, D. (2016, May 13). *Examples of policies and emerging practices for supporting transgender students.* US Department of Education. Retrieved from https://www2.ed.gov/about/offices/list/oese/oshs/emergingpractices.pdf

White Privilege

Carter Andrews, D. J. (2012, October). Black achievers' experiences with racial spotlighting and ignoring in a predominantly white high school. *Teachers College Record, 114*(10), 1–46.

DiAngelo, R. (2015, April 9). White fragility: Why it's so hard to talk to white people about racism. *The Good Men Project*. Retrieved from http://goodmenproject.com/featured-content/white-fragility-why-its-so-hard-to-talk-to-white-people-about-racism-twlm/

LaBouvier C. (n.d.). I, racist. *Those People*. Retrieved from https://thsppl.com/i-racist-538512462265

Marusic, K. (2015, June 22). Nine ways you can use your white privilege for good. *MTV News* . Retrieved from http://www.mtv.com/news/2187137/white-people-documentary-privilege-for-good/

Matias, C. E. (2016). White skin, black friend: A Fanonian application to theorize racial fetish in teacher education. *Educational Philosophy and Theory, 48*(3), 221–236.

Matias, C. E., & Zembylas, M. (2014). "When saying you care is not really caring": Emotions of disgust, whiteness ideology, and teacher education. *Critical Studies in Education, 55*(3), 319–337.

Matias, C. E., & DiAngelo, R. (2013, summer–fall). Beyond the face of evil: Emocognitive explorations of white neurosis and racial cray-cray. *Educational Foundations*, 3–20.

Matias, C. E., & Allen, R. L. (2013). Loving whiteness to death: Sadomasochism, emotionality, and the possibility of humanizing love. *Berkeley Review of Education, 4*(2), 285–309.

McIntosh, P. (1988). White privilege: Unpacking the invisible knapsack. Retrieved from http://www.deanza.edu/faculty/lewisjulie/White%20Priviledge%20Unpacking%20the%20Invisible%20Knapsack.pdf

Pang, E. (2015, July 6). Wondering what "privilege" is? This video has some answers for you. *Huffington Post*. Retrieved from http://www.huffingtonpost.ca/2015/07/06/what-is-privilege_n_7737466.html

Rakestraw, M. (2012, May 21). Thirteen resources for teaching about white privilege. *Institute for Humane Education*. Retrieved from http://humaneeducation.org/blog/2012/05/21/13-resources-for-teaching-about-white-privilege/

Sehgal, P. (2015, July 14). How "privilege" became a provocation. *The New York Times*. Retrieved from http://www.nytimes.com/2015/07/19/magazine/how-privilege-became-a-provocation.html?_r=0

Southern Poverty Law Center. (2016, summer). Why talk about whiteness? *Teaching Tolerance, 53*, 31–33. Retrieved from http://www.tolerance.org/magazine/number-53-summer-2016/feature/why-talk-about-whiteness

Southern Poverty Law Center. (2012, fall). Confronting white privilege. *Teaching Tolerance, 42*, 23–26. Retrieved from http://www.tolerance.org/magazine/number-42-fall-2012/feature/confronting-white-privilege

ARTICLES

Bemak, F., & Chi-Ying Chung, R. (2008, summer). New professional roles and advocacy strategies for school counselors: A multicultural/social justice perspective to move beyond the nice counselor syndrome. *Journal of Counseling & Development, 86*, 372–382. Retrieved from http://edresearch.yolasite.com/resources/BemakChung.pdf

Butrymowicz, S., Kolodner, M., Garcia Mathewson, T., & Garland, S. (2016, September 22). "They only kill us because of our skin color and our race." *The Hetchinger Report*. Retrieved from http://hechingerreport.org/kill-us-skin-color-race/

Caplan-Bricker, N. (2016, September 29). "My school punished *me*." *Slate*. Retrieved from http://www.slate.com/articles/double_x/doublex/2016/09/title_ix_sexual_assault_allegations_in_k_12_schools.html

David, S., & Hoppenstedt, D. (2014). Social justice: One district's comprehensive approach to increasing student engagement. *Michigan Association of School Administra-*

tors. Retrieved from http://www.gomasa.org/news/social-justice-one-district-s-comprehensive-approach-increasing-student-engagement

Dupree, M. (2015, May 4). Here's what white teachers tend to do with gifted black students; it's appalling. *Financial Juneteenth*. Retrieved from http://financialjuneteenth.com/heres-what-white-teachers-tend-to-do-with-gifted-black-students-its-appalling/

Ford, D. Y., & Toldson, I. A. Study on black, Hispanic children in special ed wrong, regressive (2015, July 5). *Diverse: Issues in Higher Education*. Retrieved from http://diverseeducation.com/article/76088/

Green, E. J., McCollum, V. C., & Hays, D. G. (2008). Teaching advocacy counseling: A social justice paradigm of awareness, knowledge, and skills. *Journal for Social Action in Counseling and Psychology, 1*(2), 14–29. Retrieved from http://www.psysr.org/about/pubs_resources/jsacp/Green-V1N2-08.pdf

Mathis, W. J. (2016, August 23). Research-based options for education policymaking—2016 collection. *National Education Policy Center*. Retrieved from http://nepc.colorado.edu/publication/research-based-options

Prangley, E. (2016, July 12). Two-thirds of public schools reported zero incidents of sexual harassment in 2013–14. *AAUW*. Retrieved from http://www.aauw.org/article/schools-report-zero-sexual-harassment/

CURRICULUM

Anti-Defamation League. (2015). *Social justice poetry*. Retrieved from http://www.adl.org/assets/pdf/education-outreach/social-justice-poetry.pdf

Ciardiello, A. V. (2010). "Talking walls": Presenting a case for social justice poetry in literacy education. *The Reading Teacher, 63*(6), 464–473. Retrieved from http://www.aiisf.org/pdf/TalkingWalls.pdf

Deshmukh Towery, I., Oliveri, R., & Gidney, C. L. (2007). Peer-led professional development for equity and diversity: A report for teachers and administrators based on findings from the SEED Project (Seeking Educational Equity and Diversity). *Schott Foundation for Public Education*. Retrieved from http://www.racialequitytools.org/resourcefiles/deshmukh.pdf

Greenberg, J. (2015, July 10). Curriculum for white Americans to educate themselves on race and racism—from Ferguson to Charleston. *Citizenship & Social Justice*. Retrieved from http://citizenshipandsocialjustice.com/2015/07/10/curriculum-for-white-americans-to-educate-themselves-on-race-and-racism/

ORGANIZATIONS

Center for Collaborative Research for an Equitable California: https://ccrec.ucsc.edu/

City University of New York Center for the Humanities: Public education, the city, and struggles for racial justice: http://www.centerforthehumanities.org/public-engagement/working-groups/public-education-the-city-and-struggles-for-racial-justice

EdChange: Bringing equitable and just schools, communities, and organizations through transformative action: http://www.edchange.org/

Gender Spectrum: http://www.genderspectrum.org

Morris Justice: A Public Science Project: http://morrisjustice.org/

National Alliance for Partnerships in Equity (NAPE): http://www.napequity.org/

The National Association for Multicultural Education (NAME): http://nameorg.org/

The One Love Foundation: What if you could help end relationship violence? http://www.joinonelove.org/

Teaching Tolerance, Southern Poverty Law Center: http://www.tolerance.org/

Transgender and LGBT Legal Organizations: http://www.transequality.org/additional-help#legal
TransYouth Family Allies: http://www.imatyfa.org
Urban Affairs Association: http://urbanaffairsassociation.org/
What's Your Issue? A national youth survey made with LGBTQ & GNC youth to lift up our experiences, priorities, & dreams: http://whatsyourissue.org/
Youth Hub: A collaborative neighborhood-based initiative working to dramatically improve youth outcomes, particularly related to career-readiness in Boston neighborhoods: http://www.youthhubboston.org/

RESOURCES

Ali, R. (2012, October 26). Dear colleague letter: Harassment and bullying. US Department of Education, Office for Civil Rights. Retrieved from http://www2.ed.gov/about/offices/list/ocr/letters/colleague-201010.pdf
Ali, R. (2011, April 4). Dear colleague letter: Sexual violence. US Department of Education, Office for Civil Rights. Retrieved from http://www2.ed.gov/about/offices/list/ocr/letters/colleague-201104.pdf
GLSEN. Claim your rights: Bullying harassment, & discrimination of LGBT students should be reported! (n.d.). Retrieved from http://www.glsen.org/sites/default/files/Claim%20Your%20Rights%20Final_GLSEN.pdf
Marilyn Gittell Digital Archive. (n.d.): http://gittell.newmedialab.cuny.edu/
New York City Department of Education. (n.d.). Respect for all: Useful links and shortcuts for teachers and school administrators. Retrieved from http://schools.nyc.gov/RulesPolicies/RespectforAll/EducatorResources/default.htm
PFLAG. Claim your rights. (n.d.). Retrieved from https://www.pflag.org/claimyourrights
Teaching Tolerance. (n.d.). Family and community engagement. Retrieved from http://www.tolerance.org/publication/family-and-community-engagement
Teaching Tolerance. (n.d.). The Southern Poverty Law Center. Retrieved from http://www.tolerance.org/
U.S. Department of Education, Office for Civil Rights. (2015, April 24). Dear colleague letter on Title IX coordinators. Retrieved from http://www2.ed.gov/about/offices/list/ocr/letters/colleague-201504-title-ix-coordinators.pdf
U.S. Department of Education, Office for Civil Rights. (2014, January 8). Dear colleague letter on the nondiscriminatory administration of school discipline. Retrieved from http://www2.ed.gov/about/offices/list/ocr/letters/colleague-201401-title-vi.pdf
US Department of Education. (2014, January). *Guiding principles: A resource guide for improving school climate and discipline*. Retrieved from http://www2.ed.gov/policy/gen/guid/school-discipline/guiding-principles.pdf
What's Your Issue? (n.d.). Resources: A short list of some of our favorite resources. Retrieved from http://whatsyourissue.org/resources/

SIMULATIONS

BaFa BaFa. Can be found at http://www.simulationtrainingsystems.com/corporate/products/bafa-bafa/
Crossing the Line. Facilitation guidelines can be found at https://my.vanderbilt.edu/vucept/files/2014/08/Crossing-the-Line-Activity.pdf
The Dance of Structural Inequality. Can be found at https://www.yumpu.com/en/document/view/49609798/dance-of-structural-inequality-in-pdf-format (see Buzzfeed video example below)
Harvard Implicit Bias Tests: https://implicit.harvard.edu/implicit/takeatest.html

VIDEOS

Bailey, M. (2014). The danger of hiding who you are. *Ted Talks.* Retrieved from https://www.ted.com/talks/morgana_bailey_the_danger_of_hiding_who_you_are

Burns, J. (2010). A message to gay teens: It gets better. *Ted Talks.* Retrieved from https://www.ted.com/talks/joel_burns_tells_gay_teens_it_gets_better

Buzzfeed. (2015). What is privilege? *YouTube.* Retrieved from https://www.youtube.com/watch?v=hD5f8GuNuGQ

Cliatt-Wayman, L. (2015). How to fix a broken school? Lead fearlessly, love hard. *Ted Talks.* Retrieved from https://www.ted.com/talks/linda_cliatt_wayman_how_to_fix_a_ broken_school_lead_fearlessly_love_hard

Choonara, E. (2014). What is intersectionality? *YouTube.* Retrieved from https://www.youtube.com/watch?v=aIoy9G3KnLE

Collins, P. H. (2013). Intersectionality. *C-Span.* Retrieved from https://www.c-span.org/video/?c4289652/intersectionality

Fukishima, A. (2013). Intersectionality matters: Alisha Fukishima at Tedx Whitman College. *YouTube.* Retrieved from https://www.youtube.com/watch?v=Iwp5rQTJi84

Gebreyes, R. (2015, June 1). How misperceptions of "aggressive" black female behavior lead to tough punishments for young girls. *Huffington Post.* Retrieved from http://www.huffingtonpost.com/2015/06/01/punishments-black-girls-aggressive-behavior_n_7484356.html

I too am Harvard. Retrieved from http://itooamharvard.tumblr.com/

Jackson, S. (2010). Intersection analysis of race, class, and education. *YouTube.* Retrieved from https://www.youtube.com/watch?v=InhCz3_Csr0

Jackson, Y. (2012). Challenging myths of educating low-income children. *Spotlight on Poverty and Opportunity.* Retrieved from http://sparkaction.org/content/webcast-video-challenging-myths-educating-

Jane Elliott: Blue eyes/brown eyes. *YouTube.* Retrieved from https://www.youtube.com/watch?v=uQAmdZvKf6M

Jane Elliot: How racist are you? *YouTube.* Retrieved from https://www.youtube.com/watch?v=XAv8JA_9uKI

Jane Elliott: *Oprah* racism experiment. *YouTube.* Retrieved from http://www.huffingtonpost.com/2015/01/02/jane-elliott-race-experiment-oprah-show_n_6396980.html

Katz, J. (2012). Violence against women: It's a men's issue. *Ted Talks.* Retrieved from https://www.ted.com/talks/jackson_katz_violence_against_women_it_s_a_men_s_issue

The linguistics of AAVE (2015). *YouTube.* Retrieved from https://www.youtube.com/watch?v=pkzVOXKXfQk

PBS. (2015). Why poverty? Retrieved from http://video.pbs.org/program/why-poverty/

PBS. (2012). Does being poor mean you will stay poor? Retrieved from http://video.pbs.org/video/2298446394/

Pilloton, E. (2010). Teaching design for change. *Ted Talks.* Retrieved from https://www.ted.com/talks/emily_pilloton_teaching_design_for_change

Porter, T. (2010). A call to men. *Ted Talks.* Retrieved from https://www.ted.com/talks/tony_porter_a_call_to_men

Rakestraw, M. (2014). Nine videos for exploring gender stereotypes and gender roles. *The Institute for Humane Education blog.* Retrieved from https://humaneeducation.org/blog/2014/9-videos-exploring-gender-stereotypes-gender-roles/

The Representation Project. (n.d.). The mask you live in. Retrieved from http://therepresentationproject.org/films/the-mask-you-live-in/

Richen, Y. (2014). What the gay rights movement learned from the civil rights movement. *Ted Talks.* Retrieved from https://www.ted.com/talks/yoruba_richen_what_the_gay_rights_movement_learned_from_the_civil_rights_move ment

Teaching Channel. (2015). Closing the gender gap in STEM education. Retrieved from https://www.teachingchannel.org/videos/stem-gender-gap-ced

TVSBSC. (2012). Intersectionality of race and gender: A framework for learning, dialogue, and change. *YouTube.* Retrieved from https://www.youtube.com/watch?v=66XEglI-EEo

Weill, J. (2015). FRAC reports on the success of school breakfast. *Spotlight on Poverty and Opportunity.* Retrieved from http://www.spotlightonpoverty.org/news.aspx?id=4144dc38-980b-4d1b9256-a198c30e936a

Zimbardo, P. (2011). The demise of guys? *Ted Talks.* Retrieved from https://www.ted.com/talks/zimchallenge

WEBSITES

AAUW. (n.d.). Find your Title IX coordinators. Retrieved from http://www.aauw.org/resource/find-your-title-ix-coordinator/

AAUW. (2016). Two-thirds of public schools reported zero incidents of sexual harassment in 2013–14. Retrieved from http://www.aauw.org/article/schools-report-zero-sexual-harassment/

AAUW. (2017, spring). The simple truth about gender pay gap. Retrieved from http://www.aauw.org/research/the-simple-truth-about-the-gender-pay-gap/

Adwar, C. (2014, March 26). Amazing new tool lets you see the racial disparities at your old high school. *Business Insider.* Retrieved from http://www.businessinsider.com/education-department-releases-school-equity-data-2014-3

Benn, M. (2014, January 31). The education gender gap is bad for girls as well as boys. *The Guardian.* Retrieved from http://www.theguardian.com/commentisfree/2014/jan/31/education-gender-gap-girls-schools-university

Boyd, N. (2015). Improving gender equality in education. *Study.com.* Retrieved from http://study.com/academy/lesson/improving-gender-equality-in-education.html

Center for the Humanities, City University of New York. (n.d.). Fight for the city: School desegregation, race, resistance, and class struggle. Retrieved from http://www.centerforthehumanities.org/programming/fight-for-the-city-school-desegregation-white-resistance-and-class-struggle

Chapman, A. (2015). Gender bias in education. *EdChange.org.* Retrieved from http://www.edchange.org/multicultural/papers/genderbias.html

ChildFund International. (2015). Poverty and education. Retrieved from https://www.childfund.org/about-us/education/

Coley, R. J., & Baker, B. (2013). Poverty and education: Finding the way forward. Educational Testing Service. Retrieved from https://www.ets.org/s/research/pdf/poverty_and_education_report.pdf

DoSomething.org. (n.d.). Eleven facts about education and poverty in America. Retrieved from https://www.dosomething.org/facts/11-facts-about-education-and-poverty-america

Education World. (n.d.). States step up efforts to reduce school segregation. Retrieved from http://www.educationworld.com/a_admin/admin/admin154.shtml

Galupo, M. P. (2007). Advancing diversity through a framework of intersectionality: Inclusion of LGBT issues in higher education. *Diversity Digest, 10*(2). Retrieved from http://www.diversityweb.org/digest/vol10no2/galupo.cfm

Gay, Lesbian & Straight Education Network: http://www.glsen.org

Hurst, M. (2015). Gender differences in the classroom: Physical, cognitive & behavioral. *Study.com.* Retrieved from http://study.com/academy/lesson/gender-differences-in-the-classroom-physical-cognitive-behavioral.html

Intergroup Resources. (2012). Intersectionality. Retrieved from http://www.intergroupresources.com/intersectionality/

Jensen, E. (2009). How poverty affects behavior and academic performance. From *Teaching with poverty in mind: What being poor does to kids' brains and what schools can do about it* (pp. 13-45). Alexandria, VA: Association for Supervision and Curriculum Development. Retrieved from http://www.ascd.org/publications/books/109074/chapters/How-Poverty-Affects-Behavior-and-Academic-Performance.aspx

National Center for Children in Poverty, Columbia University: http://www.nccp.org

National Education Association. (2015). Research spotlight on single-gender education. Retrieved from http://www.nea.org/tools/17061.htm

National LGBT Health Education Center, Fenway Institute: http://www.lgbthealtheducation.org/training/learning-modules/

Poverty USA. (n.d.). Learn about the state of poverty. Retrieved from http://www.povertyusa.org/the-state-of-poverty/

Salera, B. (2014). Intersectionality in the classroom: My experience teaching at the crossroads of ethnicity and gender. *Hybrid Pedagogy.* Retrieved from http://www.hybridpedagogy.com/journal/intersectionality-classroom-experience-teaching-crossroads-ethnicity-gender/

Save Our Schools. (2014). A nation's priority: Poverty and/or the children? Retrieved from http://saveourschoolsmarch.org/issues/poverty-and-the-effect-on-education/

Stanberry, K. (2016). Single-sex education: The pros and cons. *Great Schools.* Retrieved from http://www.greatschools.org/gk/articles/single-sex-education-the-pros-and-cons/

Teaching Tolerance, Southern Poverty Law Center. (2013). Best practices. Creating an LGBT-inclusive school climate: A teaching tolerance guide for school leaders. Retrieved from http://www.tolerance.org/sites/default/files/general/LGBT%20Best%20Practices_0.pdf

UNESCO Institute for Statistics. (2017). Gender equality in education. Retrieved from http://uis.unesco.org/en/topic/gender-equality-education

Index

About the Authors

Jane A. Beese is an associate professor at Youngstown State University in the Department of Educational Foundations, Research, Technology, and Leadership. She teaches a range of courses in the masters and doctoral degree programs. The scope of her professional knowledge base and teaching expertise is broad, spanning several areas, including learning theory and instruction, current policy issues, organizational change, leadership theory and practice, and introductory research and qualitative methods. Her research agenda focuses on feminist and social justice issues. She has co-authored *Teaching for Educational Equity: Case Studies for Professional Development and Principal Preparation, Volume 1* and chapter 2 in *Feminist Pedagogy, Practice, and Activism: Improving Lives for Girls and Woman.*

Jennifer Martin is an assistant professor of education at the University of Mount Union, previously an alternative high school English teacher for students labeled at-risk. She is the editor of *Racial Battle Fatigue: Insights from the Front Lines of Social Justice Advocacy* (Recipient of the 2016 AERA Division B's Outstanding Book Recognition Award), and co-author of *Teaching for Educational Equity: Case Studies for Professional Development and Principal Preparation, Volume 1* (Rowman & Littlefield). Her most recent edited volume is *Feminist Pedagogy, Practice, and Activism: Improving Lives for Girls and Women* (2017).

Milton Keynes UK
Ingram Content Group UK Ltd.
UKHW012000040424
440632UK00011B/129